# Against Power Inequalities

*A History of the Progressive Struggle*

New Edition

# HENRY TAM

**Against Power Inequalities**

New edition 2015
ISBN-13: 978-1499144635
ISBN-10: 1499144636

---

The 2015 edition, published in commemoration of the 8th centenary of the signing of Magna Carta, incorporates new materials and revisions to the original version (published in 2010 by Birkbeck College, London University). It provides a historical guide to the progressive struggle for power redistribution, and draws out the underlying obstacles to the development of more inclusive communities.

---

### About the author

Henry Tam is Director of the Forum for Youth Participation & Democracy, Faculty of Education, University of Cambridge; and Visiting Professor at Birkbeck College, University of London. He has written extensively on democracy, citizenship & communitarianism, and led national policies on the development of inclusive communities during his time as the UK Government's Head of Civil Renewal.

Henry Tam's other published works include:

- ❖ 'Communitarianism, Sociology of', in the *International Encyclopedia of Social and Behavioural Sciences* (Elsevier: 2015)
- ❖ *Whitehall through the Looking Glass* (a novel) (QTP: 2014)
- ❖ 'Cooperative Problem-Solving & Education', *Forum*, Vol 55 Number 2 (Symposium Books: 2013).
- ❖ *Kuan's Wonderland* (a novel) (QTP: 2012)
- ❖ 'Through Thick & Thin: what does it really take for us to live together', *Ethnicities*, Vol 11 Issue 3 (Sage: 2011)
- ❖ 'The Importance of being a Citizen', in *Take Part: Active Learning for Active Citizenship*, ed. by J. Annette & M. Mayo (NIACE: 2010)
- ❖ 'Civil Renewal: the agenda for empowering citizens', in *Re-energizing Citizenship: Strategies for Civil Renewal*, ed. by T. Brannan, P. John and G. Stoker, (Macmillan Palgrave: 2007)
- ❖ *Progressive Politics in the Global Age* (Polity Press: 2001)
- ❖ 'The Community Roots of Citizenship', in *Citizens: Towards a Citizenship Culture*, ed. by B. Crick (Wiley-Blackwell: 2001)
- ❖ *Communitarianism: A New Agenda for Politics & Citizenship* (Macmillan/New York University Press: 1998)
- ❖ *Putting Citizens First*, with J. Stewart (Municipal Journal/SOLACE: 1997)
- ❖ *Punishment, Excuses & Moral Development* (Avebury: 1996)
- ❖ 'Crime & Responsibility', in B. Almond (ed.) *Introducing Applied Ethics* (Blackwell's: 1995)
- ❖ *Citizenship Development: Towards an organisational model* (LGMB: 1994)
- ❖ *Serving the Public* (Longman: 1993)
- ❖ *Responsibility and Personal Interactions* (Edwin Mellen Press: 1990)

For more information, go to 'Henry Tam: Words & Politics': http://hbtam.blogspot.co.uk

Visit his on-line Journal: *Question the Powerful*: http://henry-tam.blogspot.co.uk

### Comments on *Against Power Inequalities*

"Henry Tam has written a book that is breath-taking in its panoramic overview of the genealogy of power inequalities and the struggles against them. But this book is much more than a compelling history of power inequalities and their contestation. In its forensic, but always optimistic, analysis of how citizens have worked in the past, and continue to work, towards a fairer, more just society, we have an inspirational example of a text that speaks truth to power." – D Reay, Professor of Education, University of Cambridge (UK)

"Tam's book is an intellectual tour de force, an erudite romp through the history of civilization that highlights the origins of power and the never-ending effort to democratize hierarchical systems through mobilized participatory communities. It bears reading and re-reading, because the issues of power and community are so fundamental, and the history so rich and evocative." – C Derber, Professor of Sociology, Boston College (USA)

"Henry Tam is a master storyteller. This is history retold as a panorama of struggle, hope and co-operation in the name of fairness and in the pursuit of an ever wider circle of respect and equality." – E Mayo, Secretary General, Co-operatives UK

"In this thought-provoking book Henry Tam demonstrates that in times in which populist movements try to pit the people against the bearers of democratic institutions, we need to reconsider the relation between democratic decision-making and community life. ... Alongside social democrats and liberal reformers, Christian Democrats ... will derive inspiration from this work of a truly independent scholar." – E M H Hirsch Ballin, Professor of Constitutional Law, University of Tilburg; former Minister for Justice (The Netherlands)

"[An] inspiring, global story of democratic struggles against concentrated power and offers guidance for progressives today. It is a broad, bold, and thoughtful manifesto for popular democratic reform." – P Levine, Research Director, J Tisch College, Tufts University (USA)

"Tam's book is a kaleidoscope of human history in which he tells a compelling story. He understands the nature of power and the negative impacts it can have in almost any conceivable culture. However he also strikes a positive and optimistic note. ... His fundamental faith in humanity shines through. This is not a book just about politics, economics or philosophy; it embraces all three." – R Spellman, Chief Executive, Workers Educational Association (UK)

"Henry Tam takes us on an epic journey spanning more than two millennia of human ideas and endeavour, and reminds us that there is nothing inevitable about inequality of power and its attendant misery, and that alternatives based on enlightened enquiry, distributed power, and constant vigilance, are always to be found." – S Wyler, Director, Development Trusts Association (UK)

"[A] breathtaking sweep of philosophy, history, and world culture. Throughout this book, [Tam] tugs with a potent blend of indignation and optimism at a single thread: What happens when people do not have a fair share of power, and how we can counter it by creating a more inclusive society." – D Dyssegaard Kallick, Senior Fellow, Fiscal Policy Institute (USA)

"Henry Tam is pivotally involved in the promotion of active citizenship in the UK and has written extensively on the subject. His latest publication, *Against Power Inequalities*, is a tour de force, providing an authoritative and widely researched account of the development of inclusive communities worldwide." – R Bolsin, Director of Education, Medway; General Secretary (2004-2012), WEA (UK)

"This book makes a thorough and compelling case for persevering with the struggle for more inclusive communities. For anyone concerned with activism and political change, it provides an invaluable touchstone to help understand the mechanics of autonomy and control." – D Tyler, Chief Executive, Community Matters (UK)

# CONTENTS

# Chapter 1
# The Problem of Power Inequalities:
# An Overview

Disparity in power

Few would dispute that reciprocity should prevail in human interactions so that none may take unfair advantage of others. Many have yet to recognise, however, that where the norm of reciprocity is most lacking is in society's power structures.

Throughout history, on every continent, in every sphere of life, whenever some have managed to amass more power than others without the latter obtaining anything sufficient to counter-balance it, the door is open to neglect and exploitation. Not everyone succumbs to the temptation to pursue one's goals without giving due regard to others' concerns, but when the opportunity to do so without any repercussion is permanently present, there will inevitably be those who seize it to advance their own agenda.

As Glaucon[1] long ago remarked, if anyone should come to possess a magical ring with the power to make him invisible – knowing he would escape censure and retaliation – the ring's owner would be less inclined to treat others with the consideration he would show were he visible to them. In reality, there is no need for any kind of magic to achieve the same kind of effect. There are many forms of power in society that can shield people from the consequences of their irresponsible actions by rendering immaterial any reactions from those they hurt. When told that others might do to him what he is doing to them, he could with callous confidence predict that they would not in fact be able to do so.

There are at least four types of power, the excessive concentration of which in a few would render others susceptible to mistreatment without any adequate redress[2].

---

[1] In Plato's *The Republic*.

[2] I use 'power' in the sense of the capacity to bring something about that can affect other people's lives. It follows that for any such given power, if some have significantly more of it than others, then the former has an advantage they can use to make gains against the latter. For an interpretation of power as the

1

First, there is what may be termed *executive power*. Any structured organisation – a business, a church, or a government – has a system of authority whereby policies are set, commands are issued, and compliance is enforced. Anyone daring to disobey what is asked of one risks being disciplined, punished, excommunicated, or exiled. Kings and emperors for centuries possessed such power in abundance until democratic resistance brought in checks and balance mechanisms to give gradually all citizens an equal share in determining the allocation of this power at the state level[3]. But not all government institutions live up to full democratic accountability; and in business, with the exception of a minority of worker cooperatives and partnership firms, senior directors still possess overwhelming executive power.

Secondly, there is *knowledge power*[4]. If what can be declared to be true or warranting belief is entirely the prerogative of one group of people, then intentionally or otherwise they can spread lies and falsehoods damaging the lives of others. The priestly elite in many ancient societies and some contemporary ones, as well as the esoteric technocracy so prominent in today's financial sector, are just two examples of how numerous people can end up having to adjust their lives to conform to particular presentations of what the world is supposed to be like. Although the Scientific Revolution has since the 17th century led to the spread of more open and empirical enquiry which distributes knowledge power more evenly to all who have relevant arguments or evidence to contribute, some groups still seek to maintain their stranglehold on fixing what is to be believed in theological, economic, or national security matters.

Thirdly, there is *status power*. In any group or society, there is a

---

ability to cause others to be affected in a manner contrary to their interests, see Lukes, S. *Power: A Radical View*, Basingstoke, Palgrave Macmillan: 2005.

[3] See, for example, Everdell W.R., *The End of Kings: a history of republics and republicans*, Chicago, the University of Chicago Press: 2000; and Bendix, R., *Kings or People: power and the mandate to rule*, London, University of California Press: 1978.

[4] For an exposition of what Francis Bacon meant by "Knowledge is power", see Urbach, P., *Francis Bacon's Philosophy of Science*, La Salle, Open Court Publishing: 1987; and on how education should address the issues of knowledge, power and democracy, see Lockyer, A., Crick, B. and Annette, J. (eds), *Education for Democratic Citizenship*, Aldershot, Ashgate: 2003.

prevailing mindset, shaped by a mix of old customs and everyday communications, that differentiates people into various status categories. In a cooperative team of workers, for example, those categories may relate to what people are best equipped to do and can correspondingly be entrusted with particular tasks. No one will be granted total deference just because they happen to be good at a few things, nor would respect be stripped away from a team member as a result of some minor, let alone irrelevant, feature. By contrast, arbitrary hierarchies emerge when over time certain types of people succeed in cultivating notions of superiority and inferiority which place them at the apex, while leaving an ever greater number further down towards the base. The halo of 'divine' endorsement, military glory, tribal-ethnic 'purity', a 'special' family name, or merely ostentatious gold hoarding, can be created to confer higher status on some; while the status of 'women', 'servants', 'the poor', 'foreigners', 'heretics', have all at one time or another been denigrated. Those with the most status power to stoke and sustain the sense of superiority/inferiority that most suit them can thus secure submission without issuing commands or threatening force[5].

Last but not least, there is *resource power*. Through the writings of Wilkinson & Pickett, Milanovich, Stiglitz, and Piketty[6], the growing inequality in resource power as measured by wealth and income has been widely documented. For centuries an elite had been able to use what might have been initially a relatively small accumulation of resources to buy up control levers that enabled them to lay claim to what eventually became a vastly greater proportion of natural and labour-generated resources than anyone else. Although in the immediate decades after the Second World War this trend was significantly curtailed[7], from the late 1970s/early 1980s on, the grab for resource power has been sharply on

---

[5] For an account of the conflicting use of status power in contemporary America, see Hunter, J. D. *Culture Wars: the struggle to define America*, New York, Basic Books: 1991; see also Sennett, R., *Respect: the formation of character in an age of inequality*, Penguin Books: 2004.

[6] Piketty, T. *Capital in the Twenty-First Century*, Harvard University Press: 2014; Stiglitz, J. *The Price of Inequality*, Penguin: 2013; Milanovich, B. *The Haves and the Have-Nots*, Basic Books: 2012; Wilkinson, R. & Pickett, K. *The Spirit Level: why equality is better for everyone*, Penguin: 2010.

[7] As we will see in Chapter 7 below.

3

the rise once more. Those with much more resource power than others often seek to justify the disparity on the grounds that it was all down to their unique ability to generate or harness resources, when in fact one of the key reasons others concede an excessive share to them is that their much greater resource power puts them in an unassailable bargaining position.

The four powers outlined above are distinct. Those with executive power may find resistance from those with status power, while those with knowledge power may challenge the claims made by those with resource power. The historical goal of democracy is to equalise power so that no individual or group can seize so much of one or more of these forms of power to subjugate or exploit others. That aspiration becomes much more difficult to achieve when all those powers are not only increasingly distributed unequally, but are concentrated in one group or a strategic alliance of powerful people. Since the 1980s those with the highest concentration of resource power have been actively buying even more influence over executive power through political campaign donations and intense lobbying; increasing their knowledge power with a greater financial role in the funding of universities and other research institutions; and strengthening their status power with their extensive ownership of the media so their preferred notions of superiority and inferiority become the cultural norm.

There are three common responses to this trend. One is to dismiss it as not inherently significant on the grounds that it is more important to let the powerful get on with what they do so they can bring prosperity and stability to everyone. Another is to declare all forms of power unacceptable and call for a radical alternative where no one has authority over anything whatsoever. And the third is to recognise the pervasive damages caused by widening power inequalities but accept its inevitability. Let us look at each of them in turn.

The consequences of power inequalities

The claim that power inequalities are best ignored have of course throughout history been consistently put forward by many who have accumulated an excessive share of power. But through cultural indoctrination, those with little power have often been conditioned into overlooking such gross disparity as well. In reality, when the powerful can get away with claiming to have superior, at times unchallengeable, access to knowledge, they effectively cut off the only reliable means of testing if any knowledge claim should indeed be believed – namely, the experience of others via their testimony, observation, deliberations. When claims and counter-claims are not settled through the respective weight of empirical evidence and cogency of arguments, but by the power of a particular disputant, mistakes stand little chance of being corrected. The judgement of the powerful becomes more questionable precisely to the extent that it is shielded from being questioned. For others, if the deprivation of critical discourse should become habitual through fear or just lack of exercise, assessment of what is to be believed would everywhere degenerate into an ill-informed and arbitrary affair. The many would either blindly accept the pronouncements of the few, or secretly harbour doubt about everything they are told to believe. Irrationality would take the place of cooperative enquiry. Opportunities to improve life would be routinely missed, and errors causing avoidable suffering would persist.

Power inequalities also corrode social responsiveness. The wider the power gap, the less likely are people to learn to accommodate and respect others, or believe that none has an inherently greater or lesser claim to help from others in times of need. The increasingly powerful find that they can stand apart and all too easily get used to being able to do as they please. At best, their sense of superiority leads them to look upon the weak as an opportunity for them to cultivate their charitable disposition and donate a minute proportion of their wealth to give some succour to those at the bottom of the pile. But their conscience would rarely extend to challenging the structural injustice that leaves others in permanent disadvantage. At worst, they switch off from the plight of the have-nots, insisting that the latter have only themselves to blame for their predicament. Some might even view abusing the vulnerable as an integral part of their power and control.

As for those with declining power, they would be caught up with the pathology of marginalisation. Feeling that they are insignificant in the eyes of those far above, some would try to cope by pushing others down to give themselves a twisted sense of worthiness. By scapegoating those who could be rendered even more vulnerable, by demanding total obedience from the weakest, by threatening those who could not protect themselves, they boost their false pride through surrendering their moral decency. Others would escape instead to alternative projections of the world where mystical

5

contemplation, indulgence in mind-altering substance, or mindless consumerism is expected to fill the void left by the faded enterprise of mutual support.

Where power inequalities persist, any prospect for genuine solidarity will crumble to dust. As the powerful find that they can increasingly get away with making decisions affecting others without the latter having a meaningful say about them, the more those decisions would neglect the needs of the wider community. Even if they could resist the temptation to go for options which benefit themselves and their allies at the expense of the voiceless – which many of them would not be able to, the longer they can take their power for granted – the absence of effective means to hold them to account would lead them to make choices disconnected with the real concerns of those who have to bear the consequences.

Instead of a bond of solidarity underpinned by the everyday relationship of equal citizens who know the value of looking out for each other, people turn inward to themselves. People compete against each other to win the favour of those with ruling power, while those in control pursue, in the absence of a genuinely shared interest, a strategy of divide and conquer. Institutional arrogance of the powerful coupled with systemic resentment amongst the powerless would thus relentlessly breed destructive tension, leaving everyone with the worthless choice between an oppressive order and anarchic chaos.

Whatever the powerful elite may say, the widening of power gaps does not bring prosperity and stability to the affected communities – at the local, national or global level. Deprived neighbourhoods are neglected by the better-off who have moved away, and plagued by gangs whose violence and disrespect ruin the lives of those left behind. Towns and cities are frightened by factions stirred up by religious and racist extremists relentlessly sowing the seeds of hatred and divisiveness. Countries are denied resources to look after the old, the sick, the poor because astronomical sums have been casually gambled away by the richest in the land. Developed nations fret about refugees heading towards their borders after they have supplied arms to fuel the very conflicts from which innocent civilians are fleeing. Top military powers warn of the threats posed to global security by terrorists and rogue regimes, even as they continue to expand their own destructive capability unaccountable to the rest of the world. Life on our planet is endangered by climate change caused by business practices, which could not be sufficiently curbed while leading polluters continue to jeopardise any international agreement to take the necessary action.

Decades of research drawing on data from around the world have shown that power inequalities are directly correlated with higher incidence of violence, poorer average levels of health, lower degrees of interpersonal trust, and more widespread prejudice[8].

For people who value fair competition as a means to achieve improvements for all concerned, power inequalities would make it impossible to have a level playing field. Hard work, innovations, or responsiveness would not count as much as the rules which are loaded in favour of the powerful. Instead of everyone competing on equal terms, some would be able to squeeze concessions out of workers, suppliers, and even the regulators because of their market dominance.

Left unchecked, the spread of power inequalities would continue to push everyone affected towards an ever-worsening state of affairs. The unenviable fate of those with little power – women in traditional societies, minority groups surrounded by intolerance, non-conformist believers, the poor and the sick under the rule of anti-welfare plutocrats, dissidents under dictatorships, citizens of economically weak countries, workers and small producers at the mercy of corporate giants – is obvious for all to see. But even for those with concentrated power, having closed themselves off from cooperative learning, their judgements will become increasingly flawed.

What can be learnt from history?

The oppressive effects of power inequalities are too pervasive to be ignored. But the reactions they engender can be counter-productive. From time to time there will be some who feel that the problem of power distribution can only be solved by discarding every form of power they come across. With knowledge power, they adopt a sceptical or relativist

---

[8] See, for example, Wilkinson, R G, *The Impact of Inequality*, London, Routledge: 2005; Milanovic, B, *Worlds Apart: Measuring International Global Inequality,* Princeton, Princeton University Press: 2005; and Kawachi, I. & Kennedy, B P, *The Health of Nations: Why Inequality Is Harmful to Your Health*, New York, The New Press: 2002.

stance, and refuse to accept that anyone can ever legitimately declare any belief as correct. Individuals are to be left to think what they want, and no one should be in a position to tell them that they are mistaken on any occasion.

With status power, they reject that there should be any kind of distinction whatsoever, regardless of people's character and behaviour. Moral praise and criticism are all considered arbitrary. Similarly, executive power is to be abandoned completely, because it is inherently authoritarian, and no one can be rightly disciplined by anyone else. As for resource power, the very notion that any individual or group can lay claim to any resource is rejected. Resources may be found or produced by people, but the latter do not thereby come to own those resources.

In theory, people living in such an anarchistic world will have no one else to tell them what they should believe, who to respect or blame, what rules or commands they must follow, and what terms they need to comply with to make use of any resource they come across. In practice, there will be no agreed basis to challenge dubious claims and irrational statements, to differentiate between those worthy of respect from those deserving censure, to issue orders that rely on collective compliance to protect the common good, or to preserve resources from those who will use them up without any thought of the impact on others.

Furthermore, out of such 'anything-goes' scenario, a few will inevitably take advantage of the lack of collective safeguards and appropriate more and more for themselves until they impose a new power structure.

The debilitating experience of being marginalised by the powerful, punctured by unworkable dreams of transcending all forms of power until they are shattered by the cunning and the exploitative, can understandably leave people thinking that a few will always have much greater power over others, and one's best hope is to get along quietly without upsetting those at the pinnacle of the social hierarchy.

What history actually reveals is that power distribution fluctuates over time. People would share power equally until some try to seize much more of it for themselves. This eventually provokes a struggle to curb the unwarranted power concentration a few have managed to secure. And the contest continues through the ages, shaped by the ebbs and flows of political activism and social movements.

It is notable that after the first major encroachment on broadly even power sharing took place with the emergence of large scale social hierarchies from around 5000-3000 BC on, the injunction to treat others as we would have them treat us – now generally known as the golden rule – became a key maxim that would feature in all cultures. The threat to power equality gave rise to a universal moral response. In both its active form which calls on us to help others as we would seek help in similar circumstances, and its restraining form which reminds us not to wrong others as we would not wish to be wronged, it has a central place in the most respected texts of ancient Egypt and India; monotheistic doctrines such as Judaism, Christianity, Islam and Sikhism; and the humanist guidance of classical Greek and Chinese thinkers[9].

Embedded in ethical codes, moral tales, and religious commandments – the golden rule reminds humankind that amidst our diversity, we share a common goal in ensuring that we show the same regard for others as we want them to show to us. This means that everyone is to be accorded equal respect, and none is to be placed at the whim or mercy of someone else. The power relations of communities at all levels should therefore be structured accordingly. Exceptional circumstances, which call for executive power to be vested in any single decision-maker, should be treated precisely as exceptional with effective plans to end the temporary concentration of emergency power.

The hyper-accumulation of wealth by some has to be reversed or at least counter-balanced by adequate tax-based redistribution for all. Citizens should be routinely engaged in the exercise of collective decision making so that none becomes permanently marginalised. Attempts to deceive people into surrendering power to an elite for the sake of the latter's interests dressed up as vital economic, military or religious goals must be exposed and rejected. The basic needs of those in the weakest position must never be passed over in any trade-off to satisfy the demands of the strong. The capacity for whistle-blowing by the few and sustained protesting by the many must be reinforced and built into the machinery of civic vigilance. In short, exclusion and domination should be progressively displaced by the

---

[9] Kainz, H P, *Ethics in Context*, Basingstoke: Macmillan Press, 1988, contains examples of 'golden rule' sayings from different cultures (pp.46-45). An extensive list of examples can also be found at http://en.wikipedia.org/wiki/Ethic_of_reciprocity.

development of more inclusive community life for all[10].

Many find this challenge daunting, if not impossible. Faced with the entrenched position of the powerful, it is easy to believe that the concentration of power is not just unavoidable, but irreversible. Precisely because the power gap has widened, the powerful would be less and less inclined to give way, while others are powerless precisely to the extent that they cannot challenge the status quo. Instead of tackling the problem of power imbalance, people are then told to dwell exclusively on the moral deficiencies of particular individuals or groups (punishing them severely if they had little power, or beseeching them earnestly if they were powerful), while at the same time accept the inevitability, even the sanctity, of power divisions such that reciprocity gives way permanently to an asymmetric relationship – the disadvantaged shall act out of deference or fear to ensure they are not even worse off, and the privileged shall act out of their generosity or mercy in granting a few small concessions.

No wonder throughout history large numbers resign themselves to living under prevailing power structures, because it is drummed into them that significant changes could never be achieved.

In reality, the progressive struggle to make communities more inclusive has periodically succeeded in reining in the powerful without conceding to new forms of power concentration. The key has been to build alliances and power-sharing arrangements so that collaboration of all on equal terms takes the place of the self-centred decisions of a few. It takes commitment to raise awareness of how unjust distribution of power could be reformed, and organise collective support to bring about those reforms. And over time, with the accumulating efforts of diverse advocates, power relations that are more balanced and thus conducive to reciprocity are attained. At different points, some would query the epistemological

---

[10] For a more extensive discussion of the inclusive model of social and political reform, see, Donnison, D, *A Radical Agenda: After the New Right and the Old Left*, London, Rivers Oram Press: 1991; Selznick, P, *Moral Commonwealth,* University of California Press: 1992; Tam, H, *Communitarianism: a new agenda for politics and citizenship*, New York University Press: 1998; Levine, P, *The New Progressive Era*, Rowman & Littlefield: 2000; and Bellah, R & Sullivan W, 'Cultural Resources for a Progressive Alternative', in Tam, H. (ed) *Progressive Politics in the Global Age*, Cambridge, Polity: 2001.

authority of dogmatists, and open up the field of knowledge to wider participation; some would question the moral authority of edicts and traditions that neglect the interests of those with little power, and promote the equal respect for all; and others would challenge the executive authority of leaders to make unaccountable decisions, and introduce more power sharing. Empiricists, rationalists, humanists, civic republicans, liberals, socialists, cooperative pioneers, progressives, democrats – they all had a part to play.

History shows that we should neither bow down to the powerful nor throw all power structures overboard. We need inclusive and cooperative power relations so that together we can expand the legitimate horizons of shared knowledge, rely on executive decision-making to sustain collective working, differentiate moral status according to the genuinely beneficial or harmful actions by different people, and secure enough resources to meet our needs and wants[11].

In the following chapters we will look at how, from the time of ancient tyrannical regimes to the contemporary global plutocracy, the powerful – acting brazenly or behind a deceptively benign mask – have tried to secure passive submission to their rule, and most importantly, what had been done to counter their attempts at domination. For civic activists, progressive reformists, and democratic campaigners everywhere, it is vital that we do not forget the pitfalls and breakthroughs of the past, lest we forego the chance of being better prepared to tackle the many oppressively divisive arrangements which are still with us today.

---

[11] For an interesting exposition of how different parts of the world have through history developed different levels of capacity to generate resources in response to changing circumstances, see Morris, I. *Why the West Rules – For Now*, London, Profile Books: 2011.

# Chapter 2
# The Origins of Power Concentration:
# Pre-history to 10<sup>th</sup> century AD

The roots of oppressive power

To understand how power which was spread evenly amongst small groups of people could become concentrated in an elite atop a vast hierarchy, we need to go back to the time when the opportunities to widen power inequalities were first discovered and rapidly exploited. Between 5000 and 3000 BC, human beings who had previously lived in separate hunter-gatherer groups with relatively minor power differences between their members were increasingly subsumed into large agriculture-based civilisations, which led to the growth of rigid and top-down social hierarchies[12]. The productive capacity of large-scale occupation and cultivation of land far outstripped what individual groups seeking food and shelter on a more ad hoc basis could ever manage.

However, the benefits from the more systematic pooling and organisation of resources were channelled more and more to the tiny minority who had secured positions of authority. These few who had by their military prowess or commanding persona succeeded in merging disparate groups into kingdoms and empires sought to consolidate their position by demanding total acceptance of their rule. In time, the alpha male became the overbearing norm at every level – the conqueror over his vanquished enemies, the tribal lord over his subjects, the master over his slaves, and the husband/father over his wife and children.

At this point, human beings had not yet developed the ability to examine critically how they could reshape their lives for the better. They found themselves in a prevailing form of life, and their instinct was to stick with it. They did not ponder the fact that some animals lived without submitting totally to a leader, others cooperated on an equal basis without any one taking advantage of someone else's hard work just by virtue of their

---

[12] See Erdal D. & Whiten A. 'Egalitarianism and Machiavellian Intelligence in Human Evolution', in Mellars P. & Gibson K. (ed), *Modelling the early human mind*, Cambridge, McDonald Institute Monographs: 1996, 139-160; and Sahlins M. *Stone Age Economics*, London, Tavistock: 1974.

size or strength, or that even the smallest insects like ants and bees could swarm formidable predators to death by acting in concert against their powerful foes. Ignorance underpinned the rising authoritarian social order.

However, given homo sapiens' cerebral potential, it was only a matter of time before some people started to reflect on how they were made to live, and consider what alternatives there might be. And at some point following the emergence of the ancient civilizations, the commands of an alpha male elicited, not a submissive nod, but an inquisitive "why", and the seeds for challenges to power inequalities were sown.

Instead of following orders in the expected manner, people began to reflect on possible alternatives. Although many pioneering enquirers were doubtless dealt a fatal blow for their insolence, not even the vicious rage of chieftains and kings could completely wipe out the propensity of the enquiring mind. And the more opportunities there were for people to show how thinking through issues led to better outcomes – these could be a superior harvest, more resilient fortification, shortened journeys to find food or shelter – the more the case for critical deliberations was made.

Unfortunately, having the capacity to consider what would be better for all concerned does not mean that it would be developed or utilised. There were too many factors holding back those who already had positions of power from tolerating, let alone supporting, the spread of cooperative intelligence. First of all, their arrogance, which had over the years relentlessly expanded without being challenged, led them to doubt that anyone else could improve on the decisions they made. Then their selfish preoccupation with getting what they wanted made them disdainful of contemplating that the interests of other people had to be taken into account. Finally, their suspicion that opening the 'floodgate' of discussions would lead to chaos meant that for them dissent must be met with the swiftest suppression.

So the first signs of the established order being questioned served as a catalyst, not for a leap in human development towards more inclusive and rational deliberations, but for an authoritarian reaction against the spread of intelligent enquiry. Since efforts to strike down every enquiring voice were neither efficient nor sustainable – curiosity was infectious and a leader could not afford to slay too many of his followers – the powerful came up with psychological tools to deflect the mind from seeking to examine how things were, or worse still, to reflect on how different they could be.

Given that human beings had generally grasped that reciprocal relationship ought to be the norm if they were to able to count on mutual support and avoid anyone being able to take unfair advantage of others, the most blatant distortion of that relationship had to be presented as something justified by a higher, deeper, unquestionable force. Playing on primal fears of the unknown and a basic yearning for security, the apologists for the powerful weaved a set of related ideas that were to become prominent from the Middle East, the Mediterranean, to India and the Orient. Central to them is the generalisation of people's basic inclination to rely on a powerful parental figure or tribal leader to look after them, to proclaiming that all must put their faith in a supreme ruler whose absolute authority over everything must be accepted.

For example, from as early as 4000 BC on, the Sumerian elite devised a system wherein monumental buildings were erected to enable sacrifices to be made to invisible gods who must be placated. The masses must bow down and serve the rulers lest the wrath of the powerful be incurred and destruction ensued. The land and other riches did not belong to the Sumerian kings – lest jealousy was aroused and questions raised about their distribution – but were held in trust by them on behalf of the gods, who were too terrifying to be questioned.

By 3200 BC, the rulers of the vast Egyptian kingdom had gone one step further and declared that they were, not mere representatives of gods, but gods themselves. Justice was defined as 'what Pharaoh loves', and evil as 'what Pharaoh hates'. They needed no code of law because they were omniscient. Whereas the general population lived in mud huts and were destined to age and die with no after life, the divine rulers commanded all to provide labour and resources to contribute to their luxurious existence both on earth and beyond – when after their physical death, they would enter the high and majestic pyramids and move to an eternal state of being.

The pattern of the powerless pressed to submit meekly to whatever was asked of them was to proliferate across the ancient world. Judaism's core concern with reciprocal respect between human beings was undermined by the notion that obedience without question to a higher authority was absolutely expected. Adam was punished for disobeying strict instruction to curb his curiosity. Abraham was rewarded because even when asked to kill his own son, he did not question the order. Noah was spared because he was utterly faithful to his God, but everyone else was to be drowned without mercy. A culture of submissiveness was thus engendered.

Hinduism's recognition of the centrality of reciprocal treatment was constrained by the power gaps between distinct castes. The higher caste, which was limited to those born into it in this life, would not have to worry about having a much better quality of life than others – for they had earned it in a 'previous' life. For those born into the lower castes, they must behave according to conventional code of following orders from above. It would in any case be their own doing in a 'past' life that they ended up in a lower caste. So long as they refrained from challenging their superiors, and remained meekly compliant, they could gradually climb up the social hierarchy through successive reincarnations after their death.

Even amongst the more secular minded people such as the Greeks to the west and the Chinese to the east, myths and folklore reinforced the value of not seeking answers beyond what one had been told. Generations of ancient Greeks were brought up on stories about the untold woes of opening up Pandora's Box – cursed were those who defied orders to leave things alone; or about Prometheus chained to eternal suffering for daring to pass on to humankind the critical knowledge of how to make use of fire.

The ideology of obedience

Indeed by the sixth century BC, China had produced the world's first comprehensive ideology of obedience which, stripping away all supernatural trimmings, set out why for the sake of harmony and order, those who were at the subservient end of any power relations should fully accept their duty to follow the lead of those in the commanding position. Its chief exponent, Confucius (551-479 BC), reaffirmed the importance of the golden rule of reciprocity, but for the sake of preserving a rigid hierarchy, he insisted that human relationships from the basic family unit to the vast imperial order required people to fulfil their assigned roles without question. In so doing, he introduced two sets of asymmetrical duties. Children, wives, peasants, servants, subjects, were to obey without question, respectively, their parents, husbands, landlords, masters, and rulers. The latter were to take care of the former to the best of their ability. Without the total obedience of those with the subordinate roles, those with the responsibilities to lead would not be able to secure a stable and comfortable life for them. So leaders must be relieved of doubts and questions to ensure they would not be distracted from their mission. Otherwise everyone would suffer from disorientation and disintegration. According to Confucius, this rigid structure of obedience, reinforced by formal rituals, was the key to the stability and prosperity of past regimes. Any departure from it would risk serious harm for everyone[13].

This ideology requires people to have a clear understanding and acceptance of their assigned role, on the basis of which they would devote themselves to doing well what is expected of them – either learning to issue firm and timely commands to deal with problems, or acting as one is told regardless of the circumstances one finds oneself in. But since this 'reciprocity' is asymmetrical, the Confucian doctrine has an in-built imbalance which inevitably tilts towards oppressive power concentration. No one could judge the powerful on whether they are doing their job of looking after the interests of all, except for the powerful themselves. If those lower down should question their wisdom or their effectiveness, they are branded as subverting the greater order and dismissed as unworthy. The powerful could therefore veer towards stupidity, selfishness, negligence, cruelty without any countering force to set things right. Worse still, they could continue to believe sincerely that they were doing what ought to be done for the greater good – as so many of them have throughout history come to equate their own whims with the supreme value for others.

By contrast, those with little power are told they should never question their superiors' actions, let alone organise themselves into reversing those actions. If they should feel that they were mistreated, or

---

[13] Interpretations of Confucius are generally divided between those who seek to defend him as a cultural icon and those who question the impact his teachings had on China, especially amongst the poor and socially disadvantaged groups like women. For a general introduction, see Yao, Xinzhong *An Introduction to Confucianism*, Cambridge, Cambridge University Press: 2000.

that opportunities were missed or mishandled by those to whom they had to entrust their fate, they had no choice but to endure passively. Unless they were prepared to break the rules and challenge their 'superiors', they would just have to put up with their lot, however bad it had become.

The Confucian ideology shows that cultivating the habit of quiet submission can be a most effective way to block the development of the potential capacity to question the reasonableness of what the powerful commands. But it would only work if continuous submissiveness delivers something other than intolerable suffering. By the fifth century BC, the collapse of effective rule under the Zhou Dynasty was leading to famine and civil war across China. Confucius had focused exclusively on getting people to remain compliant to the hierarchical order before them. He had nothing else to offer when people began to lose faith in the social and political order of the day. What he did encourage, given his fundamental premise of not challenging those with power, was the restoration of order through the establishment of another, more stable, and even more unquestionable regime.

What this doctrine of obedience tends to deliver is therefore a culture which maximises the chance for the powerful to retain the status quo. It breaks down when those at the top are so appallingly ineffective that the downtrodden are finally driven to doubt their leadership and undermine their hold on power. With nothing in place to guide the reasoned resolution of disputes, or deliberative selection of alternative decision-makers, the system breaks down into chaos, until a new set of powerful figures take control, promising that they would fulfil their duty to look after those propping up their regime. And another dynastic cycle commences. Unless there is an intellectual breakthrough which points to another way to distribute and manage power in society, the superficial stability of this supposedly benign form of authoritarianism, reinforced by the fear of anarchic strife, would go on keeping the mass of humankind docile as sheep, and enthroning wolves in shepherds' clothing.

As a potent formula that the powerful can use to marginalise their opponents, it has been retained and updated over centuries, in China and other parts of the world too[14], to not only keep the have-nots in their

---

[14] It was to appear over 2000 years later in Thomas Hobbes' *Leviathan*.

place, but make them feel grateful for the unyielding rule of their superiors. If reciprocity was to be respected in practice as well as in theory, this outlook must be challenged and overthrown.

## The first challengers

Confucianism encapsulated the authoritarian ethos wherein power would always be concentrated in an unquestionable leader who commanded total obedience. His immediate subordinates, bowing to his absolute authority, could in turn demand utter subservience from those who were beneath them in the hierarchy.

This pattern looked set to continue throughout the world until two of its key champions suffered a reversal of fortune. First, the decline of the Zhou rulers in China reached such a low point that by 500 BC states across China were developing their own policies without any reference to an overarching sovereign. They did as they pleased and they encouraged people with new ideas to put them forward so that they could learn about things that might give them an advantage in competing against other rival states. Secondly, the failure of the Persian Achaemenid Empire to crush the Greeks, especially the Athenians who had embraced Cleisthenes' (570-508 BC) reforms to distribute decision-making powers of the state to male adults with the status of citizens, meant that autocratic rule was unable to stop a radical experiment in democracy. Under these conditions, the first wave of resistance to power imbalance began to challenge how judgements for the collective good should be made.

In China, Mozi (c. 479-399 BC) led the challenge[15]. His family, unlike Confucius', was from the labouring class, and for him there was no nostalgic yearning for an aristocratic past when everyone allegedly had a good life following the traditions laid down by the powerful. Instead of grounding the legitimacy of ideas concerning how society should function exclusively on what some wise lord or king had said in the past, Mozi formulated a social philosophy, which took reciprocity as an essential guide to how people

---

[15] There are few books on Mozi (Mo Tze, or Mo Ti) in English. A good introduction can be found in Mei Yi-Pao's aptly named *Motse, the neglected rival of Confucius*, Hyperion Press: 1976. Mei also translated the Book of Mo Tze under the title of *The Ethical and Political Works of Motse*, London, Arthur Probsthain: 1929.

should live. Individuals and groups sought their own wellbeing, but their pursuit would be so much more effective if they not only avoided undermining each other's efforts, but if they actively lent support to one another. On this basis, he argued that the acceptability of any policy proposition should be subject to three tests.

First came the test of past experience. Sages, kings, soldiers, labourers, all had their experiences of different social arrangements and practices. What they found to be helpful to achieving a satisfactory life and what they found to be a hindrance should be taken into account. On this test, Mozi found that many of the proposals championed by the Confucians were not supported by past experience. The elaborate rituals the Confucians wanted to reinforce, for example, were not in fact always valued by past generations. The people of the earlier age of Hsia recorded favourable accounts of much simpler rites, which allowed people to show respect without having to use up scarce resources, especially amongst the poor, on showy ceremony. People were more inclined to behave in a dignified and mutually supportive way towards each other when they were not made to feel that only those who could afford lavish practices (matrimonial, burial, etc) could command the respect of others.

The second test consisted of current testimony. What people said, regardless of their social background, should be considered in deciding if any proposal was beneficial or not overall. If someone with authority proclaimed his way of fortifying a city against attack was the best way, and yet people involved with defending cities testified to key weaknesses of the approach, their testimony must be given weight. To allow someone to declare anything – a doctrine, a political demand, a custom – as indisputable solely on account of their powerful position would be conceding to a distortion of the truth, which must be open to the views of all if an objective decision on a claim's legitimacy is to be reached. Mozi did not just advocate open and fair deliberations as a way to settle disputes, he met with the rulers of different states to persuade them to embrace reasoned resolution instead of military aggression. For him, the offensive use of force removed any real prospect of genuine collaboration to achieve a better life. When states refused to listen to him and launched their attacks, Mozi and his supporters would directly assist with the defence of those coming under siege.

The third test built in utilitarian checks from future experience. Even if past records and current testimony suggested that a particular policy or practice would deliver improvements for people, it still would not rule it out from being changed if its impact in the future proves to be negative. On Mozi's analysis, no one can have the authority to exclude future findings from having a corrective role in on-going decision making. When the three tests are combined, we have a progressive philosophy which moved the authority to rule over people from an unquestionable elite to the continuously evolving experience of the people themselves. No one, on the evidence available to everyone, was infallible, therefore all judgements must be subject to objective consideration. And if no one can arbitrarily claim that they and their families alone should be given certain privileged position without earning them in a fair way, resources and respect would be expected to be spread in a much more even way across the whole society.

Mozi argued that the overarching principle for regulating our behaviour must be that of 'universal love' – meaning that no one should be deprived of the concern and care needed to give them a decent quality of life, because that is how each of us would want to be treated ourselves. Anyone seeking to place their demands above others must accordingly be challenged. A leader who was pressed by Mozi to rethink his approach insisted that he was the wiser one as Mozi would waste his life trying to get everyone to treat each other with reciprocal concern, whereas he would continue with looking out for himself regardless of the effects on others. Mozi told him that such an outlook was self-defeating – the leader must either let others know his attitude and live with the consequence that they would treat him with mistrust and disdain, or he must live a lie and not show his dissent from the principle of universal love.

Within a single generation, Mozi's school had become the main rival to the Confucians. Mohist adherents travelled extensively in China to spread their reform message. The Confucians detested them for suggesting the needs of all should be responded to with equal respect, instead of bowing down to the hierarchical establishment. Leaders of competing states found little of use in Mohist teachings and much to irritate them in the Mohist practice of providing armed protection where necessary to defend the weak from attempted invasions by the strong.

Mozi and his followers developed the first clear model for challenging power inequalities. Most importantly, they had formulated a coherent set of ideas on why people should strive to support each other to improve their wellbeing, by opposing the attempts of any to dominate others, and enabling everyone's experience to count in deciding what policies were to be pursued. On the basis of this philosophy, they set out a programme of action which notably included promoting the value of appointing capable individuals to key decision-making positions regardless of their class background; executing counter-offensive campaigns against any form of military aggression; and promoting to everyone the modest use of scarce resources. The last of these was particularly significant against the background of prevailing customs, which the Confucians celebrated as integral to upholding traditional values. For example, the Confucians insisted that filial piety must be reflected in lavish funeral arrangements, with the most expensive wood used for coffins, and long periods of mourning with all productive activities suspended. The Mohists sought to persuade ordinary people to ignore such notions because they would serve little purpose other than making the poor poorer still. They criticised the wealthy for indulging in such extravagant practices when they could save those resources for the good of society as a whole.

Mozi himself was acknowledged even by his Confucian critics, as someone who was utterly dedicated to pursuing the goal of a better life for all – even if they disagreed with his reasoning. They admired his courage in standing up to princes and their armies, and recognised his visible commitment in travelling to different parts of China to explain his doctrines. In doing this, the Mohist leadership was backed by a robust organisation so that actions were prioritised, planned and energetically followed through. Mohist followers were imbued with the culture of serving the greater good and reinforced each other in tackling the obstacles thrown in their way.

They were not only up against the Confucians who advocated the revival of rigid Zhou rites and hierarchies, they also had to contend with the Taoists, who suggested the best course of action was to retreat into a small community and disengage from challenging the powerful. Taoist teachings appealed to those who wanted to think only about their own peace of mind, and were all too ready to leave issues of injustice to others to worry about. There were also those (known as the 'Legalists') who declared that the strong should impose themselves on others and maintain their rule with oppressive laws and ruthless enforcement.

Against these rivals, the Mohists adapted the common cultural concept of 'Tien' (which could be interpreted variously as 'the heavenly sky', 'the power above' or 'god') and explicated it in terms of the will to secure universal love. Contrary to the authoritarian practice of claiming that the masses must do whatever 'God' asked them to do, and that the powerful on earth were the anointed interpreters of what 'God' had to say, the Mohists asserted that everyone could know the will of Tien by assessing what in any given situation would most promote universal love. Anyone trying to suggest that heaven above wanted people to serve the privileged few as opposed to the weak and disadvantaged would be exposed as charlatans. The Mohists turned the traditional tendency to bow before the establishment's use of religious language into a challenge to the establishment that ordinary people could deploy.

The Athenians also turned traditional hierarchical practices upside down[16]. Around the time the Mohists were spreading their doctrines across China, their progressive counterparts in the West, having survived the Persian attempt to subjugate them, were consolidating their democratic constitution so that, in the words of Pericles (495-429 BC), "power is in the hands not of a minority but of the whole people. ... Here each individual is interested not only in his own affairs but in the affairs of the state as well: even those who are mostly occupied with their own business are extremely well-informed on general politics – this is a peculiarity of ours: we do not say that a man who takes no interest in politics is a man who minds his own business; we say that he has no business here at all. We Athenians, in our own persons, take our decisions on policy or submit them to proper discussions: for we do not think that there is an incompatibility between words and deeds; the worst thing is to rush into action before the consequences have been properly debated."

While the Athenian democrats did not articulate their ideas in a cogently written work like the Book of Mozi, the thinking underpinning their political reforms was widely shared amongst the city's residents. Solidarity and mutual aid were best strengthened by giving all citizens an equal right to participate in decision-making concerning the policies of the state and the selection of executives to act on behalf of the people. The wealthy could not dominate others on account of their possessions. The poor could contribute

---

[16] Two contrasting introductions to Athenian democratic politics can be found in: Farrar, C, *The Origins of Democratic Thinking: the invention of politics in classical Athens*, Cambridge University Press: 1988; and Ober, J, *Mass and Elite in Democratic Athens: rhetoric, ideology and the power of the people*, Princeton University Press: 1989.

their ideas to debates regardless of their economic status. This outlook was systematically translated into a political system that spread power across the polity and guaranteed the opportunities for all to fulfil their civic duties, including payment to take particular public offices for those who could not otherwise afford to do so. Under the leadership of civic champions like Pericles, successive generations of Athenians took pride in their unique system of governance and played their part in building up a state organisation that would operate effectively to sustain the city and counter any external threat against its continuation.

While the Mohists were still criss-crossing China in search of a state to adopt their ideas for developing inclusive communities, Athens had established itself as a most promising exemplar of what a commitment to open cooperation to achieve improvement for all, based on empirical reasoning, could mean in practice. The scope for rulers or a wealthy elite to order others to do their bidding was far more limited in Athens than anywhere else in the world. Citizens knew they had a guaranteed part to play in deciding the policies of their state. Furthermore they knew they could make enquiries and discuss issues amongst themselves. In this spirit they pursued innovations without fear of arbitrary restrictions from a top down hierarchy. In science, literature, arts, commerce, technology they demonstrated how, being liberated from the oppressive power inequalities of old authoritarian societies, they could steadily better the quality of life for everyone.

However, power inequalities could only be held in check if the commitment to building reciprocal relationships was consistently applied and sustained over time. Athens had advanced beyond virtually all others in its days in terms of its redistribution of power and responsibility. But it needed to go further and become even more inclusive, and by the fourth century BC, its limitations had become terminally apparent.

Why the reform momentum was lost

Instead of questioning the adequacy of its arrangements in empowering all affected by its decisions to cooperate as rational equals, Athens became complacent. Not only were women and slaves overlooked for the part that they could and should play, the increase in commerce raised a new problem of power distribution which Athens also ignored. Leaders of business enterprise did not model their decision-making structures after their democratic state. Where they were able to amass greater wealth than other citizens, they had no obligation to share their resources with them. For the great majority of the people, in a manner that would resurface in the future whenever similar circumstances arose, the sense of becoming less powerful and important in their own country had to be countered by asserting themselves abroad.

Some of Athens' more insightful minds were acutely aware of the need to cultivate a deeper democratic culture. For them, simply inviting individuals to express their preferences over policy options without other factors being taken into account could lead to highly damaging outcomes. Euripides (484-407 BC), for example, in his play *The Suppliant Women*, made clear that while Athenian democracy was superior to authoritarian forms of society, it was not developed enough to prevent people stirred by feelings of fanned outrage and false pride to launch wars destined to be destructive for all concerned. The play was specifically about Athenians voting to attack Thebes, which had refused to release for burial two dead Athenian soldiers (who had joined in a previous attack by another state on that city). The underlying point was that democracy needed to be grounded on rational deliberations, not blind passions.

Another Athenian, Socrates (470-399 BC), raised the question of how communities could rely on the mere exchange of opinions to reach the correct answers on any serious matters. Such opinions might be poorly thought through, or they could be shaped by others' flawed reasoning, or worse, manipulative persuasion. Socrates engaged students and experts alike in examining many basic assumptions in public discourse and demonstrated that people were not always clear what actually justified their assertions. For example, when pressed, no one seemed able to explain what would render any given trait virtuous, just, praiseworthy, and so on. Socrates' argument was that unless we have a reasonable basis for applying key evaluative concepts to different circumstances, the decisions of the public might be as arbitrary as any individual ruler's.

Instead of responding to Socrates' challenge to question the foundations of and thus strengthen the development of democracy, the Athenian establishment adopted an oppressive stance and declared him a corruptive influence on the youth of the city, a crime punishable by death. Although he was given a chance to escape with his life if he would call on the financial intervention of a few aristocratic friends, Socrates insisted that his acceptance of democratic procedures was never in doubt, and he famously fulfilled his death sentence by drinking hemlock. Athenians' refusal to examine democracy along Socratic lines revealed the fragility of the system. For democracy to be a progressive force in cultivating and applying the cooperative intelligence of people who live by its decisions, it has to maintain a commitment to develop its critical and inclusive capability. The Athenians had embarked on a radical path of democratisation, but in arrogantly believing that there was no further room for improvement – in terms of safeguarding public discussions against irrational or deceptive proposals, letting women and those they enslaved to participate in civic decisions, or responding constructively to the criticisms formulated by its leading minds – they fell into the old authoritarian trap of seeking to freeze prevailing power distribution.

Most critically, Athenians neglected to apply the principle they upheld in their domestic politics to their foreign relations. 'Let no one be too powerful over the rest' had been their guiding tenet. Yet, as their naval and commercial power grew, along with their tendency to launch attacks on other states over petty and serious disagreements alike, they were in danger of becoming in the Hellenistic world precisely the kind of intolerable tyrant they would take up arms against in Athens itself. People would accept the loss of power equilibrium only if they were convinced it was absolutely irrecoverable. For Sparta, Thebes and other Greek rivals, they would rather fight to the death than allow that to become the status quo.

The Athenian drift away from developing its engagement with its own residents and the people of other states on a more rationally deliberative basis, towards a jingoistic, relentlessly belligerent outlook, was to have fatal consequences for the young democracy. Intellectually, the leadership went from Socrates, a champion of rational public discourse, to Plato (427-347 BC), the most influential amongst Socrates' pupils, and an uncompromising critic of democratic politics[17]. For Plato, knowledge claims could only be properly assessed by an exclusive group of individuals who uniquely possess

---

[17] Scholars do not readily agree on how Socrates' views should be interpreted in a distinct manner from the presentation of Socrates in Plato's writings. But it is worth consulting Guthrie, WKC, *Socrates*, Cambridge University Press: 1971; and Vlastos, G. *Socrates: ironist and moral philosopher*, Cambridge University Press: 1991.

the ability to make such judgements. For that reason, he rejected the democratic reliance on the common people as wholly inappropriate. For him, only the few with a special grasp of what truth was should have executive and knowledge power.

In the absence of any Mohist form of epistemological critique, a Platonic ruler would simply be anyone who manages to proclaim himself a philosopher-king. If the people in general were excluded from debating the real merits of different claimants to the mantle of Platonic wisdom, it would not be reasoning but tactical power play that secured the right to pass judgement on others. The slide towards arbitrary rule would be inevitable.

Politically, Athens failed to spread the ideal of democracy and became increasingly caught up in military misadventure. Within a century of Socrates' execution, Athenians were so weakened by their interminable battles with neighbouring states they succumbed to the Macedonian invasion, and lost their proud independence to a monarchical ruler who had no time for power-sharing with anyone. The culture of democratic decision-making was to be buried for the next two thousand years.

While Socrates' attempt to improve the process of public discourse came to nothing, Mozi's vision for an inclusive and cooperative society was also ultimately shattered. The Mohists were so committed to their cause that they would defend to the death – all too literally – people who were threatened by the invading troops of any aggressor.

They did not manage to win over the wider populace about how they could contribute to their own improvement, or convince them of the need to redistribute power in society. They allowed the Confucians to portray them as insensitive radicals who would destroy all that was precious in traditional culture. In their own organisation, they embraced an increasingly strict command-and-control system. They became more of a heroic rescue unit than everyday advocates for reform. After Mozi's own death, his followers were gradually wiped out by the military campaigns the Mohist leadership was determined to fight against overwhelming odds. And along with their demise, the Mohist philosophy was extinguished.

Like the Athenians, the Mohists were pioneers in opposing unjust power distribution. They were outnumbered by forces which had little sympathy with their views, and they ended up adopting the erroneous stance that if they stuck rigidly to their approaches – ruling out intellectual refinement of their core ideas or more inclusive alliances with people outside their tent – they would triumph. The beachhead they established in the struggle for more inclusive communities was remarkable in opening up the possibility of a morally worthy and philosophically sound alternative to the pervasive subjugation characteristic of power hierarchies. But without rallying enough support to establish a long term power base, or possessing sufficient foresight to develop their thinking to meet future challenges, they were too easily marginalised and then erased from history.

## Consolidation of the authoritarian ethos

From the fourth century BC on, authoritarianism struck back with a vengeance. It imposed the leadership of an alpha male as the supreme form of authority. Many were to be – to this day – completely in awe of these all-powerful figures. Alexander (356-323 BC) was branded *the Great* for imposing *his* rule over much of the West; and in establishing the most extensive empire in the East, Qin Shi Huang (260-210 BC) has been honoured as the *First Emperor* of China ever since. Under these two warrior-rulers and the regimes of the Roman and Han Empires, which succeeded them respectively, there was no clash of civilisations but a convergence towards the ethos of power concentration.

In the five hundred years leading up to the end of the first century AD, this ethos permeated authoritarian rule in every major civilisation. It was characterised by five inter-locking components. First and foremost, it was militarily aggressive against the 'others' – barbarians to be conquered and subdued. The shame of having to be utterly subservient before one's absolute ruler was to be displaced by the pride from being superior to the defeated foreign foes. Han Wu Ti (140-87 BC) and Julius Caesar (102-44 BC) exemplified the reflected glory the masses derived from the exploits of outstanding military leaders. This in turn underpinned the protection racket presented as a tax-for-security system. The powerful would warn the weak that unless they paid up they would suffer the consequences. Diametrically opposed to the concept of progressive taxation, extortionist state revenue demands were directed most heavily at those least able to meet them.

Thirdly, it would monopolise the knowledge establishment. While Qin Shi Huang used the crude method of burning all books he did not approve and burying when still alive scholars who were remotely critical of him, the Han emperors used a more sophisticated approach. Under Han Wu Ti, Confucianism – the conservative ideology of obedience – was adopted as the official state doctrine. The elements which emphasized the need for 'superiors' to be kind and supportive were pushed to the margins, whereas the importance of giving unquestioned obedience to those placed above one was made central. Nothing but Confucian ideas and writings would be promoted, and to obtain positions of power in the state bureaucracy, one would have to pass examinations based on the state doctrine.

Constantine (280-337 AD) was to lead the Roman Empire down a similar path by ending the simplistic persecution of Christians and co-opting their religion as the official religion of the state. The Christian love for the weak and vulnerable became a matter for individual kindness, while the absolute subordination to an almighty power who backed the ruling regime formed the basis of a much more thorough form of mass control. To go against the regime was to incur the wrath of God and reap the curse of eternal suffering.

Fourthly, it embraced escapist outlets for the ignorant masses. The ruling elites in Rome and China understood that authoritarian control would meet with less resistance if people were diverted into activities which numbed their political consciousness. Superstitious pilgrimage, colourful public entertainment, mystical contemplation, pursuit of private pleasures, were given due space to flourish. Epicureans in the west and Taoists in the east encouraged people to withdraw from public life to seek enjoyments in their own spheres of life. Those in charge of the public realm were more than content to see potential opposition drained of its support.

Finally, it celebrated the alpha male authoritarian ethos as the most sanctified social custom. Down the chain of command, an unchallengeable male would be installed as a mini-absolute ruler of his given domain in the imperial service, in the running of a town or village, right down to every household. Women, servants, slaves were to be the submissive fodder to give even those men at the lowest levels of the rigid hierarchy a sense of control and self-esteem. Departure from this code would be severely dealt with.

In the form outlined above, authoritarianism increasingly tightened its grip until there was no conceivable room left for any hint of opposition. Two flickers of defiance showed that the intellectual capacity was still there to map out an alternative, but also that they could so easily be snuffed out. Caesar's threat to the old Roman republican commitment to prevent any single man from holding absolute power over others was challenged by Cicero (106-43 BC) who well understood that the ethos of free enquiry and debates – essential to differentiate truth from falsehood in any discourse, above all, in any judgement concerning the public realm – was not compatible with the rule of an unquestionable individual[18]. The assassination of Caesar, however, was not enough to prevent those who wanted to pursue authoritarian rule from continuing their insidious work. Cicero, Brutus, and other republicans were no match for the combined ruthlessness of Mark Anthony and Augustus (63 BC – 14 AD), who sanctioned Cicero's murder before he eventually established his own status as the supreme Emperor of Rome.

The attempt to reform the authoritarian hierarchy under the Han Dynasty was taken up by another philosopher-politician, Wang Mang (45 BC – 23 AD), who like Cicero, had a substantial reputation of being a learned scholar, but unlike the Roman, he actually managed to take control of the state apparatus to introduce his reform programme. In 8 AD, having already been appointed regent to the infant Han Emperor Ying, Wang Mang took over the throne and proclaimed a new Dynasty under the title of Hsin (meaning 'New')[19]. His reform mission was set out for all to see. He wanted to end the extreme inequalities in society which had fuelled the exploitation of the weak by the powerful at every level. To do this, he put forward a comprehensive programme of land redistribution. The land to be allocated to each farming family would be enough for a decent livelihood, with roughly one 'ching' (approximately

---

[18] Critics of Cicero tend to argue that he was merely defending the interests of the aristocratic class, but in the context of facing up to the threat of greater power concentration advanced by Caesar, his vocal opposition was of central significance. See Rawson, E. *Cicero: A Portrait*, London, Bristol Classical Press: 1983; and Cicero, *On Duties* (ed. by Griffin, MT & Atkins, EM) Cambridge University Press: 1991.

[19] Opinions on Wang Mang have always been divided. For example, he was credited with seeking real improvements for the people (even if he failed) in Li, D.J. *The Ageless Chinese: a history*, London: JM Dent & Sons: 1965 (pp.117-121); by contrast, even his motive was questioned in Eberhard, W *A History of China*, University of California Press: 1977 (pp.91-95).

15 acres) for a family with up to eight male members. Any excess land would be transferred to others with greater need. Landlords neglecting to make use of the land in their possession would be taxed triply. The trading of slaves would cease. Local magistrates would ensure that anyone without a means of earning a living through no fault of their own would be clothed and fed. Excessive price fluctuations caused by profit seekers would be countered by government regulation.

Wang Mang understood better than Cicero that to tackle the unjust distribution of power in society, it was not enough to prevent its concentration in one single individual, but it had to be reversed at every level and every sphere in society. However, whereas Cicero grasped the need for strategic alliance to oppose vested interests – even if the alliance he forged failed to win the day – Wang Mang made the critical mistake, sadly to be repeated by others, of thinking he could achieve progressive goals by authoritarian means. Relying solely on the power he had as Emperor, he ordered his reforms to be implemented.

He did not embark on winning the hearts and minds of the people who were easily persuaded that what the 'usurper' (as he was swiftly presented by those who would lose power under his proposals) put forward would harm them. Instead of strong allies who could help advance his cause, he rapidly made too many powerful people his sworn enemies. Concentrating on his grand scheme for a new society, he neglected to learn from the difficulties it was encountering in practice, especially the abuse by local officials who simply siphoned off tax revenue to benefit themselves instead of funding the envisioned welfare provisions.

In 23 AD Wang Mang suffered the same fate as Cicero. He was murdered by troops loyal to Liu Hsiu (6-57 AD), who restored the Liu's family imperial franchise and revived the Han Dynasty. Under Liu Hsiu and Augustus Caesar the hegemonic supremacy of alpha male authoritarianism became unchallengeable. Within this system, individual women and indeed men from lowly positions might under particular circumstances obtain power, but they would use – and just as likely abuse – that power within the overall power structure established around them. For everyone, it was much more important to maintain their self-worth by ensuring they could keep those below them firmly in their place, rather than questioning the behaviour of those above. For those at the bottom, the superstitious solace of a decent after-life or an improved reincarnation made it just about tolerable to continue with an otherwise abject existence.

With the likes of Cicero and Wang Mang slain, the traditions of Socratic criticisms and Mohist mutuality long forgotten, authoritarian rule eliminated every other conceivable form of power redistribution in society. It was not at all surprising that the rise of the Islamic empire from the seventh century on took exactly the same form. 21$^{st}$ century commentators who try to paint Islam as an alien civilisation with completely distinct roots from the 'West' should focus on its structural and cultural similarities to the socio-political models of both the 'West' and the 'East' around the same period.

While the Han rulers adopted Confucianism and the Roman regime incorporated Christianity to give them a centralised belief system to monopolise the right to declare what was good and what was bad, Muhammad (570-632) synthesized various strands of religious ideas and behavioural codes of his time into the belief system of Islam. This underpinned the other familiar features of alpha male authoritarianism: the conquest against the 'kafir' – the non-believers; the demand for revenue and subjugation in return for 'protection'; the tolerance for escapism – especially in the form of mystical contemplation – which deprives opponents of potential support; and the entrenchment of alpha male-centric social hierarchy[20].

The care the powerful was supposed to show to those under their control – women, children, slaves - was a matter of voluntary kindness. They owed them nothing. By contrast, the subordination of those below them was absolutely unconditional. The ruled were expected to show gratitude towards their superiors when they acted for the common good, but if those with power were to behave irresponsibly and bring calamity to others, they should just endure it patiently. Confucian and Christian imperial apologists alike would have approved.

---

[20] Islamic religious texts resembled those of other cultures in containing both general respect for reciprocity and snapshots of ritual practices from their times. They were used, as all sacred texts tended to be in this period, to support an authoritarian socio-political system where the prize of intensely concentrated power bred ruthless contests to become the caliph. See Lewis, B. *The Middle East,* London, Weidenfield & Nicolson: 1995 (pp.61-74).

Proponents of the authoritarian ethos have ever since used this approach to block, and where possible, crush attempts to remove the power barriers to more reciprocal relationships. At any juncture where they remotely felt they had to be on the defensive, they would roll out the usual line that to concede grounds to the reformists would be insulting to their deep cultural heritage – Confucian, Christian, Islamic, British, American or any other trait. But the invocation of their faith, national or racial identity is merely a device to mask the common roots of their animosity to having a less unequal society. Beneath the surface lies their shared attachment to rule by unchallengeable leaders, the subordination of the disadvantaged, the enslavement of the unfortunate, and the utter marginalization of independent thought. So long as they prevail, the gap between the powerful and the rest will remain unbridgeable, and communities will be left in a state of oppression.

# Chapter 3
# Learning to Challenge the Powerful:
# 1054 – 1689

<u>Who can claim to know</u>

The power of the few to control the many was from the beginning bound up with their ability to make others believe that only they knew what should be done. The emperor guided by Confucian sages, the Platonic philosopher-king, the divinely anointed ruler, or their modern equivalent, would convey an air of certainty incompatible with anyone else doubting their infallibility. Conversely, the more the illusion of unquestionable wisdom could be shattered, the better the chance communities could stand together and reject divisive inequalities.

After the authoritarian ethos had taken hold across the world for nearly a thousand years since the likes of Cicero and Wang Mang were eliminated, a ray of hope came with the irrevocable schism between the Western Roman Catholic and Eastern Greek Orthodox Churches in 1054. It set a precedent for questioning mere mortals' proclamation about their exclusive right to speak for an unchallengeable deity, and by extension, to rule on 'His' behalf. A divided Europe encouraged the Islamic offensive which over the following centuries weakened Byzantine authority in Eastern Europe while rendering the Papal regime more dependent on the resources of diverse kingdoms in the west. The fragmentation of Europe's theocentric authority was to make it possible for critical civic thinking to develop again after a millennium of control-through-conformity.

European thinkers, unlike their counterparts in other countries, were never reduced to being mere interpreters of sanctified texts. Classical Greek and Roman literature, including works by Aristotle and Cicero celebrating the virtues of critical thought and civic autonomy, were not completely cut out of their historical consciousness in the way, for example, Mozi's teachings were extinguished in China. The intellectual ammunition in support of the objective scrutiny of authority were spread across a variety of works which were preserved in the eastern Roman Empire even when theocratic forces in the western

Empire treated them with disdain. By the time they started to spread to western Europe, the Catholic Church's power to regulate the dissemination of ideas had begun to be eroded by the independent-minded kings and princes in England, France, Italy and Germany.

As the faith-based, military, tribal-national, economic sources of power increasingly flowed towards, not a common supreme recipient, but a variety of contenders for allegiance, it became more and more difficult for any single individual or group to secure immunity from criticism. In this climate, the flaws of any kind of concentrated power were more readily exposed.

For example, in England, John of Salisbury (1119-1180) wrote *Policraticus*, a treatise which asserted the primacy of law in determining what was right for rulers to do. Law should be formulated in accordance with reason. Rulers who did not comply with the law but oppressed his subjects with the use of force were to be regarded as tyrants, and as such it would be lawful to kill them. John was all too familiar with power struggles. He was secretary to Thomas Becket whose attempt to assert his authority as archbishop over King Henry II led to Becket's murder. He was also a friend of Pope Adrian IV, who supported the Byzantine Emperor, Manuel Comnenus, in the invasion of Italy against the ruling Normans in 1155 in return for a united Church and Empire, but the enterprise failed and there was to be no further attempt to reintegrate Rome and Constantinople.

The proliferating power centres not only brought to the fore questions of the legitimacy of different power holders, but also allowed the likes of John of Salisbury to articulate radical answers without being blocked by any single authority. This new trend of redefining the basis of power was particularly notable in his home country when in 1215 the English King John was pressured by the leading barons of the realm to sign the Magna Carta, a legal document setting out the conditions under which he was to exercise his power in the future, and the requirement to consult the lords before he took decisions in a number of specified areas. Of course the concessions made by the King were limited to arrangements between him and the barons, and had little to offer people further down the social hierarchy. However, the Magna Carta was significant in that it set a precedent in using a legal framework to formalise the redistribution of power from the uppermost authority of the land to those who were under his jurisdiction. In practice, King John and his successors were quite ready to breach the agreement, but the formulation of the charter, as well as the ability to secure the King's assent to its terms in the first place, showed that the mindset had changed. It had become conceivable to demand the ruler to take account of the views and concerns of those he had power over. John's son, Henry III, was to discover that the barons had got a taste for checking royal power and would not readily concede to clauses of the Magna Carta being violated. Simon de Montfort (1208-1265) led a successful rebellion against him, and having imprisoned the King, called for Parliament to be convened for the first time with elected representatives from each county and selected boroughs. In so doing, he showed that there was an alternative to the absolute concentration of power in a single ruler[21].

Although the 1265 Parliament was short-lived as the escaped King rallied his troops and de Montfort was killed, it was not possible for the royalists to reverse society's collective realisation that even if the authoritarian figure at the top was too powerful for any individual to stand up to him alone, if a sufficient number were to join forces that could be enough to limit his powers. To expand that counter-powerbase, as de Montfort had demonstrated, one needed to move towards greater inclusion in offering a wider range of people a say in the shaping of policies which affected them. If no single individual could be trusted to make all the right decisions, neither could a small group of aristocrats.

A century later, the English monarch was to be confronted in 1381 with the Peasants Revolt, led by ordinary people like Wat Tyler and Abel Ker, who with the support of the outspoken priest, John Ball, put demands to the king to remove unjust taxes which placed the greatest burden on the poorest, protect them from abuses by the church and the aristocracy, and issue new charters to enable them to make a living[22]. The peasants, at the bottom of the social hierarchy, had had to endure

---

[21] For an examination of the historical context of the Magna Carta and its subsequent influence in Britain and America, see Turner, R. *Magna Carta*, Pearson Education: 2003.

[22] It remains a relatively neglected episode in history, but see Jones, D. *Summer of Blood: the Peasants' Revolt of 1381*, Harper Press: 2009.

endless exploitation, but they were ready to organise themselves and call for reforms. Richard II, like other monarchs before and after him, promised reforms and later reneged on them. However, the tide was turning against absolute domination over the powerless.

For those at the apex of the traditional ruling regimes, their best chance of preventing any momentum to oppose them from being built up was to unite all main forms of power in a single monolithic regime with no room for any alternative power base. With empires such as those of the Ottoman in the Middle East, the Yuan/Mongolian as well as the Ming in China, and the Vijayanagara in India, that was on the whole what they achieved. Unquestioning acceptance of the edicts from above thus continued to be the order of the day. But for Western Europe around the same period - the thirteenth and fourteenth centuries – power was no longer concentrated in one alpha male authoritarian. For example, neither Pope John XXII nor Emperor Louis IV had any intention of deferring to the other, and their animosity paved the way for independent criticisms to flourish.

One progressive-minded thinker to benefit from this was William of Ockham (1288-1347) who was summoned before John XXII in 1324 to defend the Franciscan position on poverty, which implicitly criticised the shameless Papal accumulation of material wealth and worldly power, when Jesus had preached humility and the simple life[23]. Thanks to the protection offered by Louis IV, William not only escaped with his life, he was able to develop his philosophical ideas, which challenged theocentric abuse of power at three levels.

At the most basic level, his nominalist views – which came to be known as Ockham's razor – suggested that theories should be stripped down to the lowest possible number of assumptions to carry conviction, running counter to the tendency of theologians to multiply unverifiable assumptions to justify their otherwise arbitrary claims about the universe, society and much besides. Next he maintained that church and state should be separated as the conflation of a simple faith in personal

---

[23] Ockham developed a wide range of ideas which influenced subsequent ages. On politics, see McGrade, A. S. (ed), *The Political Thought of William Ockham*, Cambridge University Press: 2002; on philosophy, see Boehner, P. (ed) *Ockham: Philosophical Writings*, Hackett Publishing: 1990.

salvation with a complex power structure to rule would only damage both – as his own Franciscan Order had already observed in their refusal to own property. Lastly, both the state and the church should be more accountable to those they had jurisdiction over. On the last two points, William's outlook was reinforced by the publication, also in 1324, of *The Defender of Peace*, by Marsilius of Padua (1275-1342), who argued that the Pope should leave matters of the state to an accountable monarch who would in turn rule according to the law and be answerable to the people.

The growing confidence in asserting the need to separate church from monarchical power helped to transform a mere contest for power into a struggle for legitimate authority. Theology's previous attempts to impose its esoteric notions as grounds for exercising executive political power were increasingly deemed misconceived. For the sake of legitimacy, rulers could not just rely on princes, lords, the church, or any single group for unwavering support. They had to cultivate broader, and often shifting, alliances. Consequently, there was more and more space for people to reflect on their priorities in life without a dogma-based straitjacket.

Against this background, humanist learning was able to expand across Europe. From Petrarch's (1304-1374) attack on the irrelevance of scholastic philosophy to human affairs, through Leonardo Bruni's (1369-1444) application of classical ideas on virtue and wisdom to civic governance, to Erasmus' (1466-1536) witty but no less well-aimed exposure of the errors of those who abused their privileged positions, especially those in the Church, progressive reflections shaped a new cultural outlook[24].

Whereas authoritarians had relied on the masses' unthinking acceptance of their version of the world – the one in which an invisible almighty being sanctioned the most extreme power inequalities for that was the only way – humanist scholars encouraged people to think about what the world could become, especially if they applied their intelligence

---

[24] Locating Renaissance humanist thinkers in the overall development of humanism, see Bullock, A. *The Humanist Tradition in the West*, London, WW Norton & Co: 1985 (pp.11-48); see also Mandrou, R. *From Humanism to Science 1480-1700*, Penguin Books: 1978.

to the daily activities around them. For too long, people were told to trust the way of the ancients, and that any departure from it would spell disasters. But philosophers of ancient Athens and Rome were discovered to be devoted teachers of critical thinking. Far from insisting people should blindly agree to whatever those with powerful positions put forward, they explained why anyone who truly cared about the wellbeing of themselves and others must keep a vigilant eye on claims made by the powerful and question their validity where necessary. Alternatives could and should be explored.

## The threat to extinguish dissent

By the time the 16th century Reformation further cut down the Church's power to dictate what was to be accepted in relation to all the fundamental issues in life, the infrastructure for eliminating intellectual diversity from Europe was significantly weakened. Individuals felt they could not only study works which questioned the legitimacy of different forms of authority, but put forward their own thinking on how power ought to be structured and exercised in practice. For anyone needing to escape persecution by the once all-controlling Holy Empire, Protestant states such as England and the Netherlands were all too ready to offer refuge.

Amongst the powerful elites of Europe, there were those who, like the ruling class in England for example, having embraced defiance against authoritarian forces as the basis of their own national religious outlook[25], and experienced negotiation over power distribution as part of their political culture, were relatively more inclined to adjust pragmatically to calls for cutting back oppressive arrangements. On the other hand, there were those who wanted nothing more than a swift return to the good old days of absolute rule in every aspect of life. As the 16th century drew to a close, Spain under Philip II took on the leadership to re-galvanise the authoritarian cause.

Philip's vision was simple enough. Catholic orthodoxy combined with military strength was to re-establish the holy imperial regime wherein everyone was to submit ultimately to the God-sanctioned King.

---

[25] The Church of England was founded on rejecting the authority of the Pope.

The Spanish-born Pope, Alexander VI, had already helpfully declared that the bulk of the newly 'discovered' Americas belonged to Spain. The prospect of gold from distant land, much as oil was to be four centuries on, spurred the ambitious on to eliminate any threat to their control. Spain, the superpower of its time, deployed the twin weapons of its vast armed forces and the dreaded Inquisition to crush dissent and secure the hierarchical world order.

However, by the time the Spanish offensive was launched, the culture of challenging the powerful had taken deep roots. Intellectually, even with the execution of thinkers like Giordano Bruno for heretical views on the nature of the universe, others like Galileo and Kepler continued to put forward evidence-based ideas, which questioned the Church's position on what the world was supposed to be like. The Church might insist that the sun and all other planets orbited around the Earth, but the observed movements of these bodies could be more easily and coherently explained by the hypothesis that the sun was at the centre of our planetary system. The application of Ockham's Razor would favour opting for a simpler explanation in the absence of any convincing reasons why additional assumptions about the peculiar movements of the planets should be invoked.

The Church would prefer to clamp down on dissenting views, but once the veneer of infallibility started to peel away, it became increasingly difficult to silent the doubters[26]. The tactic of striking fear into the general population by telling them not to question 'sacred truths' was undermined by the fact that the more intelligent in their own ranks could see the absurdity in denying what the scientific minded observers were proposing, irrespective of previous interpretations of 'holy' texts. At the same time, improvement in printing and transport facilitated the spread of new theories which could be readily tested for their veracity by people's own observation and experiments. The Protestant ethos of by-

---

[26] The growth of scientific ideas reinforced the mindset of challenging any authority which could not back its commands and declarations with appropriate reason and evidence. Two excellent books to refer to on this subject are: Feuer, LS *The Scientific Intellectual: the psychological and sociological origins of modern science*, New Brunswick, Transaction Publishers: 1992; and Easlea, B. *Witch-hunting, Magic & the New Philosophy: an introduction to the debates of the scientific revolution 1450-1750*, Brighton, Harvester Press: 1980.

passing the Catholic Church hierarchy and reaching out through one's own efforts to understand the truth also helped, albeit unintentionally, to encourage the outlook of finding out for oneself rather than taking the word of a Church leader for it.

The Protestant emphasis on the individual's relationship with God also encouraged a more naturalistic interpretation of what really mattered in being a good Christian, which centred on how caring one acted towards other people rather than on one's acceptance of a multitude of obscure doctrines defined by authorised theologians. After centuries of being marginalised as a minor footnote to volumes of esoteric theological tenets, the golden rule of moral reciprocity was being re-discovered by ordinary people who, not being preoccupied with running a vast multinational business involving land ownership and expensive buildings, readily sensed the essence of goodness in caring for others as one would have others care for oneself.

The more people engaged with the moral essence of being religious, rather than its divisive dressing, the less able was the Church authority to secure total compliance with its edicts, which had much more to do with their own interests than promoting the wellbeing of all. Centuries later, the resurgence of religious fundamentalism in America reflected once again the interest of the powerful to stir up doctrinaire fanaticism to deflect people from the core Christian message of doing to others what we would have them do to us.

Politically, the jurisdiction claimed by the Spaniards over their domain was already rejected by the Dutch in the Netherlands and by the English at every opportunity they could seize. The Pope might have declared that Spain could take what it wanted from its American territories, but the English, not for a moment accepting the Pope's infallibility, were convinced they could take what they wanted from the returning Spanish ships.

Given Protestant England's rise through its commercial and naval capability, it was not surprising that it became both a rallying point for defiance against Spanish authority and a prime target of the latter's wrath. The menacing launch of the Spanish Armada, followed swiftly by its humiliating defeat in 1588, marked a turning point in the struggle against power concentration. Had Spain's invasion been successful and the Inquisition was instituted on English soil to root out new thinking amongst the natives and the refugees from anti-Protestant rulers, authoritarianism might have reclaimed total control over how people were to think and live. But England stood up to the world's superpower and paved the way for succeeding generations to challenge power inequalities at home and abroad.

## Knowledge is power

Francis Bacon (1561-1626) – distinguished scholar, active politician, legal expert, and tireless correspondent with many of the leading minds across Europe of his time – developed a systematic basis for challenging the claim of the powerful to legitimate authority[27]. He rejected scholastic disputes about theological minutiae, as they were not connected with anything of substance in people's experience of life. Instead, he stressed that people who were serious about their religion should focus on the real ethical issues, which were essentially about the relief of human suffering. Doing what would be beneficial to the healthy and comfortable living of other people, unlike the fermenting of religious arguments or the pursuit of personal glory, was the only thing we could consistently encourage without excess. As for what would bring about beneficial effects, such questions could only be settled by observation and experimentation. The antiquity of a claim would confer no greater veracity on it, nor indeed would the curiosity of a novel proposition merit our inclination to embrace it. Actual evidence, the testimony of reliable witnesses, the robustness of suppositions in standing up to empirical tests, these were the means to establish what warranted our epistemological assent.

In these respects, Bacon revived key elements of Mohist thinking which had been virtually erased from history. Crucially, he took them forward through a vital approach that Mozi and his followers overlooked. That was the reliance on cooperation in reaching decisions.

---

[27] Bacon's reputation suffered a long eclipse which lasted from mid-19th to late 20th century, but has since begun to recover. Amongst the books which set out his ideas and their importance are: Urbach, P. *Francis Bacon's Philosophy of Science*, La Salle, Open Court: 1987; Perez-Ramos, A. *Francis Bacon's Idea of Science*, Oxford, Clarendon Press: 1988; Faulkner, RK *Francis Bacon and the Project of Progress*, Rowman & Littlefield Publishers: 1993; and Peltonen, M. (ed) *The Cambridge Companion to Bacon*, Cambridge University Press: 1996.

The Mohists had reacted to the attacks by aggressive enemies by adopting a rigid command structure that left little room for people to deliberate on what courses of action they should pursue. For Bacon, perhaps with the benefit of England having successfully repelled the Spanish invasion, it was important in practice as well as in principle not to exclude anyone who might have something relevant to contribute to a decision – either in terms of bringing forward pertinent evidence or assisting with the scrutiny of the claims in question. The quest for knowledge was a public enterprise, which by its very nature could not afford to keep out potentially worthy participants. This meant that whoever possessed the administrative authority to make decisions must at the same time recognise that the legitimacy of those decisions would rest on their competence in drawing on the input from others whenever that would be appropriate. Politically, no head of state should expect to command the following of his subjects without seeking their cooperation in making decisions affecting their vital interests. Although Bacon – in his official capacity as one of James I's top advisers – frequently defended the King from Parliamentary criticisms, he repeatedly reminded James of the need to engage Parliament in deciding the key issues of the realm.

Bacon observed that "Knowledge is Power", and it followed that power was ultimately derived, not from theological obfuscation, claims of lineage, or even the sword as an instrument of fear, but from knowledge of the world as it really was, and how it could be improved for the benefit of all. Once society started to apply the experimental approach to expand its knowledge, it would increase its power to generate more resources, combat others' military forces more effectively, enhance people's health and understanding, and move to a better position to look after its members than any authoritarian who would by then have little leverage to help them retain control. The power of knowing how to make the world steadily better would take over from the power of deceiving people into accepting their wretched position in the authoritarian hierarchy.

According to Bacon's exposition of the nature of knowledge, the power it would confer depended on how inclusive the process for developing it was. As knowledge was accessible only through experience, no one could reasonably claim to know that he alone possessed all conceivable knowledge. There were as many possible routes to finding new evidence and reviewing new theories as they were people. Of course some might have nothing substantial to say, some might be deluded, some might be dishonest, but they could not be ruled out *a priori* without a fair hearing had been given to what they had to say. The more a society moved towards enabling all its members to contribute to its knowledge expansion, by removing dogmas and supporting cooperative deliberations, the stronger it would become.

While the persecutions of scientific thinkers by religious authorities persisted in the rest of Europe in the seventeenth century, Bacon's vision for assessing knowledge claims by subjecting them to objective questioning, experimentation, and open deliberations, inspired in England the founding of the Royal Society, which was to receive the patronage of Charles II without losing any of its freedom to formulate and examine theories about the nature of the world[28]. The medieval culture of seeking to win scholastic arguments by getting those with senior church positions to give their endorsement (and preferably along with condemnation of rival theories) was displaced by the transparent exchange of ideas and information so that the community of scholars, which itself was open to anyone with something to offer, would judge for itself what merited their assent.

This led to a shift in the wider public perception of how knowledge was developed through the accumulative and critical efforts of numerous people rather than determined by the arbitrary pronouncements of a few powerful individuals. Bacon explained at the outset that he did not believe the advancement of learning was an enterprise that he or any individual for that matter could achieve, because it required the contributions from successive generations. He had criticised the subversion of Greek thinkers like Aristotle when they were turned into unquestionable icons to block off future enquiry. For Bacon, whatever new insight or discovery was brought forth at any time, it was vital to see it not as an end point, but as the next springboard to improve our knowledge further.

---

[28] The best introduction to how Baconian ideas shaped and were in turn taken forward by the Royal Society is to be found in Purver, M. *The Royal Society: Concept and Creation*, Cambridge, The MIT Press: 1967.

The Baconian Royal Society thus helped to promote scientific research which not only led to universally acclaimed achievements by outstanding thinkers like Robert Boyle and Isaac Newton, but sustained a culture of learning wherein even the likes of Boyle and Newton would not be regarded as having had the final say about the laws of nature. Much more was to be examined, tested, developed, and it would be down to the generations to come to improve our understanding of the world beyond current levels of knowledge. This commitment to open and cooperative learning was to become particularly advantageous in accelerating the development and application of technology to solving problems and relieving human suffering in centuries to come.

Bacon regarded the general enhancement of human wellbeing as the core object of progress. Communities should strive to be better, not in the interest of a few select individuals, but for the sake of everyone being able to live a longer, decent, more fulfilling life. His naturalistic reorientation of religious devotion towards caring behaviour and away from doctrinaire disputes gained ground through the moderation of established religious organisations as well as the proliferation of new non-conformist sects. The readiness to embrace tolerance of diverse religious views grew along with the widening consensus over what would really make a good person – the commitment to look after the wellbeing of oneself and one's fellow human beings.

Against this background, the one doctrine which still sought to impose its own theological interpretations on what God demanded – that of the Catholic Church – was increasingly rejected, to the point that when King James II wanted to restore it as the official religion of his reign, he was deposed. By contrast, sects which rejected an authoritarian belief system in favour of participatory exchanges in their religious practices, such as the Society of Friends, flourished. The spirit of the Quakers was indeed to spread beyond the numbers of its formal followers – deference was not to be shown to people solely on account of their purported status in society hierarchy, but respect was to be granted to all who demonstrated their kind intentions through their behaviour.

While Bacon advocated the importance of securing a progressive research culture backed by robust institutional arrangements, he also argued for wider political support to ensure that the potential for cooperative learning was realised. He was particularly concerned that hierarchical arrogance could force counter-productive actions such as military adventures on people who would otherwise be able to spend their time more fruitfully on dealing with the real problems they faced. He recognised that the use of force abroad and at home would sometimes be necessary, but stressed that decisions on such matters must all the more be grounded on reliable testimony and empirical evidence. He advised the monarch not only against waging wars that would drain the country's resources rather than enhance them, but also against the use of torture for it was a completely unreliable means of obtaining information. In place of blind aggression, he favoured peaceful, pragmatic methods to keep the nation's development on an even keel, resorting to force only if the evidence was to show clearly that there was no alternative. In the long term, the use of force in regulating domestic and foreign relationships was to be relegated below the use of dialogue and diplomacy. The macho alpha male was to give way to the deliberative man or woman of reason in steering the ship of state.

Bacon helped to usher in a much more inclusive form of community life. He encouraged the exchange of ideas with others regardless of their nationality or religion. He lobbied at every opportunity for reforms that would bring about a society more readily guided by experimentally derived knowledge. He exposed the irrational ideas deployed by the powerful to mislead the masses.

His rejection of the use of saintly pretensions as a method of commanding assent, however, did not shield him from the kind of character assassination to be targeted at all progressive advocates to come. For Bacon, people who ostensibly displayed the utmost purity in their conduct might nonetheless be mistaken in their beliefs about the world and erroneous in their judgement about what should be done with other people. Public figures should be judged on the soundness of their policies and the impact of their practices.

But Bacon's enemies attacked him for his personal flaws such as deserting his friend, Essex, when in fact the latter acted against his advice and threatened the security of the country; accepting gifts as a senior legal officer as it was customary of the time even though he never gave a judgement in favour of those whose gifts he had received; and lavishing money on friends and servants when he was often in debt. Wounded in his reputation, distrusted by the King's favourites, Bacon was unable to persuade James I to adopt his reform programme. Instead, the King ignored his advice and embarked on a confrontational course with Parliament. When Parliament became increasingly agitated with the King, James superficially placated them by allowing his Chancellor, Bacon, to be removed from office. Soon after Charles I succeeded to the throne, Bacon died. The collision between the House of Stuarts and the Houses of Parliament was by then unavoidable.

## The English Civil War and the Levellers' challenge

Charles I was even more obdurate than his father about his divine right to rule over his subjects. He acted as if he could accomplish what Philip II of Spain had failed to do just a few decades ago. He was blind to the fact that British intellectual and political currents were moving the country in an anti-authoritarian direction – the very opposite of what he wanted to bring about with his doctrinaire approach to imposing changes to the Church and his attempt to levy taxes without consulting Parliament. The readiness to accept what those in the most powerful positions demanded had been steadily eroded by the growing spirit of enquiry. In the end, Charles I's arrogance forced many in Parliament, including those who were reluctant to put aside long-standing commitment to monarchical rule, to declare his rule illegitimate. They were far from united about how far the prevailing authoritarian power imbalance should be corrected by distributing power more widely and fairly, but they had no doubt that concentrating power in the king was not the way forward.

The English Civil War (1642-1651) focused the minds of its participants on the question of power distribution like no other event had before in the country or anywhere else. Unlike so many bloody contests in history over who should take the throne, it raised the central question of how the power to rule should itself be structured[29].

---

[29] Two books by Christopher Hill provide an excellent overview of the ideas that led up to and further radical ideas which emerged during this period: Hill, C. *Intellectual Origins of the English Revolution*, Oxford University: 1965; and his *The World Turned Upside Down: Radical Ideas during the English Revolution*, Penguin Books: 1975. An accessible outline of the English Civil War can be found in Ollard, R. *This War without an Enemy: a history of the English Civil War*, Fontana Press: 1976.

The Royalists used what in essence was the age-old Confucian argument that if the supreme alpha male power holder were removed, the command structure would fall apart, and there would be chaos everywhere. The Parliamentarians under the de facto leadership of Cromwell maintained that subjecting the ruler to the systematic scrutiny of the leading Peers and Commoners of the land was a more reliable method to secure sound governance. It was Charles I's refusal to comply with this approach that led to civil war. A ruler's readiness to deliberate with Parliamentary representatives would bring out the best in political cooperation. His determination to remove the right of those representatives to have their say was tantamount to subverting the legitimate exercise of power and punishable by death.

Between the fierce arguments from these two sides, a group of activists who came to be known as the Levellers (led by John Lilburne, 1615-1657, Richard Overton 1599-1664, and William Walwyn, 1600-1681) put forward a challenge to both of them[30]. Following Bacon, as we have seen, there was growing recognition that decisions over what was to be believed should not be left in the hands of people who would make such decisions on an arbitrary basis, just to suit their own interests, without grounding the decisions on empirical corroboration which would be open to all who could make a contribution. The Levellers were the first to apply this insight to decisions affecting the body politic, or to use the term which came into currency around this time to denote the new focus on securing the people's common wellbeing – the commonwealth. For them, everyone had an interest to be governed well, and no one could pretend that they would look after the interest of others while they would at the same time shut them out of any deliberations about what should be done for the collective good. In a debate with Cromwell and his followers who were prepared to take power away from the King but not to pass it on to others, the Leveller, Thomas Rainsborough (1610-1648), famously explained:

"For really I think that the poorest he that is in England has a life to live as the greatest he; and ... every man that is to live under a

---

[30] Extracts of writings by the Levellers are available in Sharp, A (ed.) *The English Levellers*, Cambridge University Press: 1998. See also Brailsford, HN *The Levellers and the English Revolution*, Spokesman: 1976.

government ought first by his own consent to put himself under that government; and I do think that the poorest man in England is not at all bound in a strict sense to that government that he has not had a voice to put himself under."

The Levellers proposed to institutionalise the cooperative approach to decision-making at the heart of Bacon's vision of an open, inclusive society. To ensure that people were able to feed their experiences and views into a collective system which would henceforth take action on their behalf, everyone had to be guaranteed an equal say in determining who should run that system, and be free from any intimidation against their participation. In 1649, the Levellers submitted to Parliament their *Agreement of the People* with demands for the right to vote for all men above the age of 21, equality of all persons before the law, trial by jury chosen from the community, limiting the death penalty only to murder, abolition of imprisonment for debt, and taxation to be linked to personal property.

Cromwell, who had taken control of the country with the backing of the army (having purged it of Leveller sympathisers), firmly rejected the Levellers' argument on the grounds that the people, especially those without their own property, could not be trusted to make the right decisions. Having overthrown Charles I for being an arbitrary and unaccountable ruler, Cromwell made himself the unelected Protector of England. In so doing, he drew a firm line against further inclusion, and gave encouragement to authoritarian minded reactionaries to restore the old hierarchy.

The Levellers had thought that the reasonableness of their ideas, and their acceptance by many others in the army would be sufficient to bring about the reforms they sought. But they only reached a minority even within the army. Outside the army, their message barely registered. It was easy for Cromwell and his supporters to paint the Levellers as irresponsible agitators threatening to rob people of their precious properties. Whereas those interested in applying Bacon's ideas to improving the institutions and procedures for research in natural sciences built up an influential network which culminated in the Royal Society, the Levellers neglected to build a base for developing cooperative political decision-making. But they had nonetheless opened up a new front in challenging the status quo in power distribution. When

Cromwell was no longer in control, the question of who should be entrusted with the power to rule on behalf of all was swiftly raised again.

<u>The need for another revolution</u>

Cromwell had been able to consolidate his power because his Royalist enemies and his Leveller critics detested each other even more. But by the time of Cromwell's death, everyone had had enough of his brand of repackaged authoritarianism, and Parliament invited the younger Charles Stuart to take the throne, on the condition that he would recognise the decision-making role of Parliament, and that any attempt to submit England to an external authority (such as the Pope) would not be accepted. The broad consensus was that if the system of hereditary monarchy could accommodate a move towards power sharing with Parliament, that would achieve the desired stability. The problem was that even though Charles II was prepared to go along with that arrangement, his brother, upon succeeding to the throne as James II, declared his intention to rule as a Catholic King, answerable only to God (through the exclusive Papal communication line).

By asserting his absolute right to rule, James II inadvertently exposed the self-deception at the heart of any submissive concession made to an authoritarian power holder. So long as the hoped for better relationship is founded on the grace, mercy, or bluntly, whims, of the person who retains the dominant power, all the problems inherent in power imbalance remains. Parliament was confronted with two choices – to reopen the question of who should have a share in the power over how people lived their lives, or to accept the King's decision as final[31]. This dilemma divided the country into two camps, each with a derogatory nickname coined by the other side. The Whigs were by and large pragmatic people who at that juncture inclined towards the progressive position that arbitrary rule must be stamped out once and for all. They were convinced that one could not keep struggling with the whims of a Charles I, then a Cromwell, and then a James II in the vain

---

[31] Harris, T. *The Revolution: The Great Crisis of the British Monarchy, 1685-1720*, Penguin: 2007; and Aylmer, GE *The Struggle for the Constitution: England in the seventeenth century*, London, Blandford Press: 1965.

hope that one day power would be taken over by a wiser and more caring despot. It must be built into the system of governance that no one could impose his will on the country.

The Tories, on the other hand, embodied the alpha male authoritarian mindset. Prostrating before an absolute ruler was wholly worthwhile because it was the indispensable apex which held together a socio-political system wherein those who had power (or aspired to gain power soon) just below the very top could exact unquestionable submission from the many more people underneath them. The King might act unreasonably, but to put up with that would mean that they themselves could behave unreasonably without any risk of being challenged by their subordinates.

If the Tories had their way, half a century of struggle for greater political inclusion would have been for nothing, leaving England back where it was when a Stuart monarch could force his wishes on Parliament and the people without any serious repercussion. Fortunately, they were poorly organised. Deference to an absolute leader in times of crisis might work if he was astute and effective. James II was neither. Furthermore, many Tories dreaded the prospect of a return to Catholicism as much as the Whigs, but they could not intellectually reconcile the contradiction of being totally loyal to a King determined to impose a religion they did not find acceptable. They overlooked one of the most cogent arguments for authoritarianism to be developed since Confucius stripped religious dressing from his ideology of obedience. Thomas Hobbes (1588-1679) had set out why total submission to a Leviathan-like absolute ruler in return for peace and order was the only sensible way to move forward. It struck a chord with many who had lived through the chaos and bloodshed of the Civil War. But Hobbes' materialism alienated him from the religious minded, and the Tories did not make use of his ideas to formulate a commanding ideology.

By contrast, the Whigs were clear about their objective and swift in negotiating with William, Stadtholder of the Dutch Republic, and husband of James II's Protestant offspring, Mary. A hundred years on from repelling the Spanish Armada, the English Whigs welcomed the Dutch fleet to British shores in 1688, and ended monarchical authoritarian rule for good. William and Mary would be joint sovereigns on strict conditions laid down by Parliament and enshrined in the Bill of

Rights of 1689.

Following the so-called 'Glorious Revolution'[32] – glorious for the relative absence of bloodshed except in Ireland where many Catholic supporters of James II were slain when they fought against troops under the command of William of Orange (leaving a deep scar in Ireland which would not heal for another three centuries) – there was no going back to an absolute ruler over Britain (though as we will see later, the problem arose in relation to the British colonies in America). The only issue to be resolved was how the empirical outlook of grounding judgements on people's experiences – as opposed to basing them on indisputable doctrines asserted by a few – was to be translated in distributing power for decision making across communities of citizens.

John Locke (1632-1704), a leading member of the Bacon-inspired Royal Society, had argued that empirical examination of rival claims was the only effective way to differentiate reliable assertions from allegations and fantasies[33]. As a corollary of this, there was no evidence that kings could rule well simply by virtue of some divinely given right[34]. The people's consent to the exercise of authority was the source of its legitimacy, and could always be tested through unfettered discussions amongst the public. Locke's philosophy was to be highly influential in mapping out the course for building more inclusive communities, first in England, and later across North America and Western Europe.

At the heart of this philosophy is a notion of reason based on reflections on actual perceptions, remote from any form of absolute knowledge transcending human experiences. We come to understand any subject matter through a combination of what we experience and how we make sense of that experience. This means that no one can simply assert that something is the case – whether it is about a cure for an illness, the structural stability of a building, or how a country is to be governed – without having the backing of the relevant experience. If a hypothetical claim has to be made, because no appropriate experience

---

[32] Dillon, P. *The Last Revolution: 1688 and the Creation of the Modern World*, Pimlico: 2007.

[33] Locke, J. *An Essay Concerning Human Understanding*, New York, Dover Publications: 1959 (ed. by Fraser, AC, in two volumes).

[34] Locke, J. *Two Treatises of Government*, New York, Mentor Book: 1963.

has yet been secured, then its validity must be tested in the future in the light of experience to come. This cuts out any attempt to impose claims by invoking one's religious, monarchical, mystical, or any other credentials, if one cannot subject those claims to the court of human experience and see if they survive the critical scrutiny of open debates.

With this intellectual climate, there was to be no more blind deference to authority secured on the back of hierarchical power – backed by the church or the monarch – but a constant quest for improved understanding of the world as experienced by all. Thinkers across Europe looked upon the achievements of Newton and others as confirmation that England's more inclusive culture was particularly conducive to vigorous research and the advancement of learning. Locke had stressed that experience-based learning should inform the education of the young as well as the deliberations of adults. The commitment to empirical investigations was thus not made merely to steer a one-off research programme, but was to be embedded in how successive generations were to learn about how justifiable beliefs were to be differentiated from those which were not.

Two momentous consequences flowed from this epistemological outlook. First, given that the only grounds for persecuting people for possessing certain beliefs or customs would be that those beliefs and customs could be properly declared to be dangerously wrong, it would follow that where those grounds are lacking, people should be left alone whatever one's 'opinion' of them might be. This does not lead to a relativist licence for people to act in whatever manner they want. It is in the realm of shared experiences that we can establish if certain beliefs were erroneous, particular behaviour would be harmful, and so on. So where there is established evidence, society would be justified in stopping, for example, parents teaching their children to believe that certain 'treatment' would cure their illness when it would do more harm than good; people seeking to prevent others from having innocuous fun; or agitators promoting the fear and hatred of people with unconventional but harmless customs. But where there is no such evidence, tolerance shall be the order of the day. Prejudices, superstitions, religious dogmas which had in the past irrationally condemned people for their harmless beliefs and customs would henceforth be exposed as groundless assertions and not be allowed to play a part in interfering with those people's lives.

Secondly, if people are to be allowed to have their own beliefs and customs so long as there is no empirically defensible grounds for considering them too dangerous and harmful to tolerate, and indeed if people are to be able to develop their ideas and test them against collective experiences in order to advance human understanding without undue hindrance, then the potential for arbitrary intervention must be systematically limited. Locke and other Whigs who demanded a new constitutional settlement were able to ensure the reformed power relations were enshrined in the 1689 Bill of Rights. The clauses to disperse power included:

- Parliament's consent to be essential for the monarch's actions in matters such as suspending the laws, levying funds, or raising a standing army, otherwise they would be illegal;
- The people are to have a right to petition their ruler and any action against such petitioning is illegal;
- There shall be no interference with the free election of members of Parliament;
- The freedom of speech and debates or proceedings in Parliament ought not to be impeached or questioned in any court or place out of Parliament;
- That excessive bail ought not to be required, nor excessive fines imposed, nor cruel and unusual punishments inflicted;
- Parliaments should be held frequently for redress of all grievances, and for the amending, strengthening and preserving of the laws.

Step by step, England led the way towards the rule of law envisioned by John of Salisbury 500 years earlier. Each confrontation with the powerful had brought about improvements, sometimes these would suffer reversals not long afterwards, but on the whole, the prospect for inclusive community life with less extreme power inequalities was drawing nearer for more and more people. To be able to live without fear of arbitrary punishment, explore different ideas with reference to objective evidence, and cooperate with others without being divided by foolish dogmas, the triumph of the Whigs over James II heralded a new dawn of moral and intellectual confidence directing human energy towards practical improvements to their quality of life, and away from futile disputes. This led to technological innovations, adventurous commercial development, and greater opportunities to tackle the needs and wants of people who only a few generations ago would have accepted quiet endurance as their lot in life.

At this juncture, English political culture could have ossified in the same way as Athenian democracy had centuries ago prior to its disintegration. The ideas of Bacon, the Levellers and Locke could have been forgotten as comprehensively as those of Mozi. But a crucial factor made all the difference. A virtuous circle of deliberative transmission had come into place through the practice of cultivating wider understanding of why authoritarian concentration of power should always be challenged. Parents taught their sons, and in some cases, their daughters too; friends corresponded with each other; thinkers shared their findings with all who would show an interest; and publishers fuelled the circulation of criticisms and new theories.

Throughout the seventeenth century, many of those who were involved in the battle of the books, the armies, and in some cases, both, came to recognise that a new way of thinking about, and hence living and organising, their lives had been discovered[35]. As a philosophy of life, it was not a matter of customs if one should adopt it or not. It was not primarily an issue of how to be a true Athenian or true Englishman, or as the Mohists came to see it, if one should formally join a particular School or organisation. It was a question of how one responds to the experiences of suffering, injustice, and ignorance in a reasonable and productive manner. To help each other overcome these problems, people were learning that they must exercise their faculty for empirical reasoning so that they could improve their common understanding of what should really be done for their mutual wellbeing.

---

[35] Two books which insightfully draw out distinct intellectual currents in English thought in the seventeenth century are: Willey, B. *The Seventeenth Century Background: studies in the thought of the age in relation to poetry and religion*, London, Routledge & Kegan Paul: 1979; and Jones, R. F. *The Seventeenth Century: studies in the history of English thought and literature from Bacon to Pope*, Stanford University Press: 1951.

# Chapter 4
# Enlightenment Ethos & its Enemies:
# 1689 – 1799

<u>Contesting power redistribution</u>

By the beginning of the eighteenth century, Britain – unifying England, Wales, and Scotland in a single political system – was demonstrating how a more inclusive distribution of power could lead to greater cooperation and substantial improvements in different spheres of life. Freedom from arbitrary interference encouraged innovation and collaborative enterprise. Commerce in turn grew with the provision of more and better products. Scientific and technological development led to advancement in agriculture and medicine. Culture was enriched through the creativity of unfettered minds in art and literature. Military strength was enhanced on land and sea.

However, past attempts at building more inclusive forms of community life in ancient Greece, China, republican Rome, had shown how precarious they were. Those who had lost out would regroup to find ways to undermine and topple the reformists. Those who did not share sufficiently in the benefits would become impatient and could easily be fooled by false promises to side with the reactionaries set on turning the clock back. All the time, another authoritarian leader could be stepping forward to show how greater order and certainty could be restored with power concentrated in him.

Alongside Britain's rise in status and influence, France under Louis XIV (reigned 1643-1715) had also established itself as one of the most powerful countries in the world, but by taking a very different route. When the British monarch was executed in 1649 for daring to usurp the power of Parliament, the French attempt to assert parliamentary right against royal rule triggered a civil war (*the Fronde*)[36] which ended with the opposite outcome. Instead of conceding power to members of a political assembly, which in turn had to ground its

---

[36] For an introduction, see Ranum, O, *The Fronde: A French Revolution*, WW Norton & Co: 1994.

legitimacy in an ever expanding electorate, Louis XIV inherited a comprehensive victory against those who questioned the absolute rule of the monarch. Consequently, France took on the role Spain had a century earlier failed to fulfil – to unite in one alpha male the authority to command his subjects at home and subdue opponents abroad.

Like Augustus and other authoritarian leaders who in their time imposed order when chaos threatened, Louis XIV exploited the fear and awe his regime inspired to launch an era of courtly splendour and martial supremacy. France's culture was adorned by the works of Molière and Racine, while its army eclipsed the Spanish and the Austrian in extending French strategic interests through successive campaigns. Unlike the British who insisted that only someone renouncing the theological infallibilism of the Catholic Church could become their monarch, Louis XIV aligned himself to the 'one and only true faith' so strongly that in 1685 he revoked the Edict of Nantes which had previously granted Protestants in France religious and political freedom. Since they had hardly lost their collective memory of the 1572 St Bartholomew's Day Massacre, when thousands of French Protestants were slaughtered by Catholics who were then promptly granted amnesty, there followed a mass exodus of Protestants from France[37].

When James II lost his throne in England because of his embrace of Catholicism, Louis XIV gave him financial and military support to reclaim it. He was to do the same for James II's son to challenge the succession of the Protestant Anne upon the death of William III in 1702. Not surprisingly, the eighteenth century opened with a sustained clash between Britain and France in the War of Spanish Succession (1701-1714). Louis XIV wanted to bring the vast Spanish Empire into his family through either his son or grandson inheriting the Spanish Crown, but that would make France more powerful in territorial and resource terms than any other European country, and Britain was determined to prevent that from happening.

However, whether the culture of greater inclusion was to grow or wilt was not just dependent on the clash between two diametrically opposite political and religious regimes. The intellectual engagement

---

[37] Diefendorf, BB, *The St. Bartholomew's Day Massacre: A Brief History with Documents*, Basingstoke, Palgrave Macmillan: 2009.

between Britain and France played in many ways an even more important role in determining the future of power redistribution in both those countries and beyond.

## Emergence of the Enlightenment ethos

After debating and accepting the merits of their country's long struggle to put an end to the age old system of absolute power and total obedience, British thinkers in the eighteenth century wanted to build on the Baconian approach – pragmatic, experimental, centred on improving human conditions, developed by Locke into a sustained reform agenda. Having witnessed their own extensive redistribution of power, with those at the top being subject to more constraints over the exercise of their power, they saw nothing from France to persuade them to change their mind about how government and society should be continuously improved. They discerned no advantage in trying to rely on any political or metaphysical certainty vested in a single being, divine or otherwise. There was no evidence that anyone was capable of coming up with a complete package of answers – totally exempt from validation by practical experience – which could settle all disputes which might arise. Instead, their constitutional arrangements from the execution of Charles I to the replacement of James II by William and Mary; the growth of their scientific knowledge from Bacon's criticisms of outmoded assumptions to Newton's experimentally based theories; their enhanced moral sensitivity from the early reactions against religious intolerance to humane embrace of diverse pursuits of faith and happiness; all suggested to them that far from shutting down opportunities for new thinking by multiple minds, more doors should be opened to promote critical dialogues and fresh experimentation.

Many of the leading thinkers in Britain of the century such as Francis Hutcheson, David Hume, Edward Gibbon, Adam Smith, Joseph Priestley, Thomas Paine, Jeremy Bentham were preoccupied with confronting residual attachment to authoritarian methods of governing human relationship[38]. Hutcheson (1694-1746) exposed the shortcomings of dogmatic conceptions of morality and was the first to articulate the importance of promoting the greatest happiness of the greatest number[39]. Quietly but persistently, he brought moral commands from behind the shield of religious unquestionability to the open court of public deliberations. Centuries of sanctified assumptions about how the establishment might treat people it had little respect for – women, the poor, non-believers – were held up as lacking any reasonable basis. The justification for sanctions against any individual must be based on the impact on human joy or suffering. Bentham (1748-1832) applied this principle to the legal system and pressed relentlessly for reforms. Laws and judgments, which led to an increase in human suffering for no commensurate gain, were deplored as harmful and mistaken. The tradition of getting away with arbitrary treatment of others solely on account of one's powerful position in the land was pummelled by Bentham's demand for justification in terms of the wellbeing of all with none counting for more than anyone else[40].

Gibbon (1737-1794) reconnected the contemporary struggle against oppressive forces with the republican past by recounting how Rome descended into imperial excesses. His *Decline & the Fall of Rome* set out how the Romans, once proud of standing together to prevent anyone from obtaining absolute power, allowed authoritarian rule to prevail, and ended up losing their way as civic solidarity was swept away by individual indulgence in superstitions and mass acceptance of religious dogmas. For Gibbons, the exercise of human rationality to determine what should be done in life and the freedom from oppression were twin conditions which must be secured together to lift people out of a state of mental and physical enslavement. If people were able to think for themselves, and not forced to bow down to the arbitrary edicts of the powerful, they would stand a much better chance of working out how to

---

[38] One of the best general introductions to British Enlightenment thinking is Porter, R, *Enlightenment: Britain and the creation of the modern world*, Allen Lane, The Penguin Press: 2000.

[39] See Scott, WR, *Francis Hutcheson: his life, teaching and position in the history of philosophy*, Bristol, Thoemmes Press: 1992.

[40] For an overview of Bentham's thought, see Harrison, R, *Bentham*, London, Routledge & Kegan Paul: 1983.

improve their wellbeing.

Others applied this line of attack to specific citadels of concentrated power. Hume (1711-1776) directed his criticisms towards metaphysical teachings favoured by the Church dominated universities, and in so doing sacrificed all chances of gaining a university position himself. With clinical precision, he dissected the total lack of coherence in attempts to by-pass empirical reasoning, and argued why claims without objectively provable grounds should be rejected regardless how powerful their proponents were[41]. Priestley (1733-1804) argued that in both the natural and social sciences much more could be discovered if the shackles laid down by the old universities were removed. In his lifetime, it remained the case that only the non-conformist academies promoted scientific experiments and new learning[42].

Facing an economic system which was still overshadowed by vast landowning interests, Smith (1723-1790) criticised disruption of fair exchange caused by the interference of the powerful in imposing controls to weaken the bargaining positions of others, resulting in greater profits for the powerful, and worse offers for everyone else[43]. He maintained that the benefits of having a division of labour could only be fully realised if no one could extract a bigger share of the profit by virtue of the hold they had over the marketplace. The dominance of the political system by an unaccountable elite was at the same time challenged by

---

[41] Hume is often misinterpreted as an anti-progressive thinker when in fact his philosophy champions moderation grounded on empirical reasoning and opposes unjustifiable assertions and actions by the powerful. See Forbes, D, *Hume's Philosophical Politics*, Cambridge University Press: 1975; and Livingston, D. W., *Hume's Philosophy of Common Life*, University of Chicago Press: 1984.

[42] Priestley's writings, because of their range, are not as readily available as most of the other thinkers referred to here. One useful collection is Passmore, J. A. (ed), *Priestley's Writings on Philosophy, Science and Politics*, New York, Collier Books: 1965. For an overview of his life and work, see Schofield, R. E., *The Enlightenment of Joseph Priestley*, (2 volumes) Pennsylvania State University Press: 1997 and 2004.

[43] Smith has in recent decades been rescued from being hijacked by market fundamentalists and can now be more readily recognised for his moral philosophy linking markets and responsible social arrangements. See, e.g., Griswold, CL, *Adam Smith and the Virtues of Enlightenment*, Cambridge University Press: 1999.

Paine (1737-1809) who repeatedly rebuked the British and French rulers for seeking to prevent a more democratic system from being developed.

The overall outlook of these thinkers was captured by Richard Price (1723-1791) who set out the key components of their shared reform agenda:

"First, an improvement in the state of civil government. The dispositions and manners of men depend more than we can well conceive on the nature of the government to which they are subject. There is nothing so debasing as despotic government. They convert the governed into beasts and the men who govern into demons. Free governments, on the contrary, exalt the human character. They give a feeling of dignity and consequence to the governed, and to the governors a feeling of responsibility which has a tendency to keep them within the bounds of their duty, and to teach them that they are more properly the servants of the public than its governors.

... But, I must hasten to what I meant next to mention as an object necessary to be attended to by the enlightened part of mankind, in order to improve the world. I mean, gaining an open field for discussion, by excluding from it the interposition of civil power, except to keep the peace, by separating religion from civil policy, and emancipating the human mind from the chains of church-authority and church-establishments. Till this can be effected, the worst impediments to improvement will remain. ...

Thirdly, another great object which the friends of reformation ought to attend to is an improvement in the state of education. ... Seminaries of learning are the springs of society which, as they flow foul or pure, diffuse through successive generations depravity and misery, or, on the contrary, virtue and happiness. On the bent given to our minds as they open and expand depends their subsequent fate, and on the general management of education depend the honour and dignity of our species. ... Improvement, in this case, must be in the highest degree useful. It has a particular tendency to perpetuate itself and may, however inconsiderable at first, increase so far as to bring about an universal reformation."[44]

---

[44] Extracts from Price's *The Evidence for a Future Period of Improvement in the State of Mankind* (1787).

Price spoke for his age when he emphasised the part education must play in parallel with keeping interventions from the powerful – political or religious – at bay. He recognised that it was not enough to stop the powerful from imposing their views on what society must accept, because the vacuum could be filled by superstitious or other misguided ideas unless people learn to develop and apply their intelligence to sifting out dubious claims from what warranted assent on the grounds of the available evidence. The growing interest in education, in promoting and cultivating the ability to think critically, was a key factor in developing the ethos of resolving issues through the joint deliberations of reasonable people.

In France, reformists like Montesquieu (1689-1755), Voltaire (1694-1778), Diderot (1713-1784), Turgot (1727-1781) and Condorcet (1743-1794) considered the ideas of their British counterpart and the effects of having a more inclusive ethos in Britain. They concluded that similar changes to cultural attitudes and institutional arrangements must be brought about in their own country, and indeed the rest of Europe[45]. Rather than looking for indubitable answers – be these handed down from the Catholic Church or deduced by *a priori* means suggested by philosophers like Descartes – they looked to the plurality of ordinary people to learn through successive trial and error what should be provisionally believed.

They made use of every form of educative communications to raise understanding of the benefits of experimental learning. They published pamphlets, plays, novels, scientific treatises to illustrate how human knowledge could be expanded if oppressive interventions were rolled back. Under the joint editorship of Diderot and d'Alembert (1717-

---

[45] Montesquieu, Voltaire, and d'Alembert looked to British political institutions and the ideas of Bacon and Locke for inspiration on developing a reformist philosophy in France. In so doing, they helped to elaborate and transmit Enlightenment thinking across Europe. Some writers have maintained that Diderot and D'Holbach developed a more radical strand of thought distinct from the British. See Blom, P. *A Wicked Company: the forgotten radicalism of the European Enlightenment*, New York, Basic Books: 2010; and Israel, J. I. *Enlightenment Contested*, Oxford, OUP: 2006. For the social factors which facilitated that transmission, see Munck, T, *The Enlightenment: a comparative social history 1721-1794*, London, Arnold: 2000; and Im Hof, U, *The Enlightenment: a historical introduction*, Oxford, Blackwell Publishers: 1997.

1783), they produced their *Encyclopédie* to set out where outmoded beliefs were being superseded by the latest ideas established by objective research[46]. Echoing the Mohist triple tests of truth claims, they would root out traditional doctrines if these were not backed by objectively recorded facts, current testimony, or experiments which could challenge their validity. They met and corresponded with each other extensively to build up a growing network that served as a virtual storehouse of ideas – so that it was immensely difficult to suppress when diverse individuals could continue to fuel its activities.

At the same time, true to their own epistemological commitments, their network enabled them to subject each other's ideas to critical scrutiny and continuous improvement. Commentators who mistook their lack of a single set of uniform doctrines as a sign of weakness simply failed to appreciate their concern with not allowing any provisional belief to degenerate into unquestionable dogma. This determination to promote the cross-examination of a plurality of ideas also explained why they included in their circle individuals who did not in fact fully share their progressive outlook. Rousseau (1712-1778) was notably, like the *philosophes*, dissatisfied with many of the prevailing features of social and political arrangements, but he wanted to replace the oppressive hierarchy with a simplistic form of community where faith in a deity and a blessed lawmaker who grasps the general will, rather than the intense exchange of intelligent criticisms between fellow citizens, would guide society. Rousseau's ideal was the elimination of inequalities for the sake of regaining a form of primitive harmony in living a basic, decent life. He recoiled from sophisticated experimental reasoning being the driving force behind an ever-improving society. His instinctive belief was that it would bring misery. For the *philosophes*, it was important to note his caution, but any society that tried to freeze itself in time was doomed to degenerate in its capacity to meet the needs of its members, and miss out on the benefits its collective intelligence could bring.

In time they extended their network to princes, bishops, kings and empresses, anyone who might be persuaded to use their position of

---

[46] For a definitive guide to the *Encyclopédie*'s vision, see d'Alembert, Jean Le Rond, *Preliminary Discourse to the Encyclopedia of Diderot*, (translated by R.N. Schwab) University of Chicago Press: 1995.

power to bring about reforms. But they were also ready to confront the powerful when necessary. On many occasions, they led the charge on high profile cases to challenge and embarrass the authorities by circulating damning reports of the bigotry, inconsistency and sheer fabrications behind persecutions and miscarriages of justice. Voltaire, for example, looked into the case of Jean Calas, a Huguenot merchant, who was executed after he was found guilty of murdering his eldest son, and publicised the countless holes in the prosecution case until the Parlement in Paris admitted its error and declared Calas posthumously innocent[47].

In advancing the case for greater inclusion, the French *philosophes* contributed to the development of the Enlightenment ethos across Europe and beyond, synthesising different strands of new thinking into a general moral outlook. In the seventeenth century, the demands for epistemological, political and religious transformation had been mainly channelled through separate routes. Bacon's core critique was directed at the knowledge establishment – at those who had the power to declare what was correct learning and what was to be dismissed. His immediate followers pooled their resources and formed what eventually became the Royal Society to help mainstream the scientific approach in the advancement of learning. But they were not at the forefront of challenging the state to redistribute political executive power. If they were, it was highly unlikely Charles II would have granted their institution a royal charter.

It was left to republicans like James Harrington (1611-1677) and the Levellers to articulate the case for new forms of government. Yet they had little interest in theories concerning the nature of the world. Harrington typically had no time for scientific experimenters whose efforts to study minute details of nature struck him as a profound waste of time. Standing apart from both the experimental philosophers and the political activists were the religious humanists who, from Herbert of Cherbury to George Fox, the Quaker, sought to refocus faith away from

---

[47] Voltaire embodied how the intellectual-activist could use his writings and connections to pressurised the establishment to draw back from a wide range of abuse of power. An excellent portrait can be found in Pearson, R, *Voltaire Almighty: a life in pursuit of freedom*, London, Bloomsbury Publishing: 2005. Also well worth reading is Morley, J, *Voltaire*, London, Macmillan & Co: 1900.

dogmatic injunctions and ritual compliance to an ethics of love for one's fellow human beings. They rarely ventured into disputes about scientific methodology or political systems, but concentrated on explaining why caring for the needs of others was really the essence of living in accordance with the highest ideal[48].

It was near the close of the seventeen-century when John Locke began to draw these strands closer together in his philosophical works. Building on his ideas, the Enlightenment ethos connected them into an integrated worldview, which would inform the overall struggle to redistribute power from those who had hitherto monopolised scholastic, political or religious authority, so that everyone could be enabled to learn, decide and contribute to their understanding of the common good. The likes of Voltaire, Diderot, Priestley, Franklin, and Bentham pressed for liberation from unreasonable arrangements that had allowed power to be exercised oppressively.

Furthermore, this ethos transcended national and religious divisions. Reformists in France and Britain, and indeed other parts of Europe and North America, shared the same underlying objectives. There was not a French set of Enlightenment principles as distinct from a British set[49]. Neither established Protestant nor Catholic doctrines served as its foundations. It was transmitted by diverse intellectuals with the common purpose of encouraging all to cultivate and use their intelligence. With the rise of the Enlightenment consciousness, the struggle for inclusive communities entered its modern, cosmopolitan phase. From then on, continuous demands for reforms would be driven

---

[48] A notable exception was William Penn, a leading Quaker advocate who established the progressive constitution of the American state that was named after him – Pennsylvania. See Hepworth Dixon, W. *A History of William Penn: founder of Pennsylvania*, New York, New Amsterdam Book Company: 1903 (reprinted by BiblioBazaar).

[49] Some academics maintain that the French Enlightenment is uniquely the most important, while others prefer to focus on the German Enlightenment, with the British Enlightenment being generally (with the notable exception of Roy Porter's work) overlooked. Anyone interested in this debate should consult in the first instance Gay, P. *The Enlightenment: An Interpretation* (in two volumes), London, Wildwood House: 1973. See also, Israel, J. I. *A Revolution of the Mind: Radical Enlightenment and the Intellectual Origins of Modern Democracy*, Princeton, Princeton University Press: 2010.

by the learning and experience of successive generations. There was to be no single all-commanding figure, no indubitable text, no organisation vested with absolute power to decree what was to be done. Bacon, Locke, Voltaire, and others would be read with respect, but not as having the definitive answers for all times. There was to be no quest for some absolute 'Reason' as a substitute for an absolute 'God', but only a commitment to consider what would constitute the more reasonable course to pursue under different circumstances[50].

## Demands for Enlightened power structures

As Britain and France fought to prevent each other from securing global domination, the champions of the Enlightenment ethos on both sides were united in calling upon those in government to take the lead in reforming power structures. The values and practices which were essential for people to learn objectively, care for each other and flourish as human beings, could only be realised if governments acted in a consistent manner so that people could reason with each other with reference to observable evidence, cooperate without fear of exploitation, and free to innovate and experiment without arbitrary intervention. Writers like Baruch Spinoza (1632-1677), Frederik van Leenhof (1646-1713), John Toland (1670-1722), Anthony Collins (1676-1729), and Alberto Radicati (1698-1737) argued that toleration for diverse beliefs should not be limited to a any theologically defined set of views, but be extended to all forms of beliefs and respect granted to all citizens since everyone should be free to experiment and argue about how they should live so long as they did not threaten the lives of others[51].

An Enlightened government would accordingly not allow any

---

[50] Those who looked to deify 'Reason' later during the French Revolution, as will be seen later in this chapter, were precisely those who betrayed the Enlightenment by seeking to amass powers to themselves.

[51] It has been argued that the Enlightenment thinkers were divided between those who were thoroughly committed to toleration and freedom and those who only had a moderate inclination towards reforms. It could also be argued that there is a broad continuum rather than any sharp demarcation. For the former, see Israel, J. I., *Enlightenment Contested*, Oxford, Oxford University Press: 2006.

doctrines, which could not be openly assessed with the aid of empirical evidence and rational debates, to dictate what people must do. Any group invoking absolute religious or traditional claims to justify their demands would seek to rule out any process whereby the legitimacy of those claims could be fairly examined by others, on the grounds that such a move was inherently disrespectful to them. If such attempts to block rational public discourse was to be permitted then nothing could be resolved through evidence-based discussions. Unquestionable assertions from one side would either be arbitrarily imposed or implacably opposed by the unquestionable counter-claims from the other. To avoid this, the affairs of the state must be kept away from the church or any organisation which thinks itself uniquely exempt from critical analysis. Enlightenment advocates wanted secular government not because they did not believe in God – some of them had a deep religious faith – but because they realised that people must be able to worship in their own ways without their differences forcing the public realm to take side.

By denying public legitimacy to any doctrines which could not be openly defended on rational grounds, a government would no longer be able to invoke some indubitable set of principles to forbid the articulation of ideas in print or at public forums. Instead of hiding behind some obscure or 'holy' pretext to censor whatever it took a disliking to, the onus would be on the government to demonstrate why certain ideas should not be circulated. In France, the *Encyclopédie* project represented one of the boldest and most concerted efforts by progressive thinkers of the day to displace false representations of the world by knowledge claims grounded on observation and experimentation. Under the leadership of Diderot and D'Alembert, volume after volume of facts and arguments bombarded the fortress of 'God'-sanctioned authority[52]. To ban such publications without putting forward convincing explanations served to undermine the authority of the government itself.

In Britain, the government tried to use censorship to stop public questioning of its policies, often without even the pretence of upholding some sacred higher principles. This naked disrespect for the importance of being able to freely debate policies that affected people's lives stirred

---

[52] Diderot's thoughts on political subjects are collected in Mason, J. H. & Wokler, R. (ed.) *Diderot: Political Writings*, Cambridge University Press: 1992.

up the resolve of printers, magistrates and jurors who had nothing in common apart from their shared belief that attempts to suppress public discussions of government actions were unacceptable.

An Enlightened government would be expected to do more than just refraining from interfering with public deliberations. It would review all the enforcement and punitive instruments at its disposal to ensure that they would only be deployed where, on the available evidence, it was necessary to achieve objectives serving the interest of the community at large. Intrusion by government agents into private properties without real justification or the use of severe punishment disproportionate to the crimes in question, would need to be duly curtailed. One of the leading critics of judicial power, reflecting the spread of the Enlightenment ethos across Europe, was the Italian thinker, Cesare Beccaria (1738-1794), who exposed the callousness and futility in using torture to obtain confessions, criticised the arbitrary discretionary power of judges, and attacked the inconsistency and inequality of sentencing, especially when the accused could use their status and connections to secure a lighter sentence[53].

In clearing judicial intimidation and unwarranted criminalisation from the public domain, people would have greater opportunities to experiment and discuss responsibly issues which mattered to them, but as Richard Price had observed, how well they made use of those opportunities would depend to a large extent on the education they received. The more people had learnt to question, reason, suspend their judgement where appropriate, and weigh up conflicting evidence, the more likely they were to contribute to wider decisions in a rational manner to the benefit of all. Followers of Bacon had succeeded in persuading Charles II in giving his backing to the Royal Society. But the established universities were still a long way from embracing empirical knowledge or scientific investigations as the basis of learning. Greater patronage – i.e., endorsement and investment – was required to increase the number and capability of educational institutions to foster the new learning culture.

Contrary to libertarian misinterpretation, which took the

---

[53] Beccaria, Cesare, *On Crimes & Punishments*, (translated and edited by Newman, G. R. and Marongiu, P.) Transaction Publishers: 2009.

Enlightenment ethos to be a free-for-all demand for people to behave as they pleased without interference from those in authority, what its proponents sought was the rolling back of illegitimate intervention by those with dubious authority. Stopping governments from dictating what people must accept to be true was only a step – though a crucial one – to enabling people to explore reasonably what should be accepted in society. Alongside Bacon, whose approach to advancing learning was enthusiastically championed by the Royal Society and the *philosophes*, the humanist figure most widely celebrated by Enlightenment thinkers was Cicero. In him, they saw someone who respected reason and public duties, and who devoted himself to enlightening others about the importance of challenging superstitions, dogmas, deceptive rhetoric, and the concentration and abuse of power. Cicero did not advise against allowing Caesar an absolute say about the affairs of Rome so that individual Romans could indulge in expressing and following whatever ideas, however foolish, they might have, leaving the state with no coherent direction to follow. He wanted to see the ability to reason cultivated and used by the citizens themselves so that the state could function effectively without relying on the charisma and judgement of one or two leaders.

Enlightenment thinkers hoped that their educative activities would bring about more inclusive communities through three critical steps. First, the small ruling elite would be guided to realise that it was in their enlightened self-interest as well as the broader public interest that they ought in any case to embrace, to ground their decisions on objective reasoning, which would be strengthened through the greater input from others concerned with getting those decisions right. It would be good for the ruler to rely on logic and evidence, but it would be better still if that reliance were enriched by the contributions of others uninhibited by threats of punitive reactions from the ruler.

Secondly, a wider section of society currently outside the ruling elite would acquire the learning to consider public policy matters by means of evidence-based reasoning, and would take on a substantial share of the decision-making power from the ruling elite, connecting those decisions with a broader representation of the public.

Thirdly, the new group of decision makers would support the rest of society to secure the education, information, responsibilities, and power that should be shared amongst all citizens, so that what the government does in the name of all would really be shaped by the reasonable input of all.

For most parts of Europe, the first step was barely taken. Voltaire and Diderot tried with the likes of Empress Catherine of Russia, and King Frederick of Prussia, to steer them onto the Enlightenment path. History was to show that without the readiness for the second step to be taken, the relative enlightened minds of a few individual rulers would not be enough to reform power structures across society. In Britain and France, hopes were raised that so long as the ruler in question could be persuaded of the value of moving to the second step, a substantial redistribution of power away from the ruling elite could be made a reality. The struggle in the eighteenth century showed that step two might become all the more necessary when step one could not be taken because the ruler in question could not grasp the need to move forward. Furthermore, success at step two could become one of the biggest obstacles for step three because the new establishment decided to oppose power being redistributed further beyond them to other less powerful groups in society.

## Authoritarian response to the Enlightenment challenge

Although Britain provided a positive example to other countries like France as to how the authoritarian powers of the monarch or the church could be systematically reduced, reformists in Britain itself were well aware that they were still a long way off achieving a fair distribution of power in society.

The composition of the two Houses of Parliament posed a particular problem. In demanding that the King should share more power with the Commons and the Lords, Parliament had presented itself as the institution acting on behalf of the people. But not only did just a small minority of the people had a say in who would represent them in Parliament, even they had an extremely limited influence when many seats in the Commons, not to mention the Lords, were filled at the discretion of the establishment itself. If Parliament was truly to be a representative body, the system for determining who should have a say about who could sit in it, and what they could or could not do in relation to the monarch and his ministerial advisers, independent judges, and the public at large, would have to be thoroughly reviewed.

Growing recognition of the need to reform Parliament built up the momentum for change in the early decades of the eighteenth century. Then events took an unexpected turn. As mentioned earlier, the deposed Stuarts had been supported by France in their claim over the British throne. In 1745, Charles Edward Stuart returned from the continent to lead an army in Scotland, with the support of the Scottish Highlanders. To deal with the threat, King George II sent his brother, the Duke of Cumberland, whose ruthlessness in the ensuing battle gave him the nickname, 'the Butcher'. His reputation in safeguarding the nation's security enabled him, as numerous authoritarian figures before and after had done, to shift the concentration of power back up towards the top of the political hierarchy.

The Whigs who had engineered the Glorious Revolution to impose constitutional limits to monarchical power were marginalised. George II and Cumberland successfully exploited the fear of another foreign-backed invasion and asked the Tories to help run their government of Britain and her overseas territories. For over half a century since the 1688 settlement, the Whigs had moved Britain forward from being ruled at the whims of a hereditary king, and reformists had been counting on the Whig leadership to deliver the next step of progress by widening the civic foundations of government to more people in the country. But now the Tories, who had nothing but contempt for the wider distribution of power to the people, were firmly entrenched again, loyally serving whichever absolute master happened to be sitting on the throne; and from 1760 on, that occupant was George III, who was as convinced about his unquestionable authority to rule as his grandfather's uncle, the deposed James II.

For the rest of the eighteenth century, George III devoted himself to extinguishing all hopes of Britain progressing towards a more enlightened form of governance. He was convinced that he had the God-given right to command his people as he saw fit. When the Seven Years War was concluded with France in 1763, George III embarked on a course which struck many Britons as being too soft on authoritarian France and all too harsh on their own kin who had settled in American territories which were now securely under British control. John Wilkes

(1725-1797) directed his criticisms at the Government's position in relation to the Treaty of Paris, which concluded the war. He published *The North Briton*, the first journal that openly questioned government policies. Nominally directed at the Prime Minister, Lord Bute, Wilkes' verbal attack was blatantly aimed at the King himself[54].

George III wanted to silence Wilkes immediately. Even though the latter was a Member of Parliament, the King had him placed under arrest on a general warrant, put in the Tower, and his house ransacked. But authoritarian assault on citizens could not be so easily achieved when the outlook of the Enlightenment had been spreading fast. Instead of blindly following the King, many members of the judiciary exercised their independent judgement and concluded that the legality of general warrants – arresting people with no specific charge – was itself suspect. Public opinion, fuelled by critical journals pioneered by the likes of Wilkes, was against the arbitrary use of executive power. The Tory administration nonetheless found a way to do the King's bidding by attacking Wilkes for writing an obscene poem, removing his parliamentary privilege as an MP, and getting him condemned by both Houses of Parliament. Wilkes, however, decided to test the system by standing again as an MP. He won comfortably.

George III was not prepared to accept that. He was determined to remove Wilkes from Parliament and had him sentenced to twenty-two months in prison. But each time Wilkes was expelled from the House, the electorate of Middlesex would vote him back in. And when the Tory Government subverted the electoral process by putting someone else in the seat Wilkes had won, they only turned Wilkes into a political martyr.

Wilkes resumed his campaign of subjecting Parliamentary proceedings to critical reporting. Far from being isolated, the Supporters of the Bill of Rights Society – reminding everyone of the unfinished business of the 1688 Revolution – was formed to back Wilkes' call for reforms to distribute political power more widely. Agents were sent round the country to make speeches, the printed press was used to denounce the Government, and show up corruptions in Parliament. One of the issues which they increasingly drew attention to was George III's

---

[54] Rudé, GF, *Wilkes and Liberty: a Social Study of 1763 to 1774*, Oxford, Clarendon Press: 1962.

policy over the British colonies in North America. Infuriated by defiant commoners like Wilkes who kept his government's activities within the British Isles under relentless scrutiny, the King would not tolerate such insolence from Britons settled in his overseas empire. Not surprisingly, colonists in America enthusiastically contributed funds to aid the Supporters of the Bill of Rights Society and Wilkes' reformist cause.

George III was convinced that with the Seven Years War between France and Britain concluded in 1763, North America was under his firm control. He decided to consolidate his authority without conceding any form of political input from the colonists in return. A Declaratory Act was passed to signal the Crown's sovereign right to tax its colonies, followed by a series of import duties. Colonists who were not initially inclined to reject British rule began to question why they should accept such rule when they were denied any say over how it was exercised.

Intellectual and political leaders like Benjamin Franklin (1706-1790) and Thomas Jefferson (1743-1826), who had been at the forefront of transmitting Enlightenment thinking to others in America, located the tension between the British Crown and the people who lived in British American territories in the wider conflict over how power should be distributed to maximise people's wellbeing. When the King clearly was not going to engage in any meaningful dialogue with his American subjects' over policies that affected them, the drift towards a violent confrontation became inevitable.

The 1776 turning point

It is understandable that in reaction against interpretations of the American Revolution as a purely idealistic battle to bring democracy to all, some historians have turned to focus almost exclusively on the ambitions of many political figures in the American colonies to create their own commercial and military empire to rival that of Britain[55]. However, in reality most of the key players acted with a combination of motives. It is true that they rarely managed to escape their historical

---

[55] Two examples are: Draper, T, *A Struggle for Power: the American Revolution*, Little, Brown & Co: 1996; and Jennings, F, *The Creation of America: through revolution to empire*, Cambridge University Press: 2000.

limitations in relation to the appalling treatment of the Native Americans or the enslavement of Africans – with a few notable exceptions like William Penn, Quaker Governor of Pennsylvania – but a crucial difference between those who were solely concerned with securing power advantages to themselves and those who had a real interest in building a fairer society was that the latter wanted to put in place new arrangements which would facilitate improvement for all in the years and decades to come.

The English Revolution had shown in the previous century that when the most powerful refused even to contemplate entering into any form of meaningful dialogue about power redistribution, oppression had to be countered by determined resistance, with the use of arms a necessity if violence was threatened by the oppressor. However, it also revealed how by its very nature violent conflicts marginalised rational discourse, and proposals for greater inclusion – as those put forward by the Levellers – could be ruthlessly discarded, while new forms of authoritarian controls would assert themselves so long as counter forces were not effectively established.

As the eighteenth century entered its final quarter, Enlightenment ideas on what further reforms were needed gathered momentum. These were not demands for the creation of some utopian society, but advice on the stepping stones essential to take communities forward to become progressively more inclusive. In 1776, calls for economic, legal and political reforms reached a new crescendo. There was the publication of Adam Smith's *Enquiry into the Wealth of Nations*, which presented substantial evidence to show that when people were able to trade their labour on fair terms without anyone using their controls of the market to gain unwarranted advantages, backed by a government investing in necessary public infrastructure, which would otherwise be neglected, prosperity would increase.

In France, Turgot who had not only developed similar ideas to Smith's, but held the position of Director-General in government, submitted his radical Six Edicts to the King, including the extension of free trade in corn to benefit the public in general (if to the disadvantage of the big farming interests); the ending of restrictive guilds; and the

taxing of landowners to provide funds for the upkeep of roads[56]. Louis
XVI sacked Turgot, and France headed even faster towards a
revolutionary crisis.

In the same year, Jeremy Bentham published *A Fragment on
Government*, attacking conventional assumptions in constitutional and
legal thinking, arguing that how things had always been taken to be by
those in power in the past was no substitute for revising laws to promote
the greatest happiness of the greatest number. One of the key reasons
why the happiness of the multitude had not hitherto been taken into
account was of course down to their not having any say in the law-
making process. And the unmet demands by the Levellers a century ago
for a democratic constitution was taken up by not only John Wilkes but
others like John Cartwright (1740-1824) who in 1776 published *Take
Your Choice* advocating universal male suffrage and the secret ballot,
and set up political associations to press for reforms.

Like his French counterpart, King George III did not want to
accede to reforms that shifted power away from the top end of the
hierarchy. But before his disagreement with Britons at home came to a
head, his confrontation with his subjects in America erupted beyond
diplomatic reconciliation. Urged on by the publication in 1776 of
Richard Price's *Observations on Civil Liberty and the Justice and Policy
of the War with America* and Tom Paine's *Common Sense*, which warned
that to maintain a submissive link to an unelected head of state would
jeopardise the future autonomy of the soon-to-be united states to make
decisions for themselves, the political leaders in America decided they
must fight off the British forces so that they could develop their own
constitution with their own elected representatives[57]. They issued their
Declaration of Independence in 1776 and commenced their irrevocable
termination of monarchical rule.

The French regime, hostile to agitation for power redistribution
within its own borders, but still smarting from their defeat by Britain in

---

[56] For more on the political background, see Dakin, D, *Turgot and the Ancien
Régime in France*, London, Methuen: 1939.
[57] For more on Paine's role in the American Revolution, see Keane, J. *Tom
Paine: a political life*, London, Bloomsbury Publishing: 1996. For a detailed
exposition of his ideas, see Claeys, G. *Thomas Paine: Social & Political
Thought*, Boston, Unwin Hyman: 1989.

the Seven Years War, decided to offer substantial financial and military support to the colonists, enabling them to secure an otherwise unlikely victory. Thus, not for the first time, animosity between alpha male authoritarians unwittingly helped progressive forces advance.

For the progressive-minded across Europe, America was a political experiment in real time, testing and demonstrating how people could as equal citizens deliberate together without the intervention of an authoritarian ruler, and come up with their own institutional structures and policies. It offered hope that inclusive communities could against all odds be built after all. Such a prospect was to reverberate through Britain and, ironically but not surprisingly, even more so in France.

The paradigm of Enlightened citizens

From now on, aspirations for fairer distribution of power would be tied to a resolute commitment to improve political arrangements. Persuasion through arguments and education should continue as Enlightenment philosophers had urged, but if oppression showed no sign of ebbing, and there was no real prospect of reasoned dialogue to resolve injustice, then a different form of government had to be established.

As Condorcet, like many who had been closely following events from the other side of the Atlantic, observed, "Men whom the reading of philosophic books had secretly converted to the love of liberty became enthusiastic over the liberty of a foreign people while they waited for the moment when they could recover their own, and they seized with joy this opportunity to avow publicly sentiments which prudence had prevented them from expressing" (*Eloge de Franklin*). Turgot called the Americans who had shaken off unaccountable rule "the hope of mankind, they may well become its model."

Henceforth, there was a new paradigm for measuring progress. It was not enough to rely on governments becoming enlightened, political conditions must be structured to facilitate the development of enlightened citizens. The architects of independent America saw at first hand how the struggle for inclusive communities was checked in Britain, and how an authoritarian-minded ruler could push aside ineffective constraints when he was determined to get his own way. They knew all too well that it was necessary to guard against complacency and be prepared to change where America was found to be insufficiently inclusive itself. The treatment of Native Americans and the perpetuation of slavery were just two of the most pressing problems.

The essence of the new paradigm was summarised by the Prussian philosopher, Immanuel Kant (1724-1804), as the capacity to think for oneself. What Kant had in mind was not individuals coming up with whatever arbitrary thoughts they might have, but people exercising their skills for reasoning fully so that they could share in objective deliberations in ascertaining what they should believe, without fearing that their reasoned quest for answers would be blocked by someone just on account of the latter being more powerful.

Whereas people like Rousseau, who looked idealistically upon the primitive past, would suppose that it was up to some kind of Platonic philosopher-legislator to grasp what the General Will was and impose it, regardless of what fickle individuals might think, Kant valued the rational potential of all human beings. It is because they wanted to nurture this potential for a more sophisticated future, not to regress it to an infantile past, that the authentic torchbearers of the Enlightenment wanted citizens to deepen their capacity for understanding. Furthermore, this is not a purely logical understanding of premises and conclusions, but an emotionally rich understanding of the needs and feelings of other people. For Kant, Adam Smith, Condorcet, and other champions in the late Enlightenment period, the abilities to reason out causes and effects, to see why others may embrace or abhor different experiences, to work out what one should do in life, were all parts of an enquiring mind – sensitive and critical – on the basis of which citizens acquired their sense of responsibility and reciprocity to each other[58].

Kant envisaged that where countries moved towards the enlightened model of governance in which citizens were able to determine their collective actions through reasoned discourse, perpetual peace amongst nations would be a realistic goal. If power were taken away from vengeful, arrogant, irresponsible leaders who had no qualification to rule but an arbitrary hereditary-based claim to the throne,

---

[58] For more on Kant's ideas and responses to them amongst German thinkers during and after the eighteenth century, see Schmidt, J (ed), *What is Enlightenment?* University of California Press: 1996.

and placed instead in people who would have to bear the consequence of their decisions, dialogue and diplomacy would become the norm in international relations as they would have done at the national level.

Citizens should therefore be given the twin support of education to develop their rational abilities, and protection from arbitrary control by the state and any powerful body. Religion was to be kept out of the public domain as any refusal to let objective reasoning question subjective faith would have made it impossible for discussions to be settled through rational means. Instead of being ordered to live in accordance with unquestionable doctrines, citizens should reason and experiment responsibly themselves to discover what would bring them and others a fulfilling life.

Against the Puritanism ascendant in 17th century England and repressive morality promoted by the Catholic establishment elsewhere, Enlightenment philosophers attacked attempts to foster guilt over the pursuit of innocent pleasures and fear to block healthy engagement with curiosity. The non-conformist academies in Britain, led by philosophers like Joseph Priestley who combined religious piety in his personal faith with rational objectivity in his public activities, showed how an increasing variety of subjects could be taught to anyone irrespective of their backgrounds so long as they had an interest in learning.

One of the most important implications of this gestalt change concerned the treatment of women in traditional alpha male dominated communities. For thousands of years authoritarians had given their male subordinates a relative sense of 'self-worth' by reinforcing the social system that subjugated women to men. Women were to be totally submissive to and dependent on men – fathers, husbands, masters. They were not to seek knowledge, pleasures, least of all an equal share of power to determine their lives. At the most extreme, if a man violated a woman sexually, it would be the woman who was considered to have brought shame upon herself. And where independent minded women from the poorer sections of society came to be seen as a threat to men's 'natural' order, beliefs in the supernatural could be invoked to burn them as witches. Progressive-minded humanists from the time of the Renaissance had already started to distance themselves from such repulsive customs. The inclusion of women in the paradigm of enlightened citizens moved this much further forward and demanded that women be given the same opportunities as men to cultivate their rational capacity and lead a fulfilling life without preconceived limitations. Condorcet (1743-1794) viewed such a development as integral to the progress of human communities from their primitive state of ignorance and repression, to ever improving social arrangements whereby everyone could find a responsible and effective path to happiness[59].

Mary Wollstonecraft (1759-1797) seized the growing awareness that arbitrary rule over the powerless was unacceptable and asked why it should be tolerated when arbitrary rule was exercised by men over women. She argued that there was no coherent reason why women should not have the same social status, respect, and educational opportunities as men. She did not base her arguments on some romanticised idealisation of women – for history had readily shown that women could be just as ruthless and arrogant as any men if they took up 'alpha male' positions in exerting macho dominance – but on the empirical understanding of women's equal capacity for learning and organisation. The marginalisation of women was exposed as nothing more than another piece of the pernicious collection of prejudices, superstitions, dogmas, which had built up over the centuries to deprive the powerless of their self-esteem, and desensitise those with power in their treatment of those at their mercy[60].

Along with women, there were of course the 'others' who were also marginalised by authoritarian communities. The Irish had long endured the arbitrary rule of the British. The more recent colonisation of India brought millions of people into a regime that regarded them as inferior beings. British and other European settlers in America, with the singular exception of the Quakers, were contemptuous and treacherous towards the Native Americans[61]. The Virginians took the land of the Powhatans, the South Carolinians exterminated the Yamasees, the Marylanders helped destroy the Susquehannocks; and New Englanders were responsible for the ethnic cleansing of Pequots and Narragansetts.

---

[59] Williams, D, *Condorcet & Modernity*, Cambridge University Press: 2007.

[60] An edition which combines original text and critical comments is Wollstonecraft, M, *A Vindication of the Rights of Woman*, (ed. by Poston, CH) New York, WW Norton & Co: 1975.

[61] Debo, A, *A History of the Indians of the United States*, London, Pimlico: 1995.

At the same time, Africans were captured, transported in the most inhumane manner even by the standards of the time, and made slaves in a far-off land. To sustain the authority of those higher up the hierarchy, they were told to be thankful for the kind treatment of them if it should ever be forthcoming, and reminded of their worthlessness when they were scolded, beaten or killed for not complying with what their superiors asked of them.

All such gross inequalities would be exposed in a new light, radiating from the promise of the American Revolution. As more and more citizens acquired an enlightened perspective, it would lead to more widespread realisation that there was no coherent reason why others currently excluded should not also be given the opportunities, indeed educational support, to become enlightened citizens too. This virtuous circle, on which Enlightenment champions of the late 18th century were pinning their hopes, depended crucially on no individuals or groups securing a permanent power advantage to prevent demands for improvements from being met. This in turn is why constitutional arrangements have always been fundamental to cutting back power inequalities.

In Britain, the authoritarian arrogance, which caused the loss of the American colonies, also brought home the utter lack of progress over a century on from the Levellers making the case to extend the franchise. Politicians like Charles James Fox (1749-1806) and forums such as the Conversation Club in Liverpool continued to press for parliamentary reform. It was not until 1785, when the Prime Minister, William Pitt, presented a Bill for Parliamentary Reform, which was swiftly if unsurprisingly defeated. It provoked the formation of a broader alliance between middle and working class reformists. By 1792 every town in Britain had its own club for Constitutional Information. Thomas Hardy (1752-1832) who led the London Corresponding Society, asserted that Members of Parliament were "falsely calling themselves the representatives of the people, but who were, in fact, selected by a comparatively few individuals, who preferred their own particular aggrandisement to the general interest of the community."

Unfortunately, the French Revolution, which broke out in 1789, was becoming increasingly violent and destructive, and any vague association of activities in Britain with calls to redistribute power more fairly was condemned as subversive. In 1794, the Habeas Corpus Act was suspended. Later that year, Hardy himself was brought to trial along with other activists on the charge that they were guilty of treason as they organised meetings where people were encouraged to disobey King and Parliament. The jury returned a verdict of 'not guilty' in the absence of any concrete evidence. But repression was only just beginning. Pitt secured the passage of the stringent Treason & Sedition Acts of 1795 and 1799 – making the combination of working people in clubs and societies, for the sake of improved working conditions and wages, punishable on grounds of conspiracy. Manufacturers could keep down wages even though the price of food was rising. Workers, without the power to vote for their own representatives or any effective means to register their discontent, were left in complete frustration.

In America, the virtuous circle had barely commenced when contests over what constraints should be placed on different holders of power threatened to throw the newly independent country into constitutional turmoil. Getting rid of the unaccountable and overbearing George III was relatively easy compared with having to decide who should have power instead. Following Montesquieu, the horizontal distribution of power amongst the executive, legislative and judicial branches of government was broadly accepted. But the vertical distribution turned out to be much more problematic.

On the one hand there were those who, in possession of ruling power in their own state, were not well disposed towards conceding any control to an inter-state, or federal, level of government. This was particularly true in the case of the southern states who knew that their continued practice of slavery was frowned upon by their northern neighbours. On the other hand, there were politicians who were already thinking ahead to how the American states would need to collaborate together to compete commercially and militarily with the much more established European nations. They anticipated that unless there was an overarching government for all the states, there would be a high risk of them going to war against each other, and they would in any case miss the opportunities to pool their resources to establish a joint financial system and a common military regime.

Then there were the progressive minded advocates like James Madison and Thomas Jefferson who were aware that having *both* Federal and State government institutions was potentially a key part of any strategy to guard against the concentration of power. But for them, getting that balance right was crucial. Criticised for fluctuating between pro-Federalist and pro-State positions, Madison and Jefferson were in fact consistently scrutinising and pressing for more effective safeguards on both sides[62]. They appreciated that injustice perpetrated by a state might require a higher level government to rectify, and were ready to exercise as President the federal power at their disposal to meet the needs of American citizens beyond what individual states could offer. However, they were also amongst the most insistent in putting constraints on that federal power. They led the campaign against the draft American constitution of 1787 because it gave too much power to the Federal Government without giving citizens protection from the abuse of that power. As a result of their vision and efforts, the Constitution was amended with the Bill of Rights in 1791.

The vital amendments included the right to exercise one's own religion, or no religion, free from any government influence or compulsion; protection of speech, press, petition & assembly – all essential for shared public deliberations and debates – from government suppression; the right to be free of unwarranted and unwanted government intrusion into one's personal and private affairs, papers, and possessions; and the right to be treated fairly and equally by the government whenever the loss of liberty or property is at stake, and regardless of social status. Given that it could not be left to the government to decide if its activities were in compliance with these requirements, it further led to the development of the Supreme Court as the independent arbiter of the constitutional legitimacy of government actions.

Although the critics of Madison and Jefferson dismissed their reservations about the risks of excessive federal power, they were to see the dangers for themselves when John Adams became President. In 1798, when an ordinary citizen, John Fries, led a protest against the imposition of a tax that eastern Pennsylvania objected to, Adams sent in Federal troops to crush the unarmed 'rebellion'. Fries was charged with

---

[62] Jefferson's wide ranging political ideas are gathered in Appleby, J & Ball, T (ed.) *Jefferson: Political Writings*, Cambridge University Press: 1999.

treason and sentenced to death, although intense public protest did secure him a pardon. It was not an isolated incident. Strongly opposed to the republican-democratic ideas fermenting in revolutionary France, Adams took up the position that aligned him with Britain's reactionary government – and at odds with the likes of Jefferson who sympathised with those agitating for political change in France. He signed into law a series of Alien and Sedition Acts which gave him the power to deport all such aliens he considered dangerous, and punish with fine and imprisonment any "false, scandalous and malicious writing or writings against the government of the United States … with intent to defame the said government." Adams used it to imprison editors who were critical of his actions. At least with America, the electorate could remove the head of state by voting him out – which they duly did in 1801. In France, it appeared that change would not come until the head of the king was removed.

## Authoritarian temptations and betrayal of the Enlightenment

For all the Anglo-American panic against the threats posed by revolutionary France, it should be recalled that a key moment in the progressive struggle was the English Parliament's decision to execute King Charles for abusing his power and acting against the interest of the people. The use of force against an incorrigible authoritarian regime was always an option, and at times, a necessity. The test was whether, when resorted to, it could be deployed in a way to avoid interminable chaos ensuing until another authoritarian stepped in. Apologists for authoritarianism from Confucius down had warned that once the established hierarchy was shattered, order could only be restored by another wielding absolute power.

     The temptations are undeniably always there. But the more widespread the ethos of inclusion and Enlightenment, the more likely others would come forward to check the excessive concentration of power and help clear a peaceful path to future reforms without further resort to violence. Cromwell was only an interim figure before the 1688 settlement moved Britain forward to a peaceful regime, which took absolute power away from the monarch. Those who sought to develop what could have been an excessively powerful central government for the United States after their revolution against the British found that they had to concede to those who succeeded in adding the Bill of Rights amendments to the American Constitution. Transition to a new peaceful, deliberative order could be done.

When it began, there were positive signs that the French Revolution could also go through a violent confrontational phase and move on to an open and peaceful regime where citizens could expect protection from the arbitrary exercise of power against them, and equal respect before the law[63]. King Louis XVI, unlike his grandfather who managed to unite all those with an interest in maintaining the oppressive status quo under his flamboyant regime, was at odds with the Aristocrats, the Clergy, the provisional parlements, all of whom were in turn in disagreement amongst themselves and with one another. Louis XVI thought he would cut back on the privileges of the Aristocrats which would benefit the majority of the people, but many in the aristocracy had the support of the parlements in opposing the King. At the same time, other Aristocrats backed by some Clergy were pressing for even more radical termination of privileges and were appealing to the interests of the citizens in general.

With such divisions amongst those with established power, when the Third Estate of representatives of ordinary people declared itself the National Assembly, there was every prospect that it would produce a constitution to underpin the fairer distribution of power across France. From 1789 on, a series of reforms were introduced. All public offices in Catholic France were opened to Protestants, the rights of citizenship were granted to Jews, the press and the theatre were freed from state control, fathers' absolute authority over their children was limited to those under the age of twenty-one, reactionary parlements which insisted on retaining the use of torture were replaced by courts ready to apply the new criminal laws freed from state-sanctioned mutilations.

Of course the reformists did not manage to get as far, or as fast, as they would like. The proposal to abolish slavery in the colonies did not go through. Changes to the laws on inheritance were limited. And

---

[63] For a history of the French Revolution, see Hibbert, C, *The French Revolution*, Penguin: 2001; and Schama, S, *Citizens: a chronicle of the French Revolution*, Penguin, 2004.

associations of workers, instead of being supported, came to be strictly prohibited. But overall, authoritarian controls were gradually being cut back. There was always hope that as the citizens-focused constitutional system was brought into place, rational discussions and mutual respect would lead to more inclusive outcomes.

Unfortunately, the reformists who held out this hope for steady improvement – the *Girondins* and their supporters – were not sufficiently aware of the risk of authoritarianism resurfacing in new forms. Condorcet, a leading *Girondin* himself, agreed with the Jacobins in rejecting a bi-cameral legislative structure on the grounds that the will of the people would be indivisible. In reality, people had many diverse, and often conflicting, interests and preferences, and they needed fair and inclusive arrangements to develop their understanding and resolve their differences through sensible trade-offs and negotiated compromises. To suppose that decisions in the interests of everyone could be made in a single forum by a single group of people was to invite the authoritarian-minded to take over that forum.

By 1793, the Jacobins under the leadership of Robespierre, backed by the ruthlessly efficient Saint-Just, had achieved the twin objectives of eliminating their potential opponents – Louise XVI and the *Girondins* alike – and concentrating decision-making power in the Committee for Public Safety. Swiftly they went about with the rapid executions of anyone suspected of being opposed to their regime, silencing of the media over any critical views they might express, and diversion of the public towards a new form of worship. Lacking any sense of irony, they deified 'Reason', turning the notion of critical examination into an unquestionable object of thoughtless admiration.

Whereas the United States had built a system which spread power across different federal institutions and between the national, state and local levels, France was plunged into a nightmare of power being concentrated in the hands of men with no compunction about sending countless innocent people to their death – via the guillotine or endless military campaigns.

These men might claim that they were pursuing the same values championed by Enlightenment philosophers, but by their deeds it was all too clear that they put their inner certainty above open dialogues, their personal sense of righteousness above public wellbeing, and their desire to be in total control above any reservations others might wish to express. It did not matter that some might claim that they acted out of deference to Enlightenment values, by their action they revealed themselves to be complete traitors to the progressive cause[64].

Whereas in the last decade of the 18th century, Jefferson and Madison turned America at a critical point of its history away from a revival of authoritarianism, Robespierre and Saint-Just pushed France down the authoritarian slope of alpha male dictatorship once more. The violent excesses of the leading Jacobins were only cut short by an application of their own prescription – the guillotine. The fear and instability they created gave rise to unscrupulous manipulations by political leaders and increasing reliance on the army to keep control. By 1799, Napoleon Bonaparte took centre stage and completed the final act of the comic-tragedy of the Jacobins' delusional presentation of themselves as restorers of ancient republican virtues by establishing himself as First Consul. It was only a matter of time before he, emulating the tradition of Roman Caesars, proclaimed himself Emperor.

Enemies of the Enlightenment

For the enemies of the Enlightenment, the terror, the breakdown of law and order were 'inevitable' consequences of questioning established traditions. Following the well-trodden Confucian path of defending authoritarian arrangements as the only safeguard against chaos and bloodshed, Joseph de Maistre (1753-1821) led the attack on criticisms which irresponsibly undermined age-old cultures and customs, weakening them to the point that they crumbled and gave way to destructive anarchy. Even Edmund Burke (1729-1797), who had in the

---

[64] Some writers insist that the radical idealism, especially towards the creation of an egalitarian society, which drove the French Revolution forward would inevitably lead to totalitarian rule (see, for example, Talmon, J.L., *The Origins of Totalitarian Democracy: political theory and practice during the French Revolution and beyond*, Penguin Books: 1952). But others have more convincingly distinguished between Enlightenment values opposing oppressive inequalities and the use of oppressive measures to pursue allegedly Enlightenment goals (see Bronner, S.E., *Reclaiming the Enlightenment: towards a politics of radical engagement*, New York, Columbia University Press: 2004)

past spoke up against the abuse of monarchical power, decided that Enlightenment arguments for progressive reforms must be rejected when they went against the established traditions of a society. As far as the opponents of the French Revolution were concerned, the belief system which underpinned the hierarchy guaranteeing the powerful their entrenched positions – over their subjects, peasants, servants, wives and children – was one to be preserved at all costs. To question it was to unleash all the worst possible scenarios in an otherwise divinely endorsed alpha male universe: a displeased God; inability to retain absurdly large property holding; women who did not need to submit to men to have a roof over their heads; people in authority having to justify their action with reference to objective evidence and reasons; or the replacement of intense primitive tribal feelings by a broad cosmopolitan sensibility and respect for human beings in general regardless of their race or religion.

The antipathy to the Enlightenment was to become a central feature of the authoritarian outlook. It would manifest itself in any traditional society when calls for the powerful to be challenged started to be heard. Some outside Europe and America have even tried to dismiss Enlightenment ideas as an alien Western approach to life which as a matter of their own cultural pride they should reject.

It might not have occurred to them that the vehement denouncement of Enlightenment thinking was itself first invented in the West as a tool for suppressing intellectual and political development. Proudly anti-Western autocrats in fact had no problem embracing Western authoritarian techniques, nor indeed did they reject the benefits of many products of Enlightenment reforms such as medical advancement based on experimentation rather than superstitions or religious dogmas. In truth, the smokescreen of rejecting 'Western' model of inclusive communities was only put up to help the powerful maintain their control over the masses they wanted to keep ignorant and compliant.

Instead of characterising the emergence of modernity in the 18th century as the moment a distinctive 'Western' civilisation split from a diametrically opposed 'non-Western' way of life, we should recognise that the spread of Enlightenment ideas and the reactions it engendered were catalytic in revealing the ideological differences between people who want to hold on to exploitative dominance over others, and those who believe that a more inclusive and rational society could and should be brought about. Far from dividing into geographical camps, their advocates were, and have continued to be to this day, found in every part of the globe, locked in the struggle over power inequalities.

# Chapter 5
# Resisting the Abuse of Power:
# The 1800s

<u>Revolutionary Legacies</u>

The American and French Revolutions left behind four key lessons concerning how power inequalities could be curtailed. First and foremost, any significant power gap must be relentlessly challenged, since even the most benign gesture from the powerful one day could be followed swiftly by ruthless oppression the next.

Secondly, the abuse of power is not inherently associated with any family, tribe, or dynasty, but is an integral danger of any form of power imbalance. Revolutionaries who speak most eloquently about ending injustice are just as likely to abuse their position of power if they were to become so much more powerful than the rest of society. To hold back from imposing safeguards against them when there is a chance to do so could mean that they would be able later on to trample on the lives of vocal dissidents or even total bystanders. Clear limits must be set and upheld to stop power from being abused.

Thirdly, the spread of Enlightenment consciousness revealed that power inequalities existed not just between a country's ruler and his subjects, but between all groups divided by the concentration of (executive, knowledge, status, and resource) power, which favoured one side over the other – men over women, business owners and employers over workers, military aggressors over the conquered, prison and asylum warders over those detained.

Finally, to correct power imbalances without engendering new forms of power abuse would require decision-making systems that enable those affected by the exercise of any form of power to be democratically involved in determining how that power is to be used. Sharing out power so that all could have an equal say is the only reliable counterweight to any individual or group entrusted with substantial power.

The progressive struggle for more inclusive communities would henceforth be shaped by the extent to which these four lessons were taken on board. To take only some of them seriously while ignoring the others would often hinder the overall cause. It was the Enlightenment ethos that continued to integrate all these lessons in a sustained drive to redistribute power from epistemological, political, economic and cultural authorities. Advocates for the Enlightenment were easily distinguished from not just the authoritarians who detested them for promoting an alternative to alpha male hierarchies, but those who would readily betray its values by taking on authoritarian powers themselves.

They would use their influence as writers, teachers, preachers, and reformists, to persuade both those with power and the wider public to move away from power inequalities. That would lead to, they argued, an improved understanding of the human condition and how it could be made better through cooperative enquiry and mutual support without the oppressive distortion brought about by those with concentrated power.

The revolutions in American and France had deepened reformists' understanding of the dangers of being trapped by authoritarian controls and how they were to be addressed. Both government and citizens must play their parts. Structurally, political institutions should be allowed to take concerted action, but only if effective checks and balances were in place. Socially, citizens should not be divided by status and education to such an extent that they would not be able to hold to account those who might seek to disregard the interests of others. Above all, power should not be handed over to any individuals on the basis of their apparently unimpeachable character – for no one could ever be assumed to be divinely incorruptible and omniscient.

If Robespierre was not enough of a warning, Napoleon Bonaparte demonstrated how in the name of saving the French Republic he would crush all opposition and place the country under his absolute rule. Undoubtedly some of the reforms he introduced in France and in the countries he conquered had beneficial effects, but his mistakes were numerous too, and no one could correct them no matter how many were hurt and killed as a result of his unaccountable decisions[65].

---

[65] Napoleon nonetheless has many admirers and defenders for his concern with advancing what he regarded as the core values of the French Revolution. For a critical account of the views from both sides, see Geyl, P, *Napoleon: For and Against*, (translated by Oliver Renier) Penguin Books: 1965.

Alongside vain emperors, there were also new authoritarians created by the Industrial Revolution. As James Bronterre O'Brien wrote in 1834 in the *Poor Man's Guardian*, "Take a factory for instance – and is not the proprietor a sort of petty monarch? ... Is it right that one man should thus hold the lives of hundreds at his pleasure, or that he should be able to say to one man – 'stay and accumulate for me upon my terms', and to another 'go and starve for I do not want your services'?"[66]

But who could correct the power imbalance between business owners and workers, and indeed between other groups, without ending up with too much power themselves? Reformists had to find a way to make sure political leaders and state institutions would not become too powerful that they could destroy people's freedom to lead a mutually beneficial life, and yet not enfeebled in its ability to tackle those who could use their wealth to control the lives of the powerless[67].

At the dawn of the nineteenth century, they faced the challenge of giving people greater freedom from the abuse of power by business interests without handing power to the likes of Robespierre, amongst whose posthumous admirers were Bronterre O'Brien and other radicals who enthusiastically recalled the deeds of revolutionaries while forgetting their callous disregard of the lives of innocent people.

To combat the threat of power inequalities, reformists must oppose *all* authoritarians, be their powerbase old or new, irrespective of their reactionary or revolutionary inclinations. Any attempt to concentrate power in anyone, however charismatic or meek they might seem, in a practically irrevocable manner was in essence incompatible with the purpose of inclusive community life itself.

By the time Napoleonic megalomania was finally defeated in 1815, it was clear that if the greatest happiness was to be attained for the

---

[66] For an introduction to the development of opposition to workers exploitation, see Thompson, EP, *The Making of the English Working Class*, Penguin Books: 1980.

[67] The challenge of balancing the need to grant democratic government enough power to act on behalf of the people with the necessity of setting effective limits against potential abuse of that power was extensively addressed by Thomas Jefferson in his political writings and his Presidency. See, Elkins, S. & McKitrick, E., *The Age of Federalism*, New York: 1993; and Matthews, R.K., *The Radical Politics of Thomas Jefferson*, Lawrence: 1984.

greatest number, then the greatest number would have to be involved in securing a fairer distribution of power.

Rallying against oppression

Following the French Revolution and the final defeat of Napoleon at the Battle of Waterloo, the Government in Britain continued to maintain a firm stance against attempts to challenge prevailing power structures. Progressive advocates were conscious that little had been achieved since the spectre of chaos had been invoked in late eighteenth century to shut out calls for reforms. It was time for persuasion to be backed by mass protest. In 1819, thousands of people gathered in St Peter's Field in Manchester to show their support for parliamentary reform (estimates varied between 60,000 and 80,000). They listened to why they would stand a much better chance in improving their lives if they could decide who would run the government, and influence the deployment of public resources to solve public problems. It was a stirring but nonetheless peaceful event. However, magistrates called in troops that attacked the unarmed crowds, leaving some dead and many more injured. The event was swiftly dubbed 'Peterloo Massacre', and it provoked angry reactions. In his poem, 'The Masque of Anarchy', Shelley (1792-1822), issued a rallying cry:

> "Rise like Lions after slumber
> In unvanquishable number,
> Shake your chains to earth like dew
> Which in sleep had fallen on you –
> Ye are many – they are few."

Shelley, an admirer of Bacon and Enlightenment philosophy, reflected the changing relationship between reformists and the public[68]. The Mohists, Cicero and the other anti-Caesar republicans, the Enlightenment philosophers, all valued the rational and moral capacity of ordinary people without systematically engaging with them. They

---

[68] On Shelley's politics, see Foot, P, *Red Shelley*, London, Sidgwick & Jackson: 1980.

viewed them as human beings deserving of equal respect, but did not strive to involve them as fellow citizens in the progressive struggle. Shelley deliberately adopted the language of 'freedom versus enslavement' to show how citizens must stand together to keep coercion by the powerful at bay. Without a real solidarity – rooted in collective action, individuals would be picked off one by one, and none would be able to exercise their judgement sensibly and determine how they should live. They would be at the mercy of others, at risk of being trapped in the most unacceptable form of human existence – a slave.

A crucial test of any call for the establishment of a common front was its application to all people without distinction. Even the French Revolutionaries held back when it came to the question of slavery, thus allowing the slave-owning interests to tarnish, in France as much as it had done in America, democratic aspirations. But the spread of liberal consciousness in nineteenth century Britain was to rally opposition to power inequalities more systematically than ever before.

Charles James Fox (1749-1806) whose reform efforts had been repeatedly blocked by Tory Ministers in the service of George III, found that the Enlightened ethos was at last beginning to turn the tide[69]. Even though the majority of Tories still wanted to preserve existing power structures, notable exceptions like William Wilberforce gave their support to Fox, who in 1806 succeeded in getting Parliament to accept legislation to abolish the slave trade within the British Empire. Others like Thomas Fowell Buxton (1786-1845) recognised that the case must be put to other nations too and their pressures paid off in 1815 when France, Spain and Portugal also agreed to stop the slave trade. By then, Buxton was convinced that not just the slave trade, but slavery itself must be ended. In 1823 he helped form the Society for the Mitigation and Gradual Abolition of Slavery. A decade later, Parliament passed the Slavery Abolition Act to give all slaves in the British Empire their freedom. Slave owners were given compensation, funded by taxpayers. The most unjust form of power arrangement had been dismantled in all

---

[69] Fox was one of the most vocal politicians in championing a fairer distribution of power through electoral reform, ending of slavery, and opposition to oppressive foreign policies. See Mitchell, LG, *Charles James Fox*, Penguin Books: 1997.

British controlled territories – which ironically meant that America, having broken away from British rule, would persist with the oppressive practice until it threatened the unity of the United States itself and pushed it into a civil war.

In parallel with the rejection of slavery, the advocates for reforms in Britain were aware that what made enslavement so pernicious was people being deprived of the opportunities to develop their capacities to think for themselves, shape their own lives, and contribute to the common good. Progressives therefore wanted to end all forms of deprivation[70]. The Peterloo incident brought out clearly that a new level of concerted action was necessary to break down resistance to reforms. If people did not have a vote, they could not expect the government to look after their interests when economic powers were increasingly being concentrated in business leaders at the expense of ordinary workers. The extension of the franchise, as the Levellers had long ago argued, was essential to pave the way for fairer power distribution.

When the 1832 'Great Reform Act' was finally passed, it was because a rapidly growing number of people were coming to the conclusion that the constitutional status quo was unacceptable. The Tory argument, echoing centuries of theological-authoritarian propaganda, that all was already for the best, increasingly rang hollow. This line of defence was mercilessly mocked by Voltaire a generation ago. Now Benthamites like Henry Brougham (1778-1868) actively promoted the progressive counter-view and encouraged those who shared it to raise their voice in demanding change. The Tories became so isolated that they could not gather enough support in Parliament to answer the King's call to form an anti-reform government. William IV had to turn reluctantly to the Whigs on their terms to form a government committed to improving the electoral system of the country.

It is not surprising that the 1832 Act should at once be a major landmark in advancing power redistribution and a disappointment[71]. Pressurising the political establishment to give way after almost two centuries of implacable stonewalling over parliamentary reform

---

[70] See, for example, Halevy, E, *The Growth of Philosophic Radicalism*, Faber & Faber: 1928.

[71] Brock, M, *The Great Reform Act*, HarperCollins Publishers: 1973.

undoubtedly counted as a breakthrough. To achieve it without disjointed riots turning into a full-scale violent revolution was also commendable except for those who craved for glory in bloodshed. However, throughout history those who gain power are all too often inclined to refuse to share their newly acquired power with anyone else. The beneficiaries of the 1832 settlement were swift to line up behind both the Whigs and Tories in declaring an end to the reform process. Their attitude was epitomised in the callous sentencing in that same year of the workers later to be known as the 'Tolpuddle Martyrs' who were deported to distant Australia for daring to set up their own Friendly Society of Agricultural Labourers[72]. Their crime was not to agitate for violence, but simply to take a stand on seeking a subsistent wage.

Events in Britain were mirrored by development in France, where the restored Bourbon regime, especially under Charles X, was going backwards instead of forward in building a more enlightened society. For example, to make profanation of sacred objects punishable by hard labour or even death was adding insult to the anti-republican injury. In 1830, Charles X was forced to abdicate, but Louis-Philippe who took over was above all concerned with consolidating his powerbase along with the social and economic elite of his time. The last thing on his mind was to redistribute power to those in the lower reaches of society.

These flagrant moves against the development of a more inclusive society fuelled bitter resentment and consequently diverted energy for reform in Britain and France towards militant confrontation rather than deliberative resolution. Revolutionary tyrants came to be romanticised as courageous warriors – they were the models to follow for radical leaders whose credentials were to depend on their readiness to fight for an idealised working class. The interests of workers embodied the interests of all oppressed people, and they were to be expressed through a vanguard that uniquely grasped how these interests were to be served.

Throughout the 1830s and 1840s, agitation grew for true radicals, socialists, and republicans to use force to bring about a society without any form of oppression. The philosophical radicalism of Jeremy Bentham (1748-1832) was dismissed as no longer relevant in Britain,

---

[72] For an account of the events, see The UK TUC, *The Book of the Martyrs of Tolpuddle 1834-1934*, Tolpuddle Martyrs Memorial Trust: 2000.

and the liberal gradualism of Benjamin Constant (1767-1830) was considered ineffectual in moving France forward[73].

The hope of building inclusive communities was in danger of being crushed between reactionaries who did not want to weaken traditional authoritarianism any further, and self-styled radicals who were determined to change the world using their own authoritarian methods. The progressive cause was at this point given a vital boost by John Stuart Mill (1806-1873), who developed a coherent philosophy which, taking all the key post-revolutionary lessons seriously, would provide a guide to a fairer distribution of power while firmly guarding against temptations to embrace new forms of tyranny[74].

John Stuart Mill's liberal philosophy

J. S. Mill reminded everyone of the epistemological basis for rejecting power concentration. In *A System of Logic*, he explained why intuitive arguments – claims that something could be known to be true solely on account of the claimant's own sense of certainty irrespective of any supporting evidence – could never be a substitute for methodological procedures which would systematically check provisional claims against evidence. Drawing on the experimentalist ideas of Bacon and subsequent theorists of scientific reasoning, Mill showed how the feasibility for testing the veracity of a claim against objective factors opened to anyone to discern was essential to resolving contested claims. If the basis for accepting truth claims was simply their confident assertion, then contradictory claims made by people who would not – in some cases, could not – doubt themselves, would all have to be accepted. The alternative to allowing the anarchic nonsense of licensing everyone to declare true whatever carried their inner conviction, was to make the

---

[73] Fontana, B, *Benjamin Constant and the post-revolutionary mind*, Yale University Press: 1991.

[74] Mill's writings are widely available, including all those mentioned in this chapter. There are also many good introductory books on his philosophical and political ideas. See, for example, Robson, JM, *The Improvement of Mankind: the social and political thought of John Stuart Mill*, London, Routledge & Kegan Paul: 1968; Ryan, A, *The Philosophy of John Stuart Mill*, Macmillan Press: 1987; and Skorupski, J, *John Stuart Mill*, London, Routledge: 1989.

basis of knowledge a public platform where only claims which stood up to scrutiny and experimental testing would be accepted.

Mill's empirical approach meant that any subjective invocation of "God created us to do this", "I know this is the destiny of our nation", or "trust me because I am for the working class" would carry no weight in deciding if its claimant should be believed. In the nineteenth century – and as we will see, it was to be again from the late twentieth century on – such invocations, especially by bringing 'God' into the picture, was still a potent force in leading people to go down some dubious paths.

Mill, in his *Essays on Religion*, argued that although as a source of inspiration to strive to be a better person and care for the needs of others, religion could be immensely valuable, it risked distorting what we should believe and what actions we should pursue in life if it was tied to dogmatic claims about the world. On the point of what divine design might be behind the world we lived in, Mill suggested that Darwin's explanation as set out in the *Origins of Species* might prove to be an effective guide to how the different biological features in nature came to be as they were without a conscious designer. Thomas Huxley, in defending Darwin's theory against intuitionist critics who just 'knew' it to be wrong, referred to Darwin's meticulous application of the evidence-based methodologies Mill had championed as the only coherent basis for settling contested claims. As history was to show, subsequent scientific development in geology, zoology, and genetics produced information to refine Darwin's theory but none contradicted its core contention.

One of the reasons why so many establishment figures, including Gladstone who was otherwise a strong supporter of Mill's outlook, came out ferociously against Darwin was that in their mind, a deliberate design was essential to give the universe a moral purpose. To argue that all living creatures, not excepting the human race, developed from more basic species without any pre-conceived plan was tantamount to the abandonment of our ethical compass. But for Mill, religion was not important because it helped to discover the ends we should pursue, its true worth rested with its effectiveness in promoting appreciation of the moral goals which were independently identifiable through enlightened human reflections.

As Ludwig Feuerbach's (1804-1872) *The Essence of Christianity* showed, religious doctrines tended to layer on top of the core concern with the wellbeing of our fellow human beings, dogmas that added to the superficial complexity of a faith but actually detracted from our real moral purpose. Once the dogmatic elements were stripped away, maintained Feuerbach, the essence of what really merited our devotion would be revealed – to love, care for others as we would have them love, and care for us. Religion at its best projected the reciprocal concern amongst fellow human beings as the overarching value[75]. The commitment to maximise the wellbeing of all – call it the flourishing, fulfilment or happiness of humankind – was what we should aim for irrespective of what any supernatural designer might have planned. Indeed as Socrates long ago explained, a divine being is worthy of our worship if it endorses the right moral objectives, but the correctness of moral objectives is not derived from what a divine being may happen to command.

The human appreciation of reciprocity in securing the betterment of all was found by anthropological studies to be embedded in diverse ethnic and cultural groups. Religious – and increasingly, ideological – dogmas may seek to introduce variations to present incompatible differences to create an unbridgeable gulf between Catholics and Protestants, Christians and Muslims, white and non-white groups, middle and working class people, and so on, but as human beings the moral sensitivity we have in common is too resilient to be wiped away by fixation on our differences.

In *Utilitarianism*, Mill developed the recognition of the moral goal of promoting the greatest happiness of the greatest number into a general philosophy of life. Many philosophers have preoccupied themselves with disputing if Mill intended the utilitarian principle to be applied to individual acts or general rules. Given Mill's concern with social and political reforms, it is likely that while he would be content with individuals deciding which course of action they would undertake when the consequences on those affected could be fairly reliably assessed, his focus would be more on how rules, policies and institutions affecting

---

[75] On Feuerbach, see Wartofsky, M.W., *Feuerbach*, Cambridge University Press: 1977; and Harvey, V.A., *Feuerbach and the interpretation of religion*, Cambridge University Press: 1995.

large numbers of people would be evaluated. Evidence, once again, drawn from historical records, experimental findings, and witnesses' reports, would be crucial in considering the likelihood of particular rules and institutions impacting, not on some specific occasion, but on the population in general. While what might happen on one chosen day, for example, as a result of a new law could be extremely difficult to predict, the effects of that law over a period of time would be easier to estimate based on the experience of similar laws or components of the law in previous policies. Since such estimates could turn out to be wrong, it would follow that one should be prepared to revise the rules or reform the institutions in the light of new evidence. The underlying aim of the liberal reform agenda is thus not to bring about the perfect society, but to facilitate continuous improvement by responding to changing circumstances and emerging information.

A key implication of this approach is power relations in society must not be so structured as to prevent this from happening. Mill's *On Liberty* developed this theme and explained that if any individual, group or institution – a tyrant, a majority of the public on a given issue, a government – had enough power to command others to behave in particular ways without the due epistemological process of testing and validating the basis of their claims, then it would open the door to the arbitrary subjugation of people. The tests which should be essential in verifying the legitimacy of any command were empirically-based ones examining if a proposed requirement to act in certain ways (or to not engage in a type of acts) would lead to the greater happiness of the greater number.

Far from asserting that governments must in general leave individuals to act as they pleased, Mill's formulation suggested that if there was reasonable evidence to suppose that certain activities of an individual or a group of them would lead to greater suffering – through spreading a highly infectious and harmful disease, taking away others' chance to earn a livelihood, or inciting others to victimise an innocent person – then there could be grounds to use the coercive power of the state to prevent those activities from taking place, provided any sanctions were proportionate. What Mill did explicitly rule out was the legitimacy of overriding an individuals' judgement of what the outcome would mean for them, so long as they were of sound mind. People's personal trade-off of pain against what they would regard as gain could be odd, indeed unfathomable, to others. But so long as their actions do not carry negative consequences for others, they should be left to decide for themselves.

Mill was insistent on this position because it followed from his experimentalist conception of knowledge that people needed to have the opportunities to reflect on their experiences and learn from the testing of their suppositions against the actual consequences to come to a better understanding of reality. This applied as much to refining their own judgement of what would give them real fulfilment in life, as to giving due consideration to radical new ideas which, like Darwin's at the time, shocked many people upon first hearing them. Actions that could demonstrably cause harm to others should be scrutinised for appropriate intervention, but otherwise the more people could review the pros and cons without undue influence from others the greater the chance they would come to the correct conclusions. For those impatiently demanding that people should be made to accept the correct conclusions instead of wasting time over prolonged deliberations, Mill would reply that the only way to determine the correctness of any conclusions was by means of the open contest and objective evaluation of rival claims. Attempts to short-circuit this process would slide towards the abuse of power.

This brings us to Mill's conception of the development and participation of enlightened citizens in self-governance. In *Representative Government*, he set out how power should be shared out so that all citizens could develop their rational capacity, moral sensitivity and exercise their political responsibility. He did not believe that all citizens could be directly involved in the many decisions that had to be dealt with by a government covering the whole of Britain. At the national level, decisions would have to be provisionally entrusted to political representatives, subject to periodic elections, to consider the issues in depth and make their judgement.

Below the national level, where local matters could be addressed effectively without being escalated to Parliament, there should be opportunities for all citizens to gain experience on local government bodies, and learn how to balance competing expectations and strive to achieve the greater good for the greater number. Both through making decisions on local matters and selecting representatives to deal with national issues, citizens would acquire the skills and confidence to contribute to shaping public policies. The alternative for Mill was to risk creating a nation of obedient sheep, incapable of assessing or articulating their interests.

Mill's fears were not directed at some distant dystopia[76]. They were provoked by the political status quo in Britain and the rest of the world. Although he has been frequently criticised for being elitist in suggesting that only those who were mature and educated should have a vote, it should be remembered that for him, authoritarian rule had left largely obedient and sheepish people, who might be roused to kick out at women or minority groups lower down the social hierarchy, but would rarely question methodically the decisions of their 'superiors'. Mill did not want to keep them out, only to accelerate their educative development so that they could be ready to take part as citizens in their own governance[77]. Only those who were blind to the excluded masses' susceptibility to manipulation – or who saw it as a positive advantage to line up fodder for their cause – would insist that a culture for civic development was unnecessary for building a truly democratic form of government.

For Mill, the cultivation of an inclusive culture in support of enlightened citizens must address prevailing socio-economic barriers as well. One of the most absurd barriers was that reflected in the title of his book, *The Subjection of Women*. Building on the arguments that Wollstonecraft and Condorcet put forward at the end of the eighteenth century, Mill set out how existing laws and customs forced women to be dependent on men in every key aspect of their lives. They could be deprived of any means of making a living if the men in control – fathers, husbands, landlords – chose to marginalise them or simply neglected their needs. They could be physically or mentally abused without any recourse to protection. Yet with education and support, girls and women could on all the available evidence develop their capacities to reason, cooperate and contribute to society. Mill maintained that the legal

---

[76] 'Dystopia' was a term coined by Mill himself to denote a totally dysfunctional society – the opposite of a 'utopia'.
[77] Garforth, FW, *Educative Democracy: John Stuart Mill on education in society*, Oxford University Press: 1980.

obstacles and cultural prejudices against women's development as human beings and citizens must be henceforth removed.

In addition to attacking the unjust treatment of women, which had for centuries been a core part of the alpha male authoritarian tradition, Mill also exposed new problems stemming from the rise of alpha male 'petty monarchs' in commanding the industrialising economy. The fixation on economic growth through business leaders' abilities to get workers to produce more and the public to consume more, while they secured an ever-larger share of the profits, was creating a new kind of dependency. The growth and concentration of resource power in the few was causing more people to have to strive to keep up with productive and consumption demands, leaving them less time and capacity to develop themselves, and depleting human happiness overall.

If economic improvement was to support the development of enlightened citizens, so that they could be both more capable of judging and pursuing what is valuable in their own lives, and acting collectively with others to ensure sound public governance prevails, then people's dependency on business chiefs must be drastically reduced.

Mill pointed to three factors. First, through technological innovations more and better products to meet our needs could be achieved without the same reliance on basic human labour. Instead of insisting that a large, even increasing, amount of human energy must be expended on mentally unrewarding tasks to fuel production, we should encourage the expansion of experimental science and technology to relieve people of menial chores and the burden of coping with human frailties.

Secondly, there needs to be increased security of person and property. For men and women, capital owners or wage workers, the economic system should not be so imbalanced as to leave some at the whimsical mercy of others. People should be protected so that they could match their skills to opportunities as equal citizens, and not accept offers made to them under economic duress.

Thirdly, reduced inequalities should pave the way for greater cooperation between people committing themselves to a shared enterprise. Cooperatives, as we will see, were emerging in the nineteenth century as a democratic form of business association so that all who worked in them had an equal vote in determining the direction of the business and the distribution of any surplus attained. People operating with such cooperative arrangements could decide that some would have more executive authority than others, some would earn more for their exceptional talents in delivering results to benefit all, and some would be given extra support should they fall ill. But in all cases, they would have the same power to decide as equal members of the cooperative.

Observations on how society had been developing convinced Mill that these factors were critical in connecting a productive economic system with the cultivation of the progressive vision of inclusive communities, wherein freed from the shackles of dependency, people would build relationships of interdependency and mutual respect. He was clear that, just as with individuals, the actions of businesses in the marketplace should be left alone by government unless there was good evidence to suggest that intervention would lead to greater happiness for the greater number. What was for the good or otherwise of any given business leader should be left to him to judge, but if his decisions would otherwise adversely affect others – employees, customers, local communities, investors – then the government should take steps to improve the situation. By means of regulation, taxation, and education, government could, and should, remove the barriers to a better form of community life for all. These ideas were set out by Mill in his *Principles of Political Economy*, which was first published in the politically explosive year of 1848.

The 1848 crossroad

Two hundred years on from Charles I becoming the first monarch to be put on trial by elected representatives of the people, and Parliament itself being asked to share the power it had taken from the King with the rest of the population, the political descendants of the Levellers converged in London in 1848 to make the case for universal male suffrage. Disappointed with the limited changes brought about by the 1832 Reform Act, the Chartist movement grew out of an uneasy alliance between those who followed William Lovett, a progressive radical who believed in the use of education and non-violent protest to build up popular support for democratic reforms; and Feargus O'Connor, an advocate for militant confrontation to break down the resistance of those in charge of the country[78].

They presented the petition for the People's Charter to Parliament, calling for the widening of the franchise and making the ratio of elected representatives to constituents similar across the country. Expectations were high with Parliament facing a combination of mass support for the petition and threats of militant action. However, once again Parliament rejected the demands. It was a defining moment. Those who opposed prevailing power structures were left with a choice. They could jettison their liberal qualms and resort to force to bring about what the leading agitators had no doubt whatsoever would be the only alternative. Or they could redouble their efforts in working with potential supporters, with or without power, to formulate a shared strategy of cooperation, moral appeals, sustained protest, and civil disobedience to achieve their reform objectives.

The first route was trumpeted with the 1848 publication of Marx and Engels' *Communist Manifesto*, calling for radicals everywhere to position themselves as the champions of the working class, and unite in overthrowing the powerful so that they could take control to remodel society in line with their unique vision[79]. While their analysis of the exploitation of workers and the shift in economic powers was not dissimilar to the socialist writings of 19th century Britain and France, Marx and Engels introduced a theoretical element that supposedly revealed how human history must unfold. Its structure was identical to theological dogmas which authoritarians had for centuries used to justify their unquestionable actions. Like the priestly class who had privileged access to God's will, and therefore had no need to consider objective evidence or concern for open validation through critical discussions, the Marxist brand of communism was based on a special grasp of History (a depersonalized God) and where it would lead us regardless of what we might individually prefer.

---

[78] A short introduction to the Chartist movement can be found in Briggs, A, *Chartism*, Stroud, Sutton Publishing: 1998.

[79] For a sympathetic interpretation of Marx, see McLellan, D, *Karl Marx: his life and thought*, St Albans, Paladin: 1976; a highly critical assessment is provided by Schwarzschild, L, *The Red Prussian: the life and legend of Karl Marx*, Hamish Hamilton: 1948; and a most readable biography, Wheen, F, *Karl Marx*, London, Fourth Estate: 1999.

Knowing that the 'working class' – the chosen people – would overcome all other classes and bring about a society without oppression, the only question left was whether we would resist History and end up being reluctantly dragged along, or stand at the vanguard of this movement and helped to bring us all to our inevitable destiny. Evidence which might point to unresolved differences amongst workers, the consolidation of business powers rather than their imminent demise, the likelihood of revolutionary leaders usurping authoritarian power instead of stepping back before the natural emergence of an ideal society, were all to be dismissed as the work of bourgeois reactionaries (the Marxist equivalent of the Devil)[80].

On the basis of their own inner certainty, revolutionaries could then push aside existing socio-economic and political arrangements even though they had no coherent or tested alternative for what might replace them. Marx accused those who promoted a non-violent, gradualist approach to reforming power inequalities of being utopian, but he himself was naïve in assuming that agitators who were inclined to crush any opposition from the existing regime would not also be inclined to crush any opposition from the public when they became their new rulers. Like Bronterre O'Brien and other radicals of their generation, Marx was not at all disturbed by the effects of power concentration achieved by the Jacobins. For all his alleged grasp of History, he could not see the connections between the institution of unquestionable authority, the dynamics of 'the Reign of Terror', and the inescapable subjection of ordinary citizens.

Although in Britain the Chartists refrained from using violence to bring down the government, radicals in the rest of Europe in 1848 embraced the revolutionary approach. Ruling families all over the continent found themselves on the defensive. In France, Louis-Philippe abdicated and the Second Republic came into being, bringing with it

---

[80] Opinions on Marxist ideas diverged widely. At one end of the spectrum they are regarded as totally irrelevant and should drop out of any serious political consideration, while at the other end they continue to be treasured as the basis of a fundamental critique of capitalist and liberal society. Anyone wishing to learn more, should see Therborn, G, *From Marxism to Post-Marxism*, London, Verso: 2008; and Kolakowski, L, *Main Currents of Marxism: The Founders, the Golden Age, the Breakdown*, WW Norton: 2008.

universal male suffrage and the right to work. But no cooperative relationships had developed to underpin the initial republican alliance. The poor in the countryside, the workers in Paris, the enemies of church and monarchy, did not share a common concern with building more inclusive communities. Instead, it was the conservative opposition to the revolution that was united by their quest for strong top-down order.

Louis-Napoleon, nephew of Napoleon Bonaparte, played on his lineage in the restoration of order and glory, and offered himself as a candidate to be President of France, knowing that the conservatives would back him to go further. Proving that merely giving every male adult a vote without, as Mill had argued, the cultivation of civic values or embedding liberal safeguards in political institutions, was far from a sure path towards democracy, Louis-Napoleon waited less than three years before he sought and secured the support of the voters in abolishing the republican constitution, and crowned himself Napoleon III. The revolutionary hopes were dashed even more quickly in other European countries. By the end of 1848, the old authoritarian regimes were on the whole back in control. Insurrection had been countered by repression.

By contrast, the second option was favoured by liberal reformists in Britain and America, where the route to greater inclusion was more consistently followed. They believed that although blunt resistance from those in power might make their cause seemingly a hopeless one at times, building alliances through real engagement with a growing circle of thinking and caring citizens would nonetheless be more likely to deliver social improvements than attempting to seize power without evidence-based ideas on how that power should be used. Two examples from 1848 illustrate this development.

One of the major problems facing the poor in cities in 19th century Britain was the utterly inadequate sanitation that left many in dire health. Edwin Chadwick (1800-1890), an associate of Jeremy Bentham and John Stuart Mill, commissioned scientific studies to examine what were the causes and what solutions might eradicate the health problems afflicting the poor. The studies pointed to the need for a reliable supply of clean water along with an effective sewerage system to get rid of waste materials. Chadwick's proposals were blocked by Peel and the Tories (now renamed the Conservative Party), who did not want to put resources into helping the poor. However, he pressed his case with the

Liberal Opposition and when they came into power under Lord John Russell, they passed the 1848 Public Health Act which transformed the state of health for those living in the most squalid conditions[81]. The Act also created local boards, which later in the century were developed into locally elected authorities providing the kind of civic engagement Mill had promoted.

Another example came from liberal campaigners in America who already shared a common cause in calling for the abolition of slavery. In 1848, one hundred of them, including Elizabeth Cady Stanton (1815-1902), Frederick Douglass (1818-1895), and Lucretia Mott (1793-1880) signed the Seneca Fall Declaration of the Rights of Women[82]. They held up a mirror to American society and reminded it that since governments were instituted to secure the rights to life, liberty, and the pursuit of happiness, deriving their just powers from the consent of the governed, it could not arbitrarily leave women out of the process. They warned that "whenever any form of government becomes destructive of these ends, it is the right of those who suffer from it to refuse allegiance to it, and to insist upon the institution of a new government, laying its foundation on such principles, and organizing its powers in such form, as to them shall seem most likely to effect their safety and happiness." Their resolution to brush aside hostility and ridicule, and readiness to resort to civil disobedience, if necessary, established their reform agenda. It was the beginning of a long campaign, and of the signatories, just one of them lived to cast her ballot in the first American elections open to women voters in 1920.

Liberation from power inequalities

By the middle of the nineteenth century, people who valued the ethos of inclusive communities were becoming acutely aware of two aspects of social development. The first was that not only old forms of power

---

[81] Lewis, R, *Edwin Chadwick and the Public Health Movement 1832-1854*, Longman: 1952.
[82] DuBois, EC, *Feminism and Suffrage: The Emergence of an Independent Women's Movement in America, 1848-1869*, Ithaca, Cornell University Press: 1999.

inequalities were persisting, but new ones were fast emerging with the rapid economic and technological changes taking place. While De Tocqueville (1805-1859) had observed in earlier decades that the democratic vitality he found in America was closely related to the broad equality of economic conditions and social status of its inhabitants, the capitalist mode of intense wealth accumulation and consequent vast wealth-based power differentials meant that increasingly people were no longer able to relate to each other with equal respect as fellow citizens[83].

At the same time, liberal champions of reforms were conscious of the solidarity they themselves were helping to spread across traditional class, gender, national and religious divisions. Enlightenment philosophers had been a cosmopolitan group who were proud of being citizens of the world. But their nineteenth century successors extended the circle of mutual support even more widely. Christian socialists, Quaker reformists, secular campaigners, working class trade unionists, liberal-minded aristocrats, middle class lawyers, merchants and factory owners who opposed exploitation of the weak, all felt at one with each other's outlook on improving societies in terms of prosperity *and* fairness. They shared a commitment to tackle the impoverishment of human life caused by others through ignorance or callousness, or both. Despite their own differences, they recognised they needed to join forces to overcome the considerable opposition they faced from those who wanted to preserve oppressive inequalities to safeguard their personal advantages[84].

At the same time as their collective influence was expanding – leading to the period being often referred to by historians as the age of reforms – other outlooks less sympathetic to tackling power inequalities were also emerging. Along with Marxist radicalism there was the technocracy of Comte, who had in common with Marx the unwavering belief that a small group of people could through their unique knowledge guide society to the 'promised land'. Where Marx believed it was the grasp of the Dialectic of History which entitled the revolutionary vanguard to dictate to all on behalf of the ignorant working masses,

---

[83] See his *Democracy in America*, Wordsworth Editions: 1998.

[84] Many examples can be found in Briggs, A, *The Age of Improvement 1783-1867*, Longman: 1979.

Comte insisted it was the exclusive understanding of scientific principles and applications that qualified his elite to take full control of society. Comte abandoned the Baconian injunction that the quest for knowledge was an on-going cooperative enterprise for all to participate in, and turned towards the rule by experts. He even went so far as to propose institutionalizing religious forms of worship to reinforce the deference of the people towards the new priestly class who would control their lives. Mill rightly warned against the Comtean approach as a betrayal of the scientific spirit and a slide towards illiberal subjection of the public by an unaccountable authority. Once the people affected by the decisions made by those placed in charge were cut off from effectively questioning those decisions, the reliability of the decision-makers would deteriorate[85].

Unfortunately, technocracy – without necessarily taking the quasi-religious form favoured by Comte – was to become an attractive proposition for alpha males who could thereby carve out their own domains where their supposedly exclusive expertise entitled them to make judgements and take action without having to account for them to the people affected. The risk was particularly prevalent in the emerging industry of control – prisons, police forces, mental asylums, work houses, orphanages – giving those in charge an officially endorsed authority to alter the lives of others without having to justify themselves. The utilitarian aspiration for greater happiness for all was subverted into a process of regulation for an arbitrarily defined 'greater good'.

The worst instrument of control was the death penalty because it inherently disallowed its mistaken application from being rectified. The challenge for liberals was that even in a leading liberal country like Britain, the legal system at the beginning of the 19th century contained 220 offences which were subject to the death penalty, most of these were directed at the poorest in society. By attrition, reformists cut this down to 80 by 1832, and down to just five in 1861. The campaign to abolish it completely was to continue into the next century.

In the meantime, imprisonment as an alternative to execution brought its own problems. Treating those sent to jail as deserving no

---

[85] For Mill's critique of Comte, see his *Auguste Comte and Positivism*, Bristol, Thoemmes Press: 1993.

respect whatsoever, the prison establishment was a microcosm of the most unrepentant authoritarian regimes. Elizabeth Fry (1780-1845), who was from a Quaker reformist family, saw for herself the conditions under which prisoners, especially women and children, were kept. She set up the Association for the Improvement of the Female Prisoners in Newgate, which helped to provide training and education in prisons. It inspired similar groups to be set up in Britain and the rest of Europe. Fry's efforts were supported by her brother-in-law, Buxton, the anti-slavery campaigner, who investigated Newgate prison and published *An Inquiry into Prison Discipline,* triggering prison reforms aimed at improving offenders' potential to lead a crime-free life in the future. Fry and Buxton made it clear that society had an interest in how prisons were run, and those with decision-making powers within prisons must subject their actions to wider scrutiny and make improvements considered by the wider community[86].

The liberal concern with people suffering from multiple disadvantages in life and their preoccupation with reducing power inequalities would rile Nietzsche whose philosophy marked out another battleground. Although he did not shape the development of any groups or organisations directly, Nietzsche represented a new current of thought that helped to confer intellectual respectability on an otherwise morally bankrupt outlook[87].

Instead of accepting the presumption that worse-off people should get more attention and support, he turned the golden rule of ethics upside down and asserted that individuals should strive to become more than they were, and anyone failing to do that should be left to their own fate. Sympathy for the weak was for him a sign of weakness itself. Nietzsche stressed that those who could only assert their strength by picking on the weak were feeble too. But whatever nuanced conception he might have in portraying the ideal form of self-development, he was unequivocal that our attention should be moved away from those unable to make

---

[86] Pitman, ER, *Elizabeth Fry*, BiblioBazaar: 2007.

[87] Some extremist racist and nationalist views have in the past been unjustifiably ascribed to Nietzsche, but his essential philosophy is nonetheless incompatible with any moral concern for reciprocity. For a sympathetic interpretation of his ideas, see Kaufmann, W. *Nietzsche: philosopher, psychologist, antichrist*, Princeton University Press: 1974.

something of their lives to exclusively what we would make of our own lives.

The anti-compassion outlook was to become mainstreamed as a 'heroic' attitude worthy of people who had attained superior positions in life. It would validate the mindset of those who despised the concern shown to people at the bottom of society. The corrosive effects of such an outlook could be seen most vividly in America where, despite the founding fathers' proclamation of democratic equality for all before the law, slavery had continued well into the nineteenth century when Britain had long outlawed the practice, and even Russia had emancipated its own serfs.

The slave-owners of the southern states, far from finding it difficult to reconcile their professed belief in the religious values of loving all humankind with the repugnant practice of enslaving others, viewed their way of life with pride and detested the animosity towards slavery in the northern states as a sign of their weaker character. Domineering alpha males should not be uncomfortable about the fate of those who were conquered, captured and subjugated by their 'masters'.

Jefferson and Madison had long ago foreseen that even though the powers of an overarching federal government had to be held back from unjustifiable interference against state governments, those powers could also be necessary when individual states abused their power against people living within their borders.

The first half of the 19th century had witnessed the turning of the tide against slavery across Europe, with America's proclamation of democratic equality increasingly ringing hollow. And the longer the US government tolerated slavery for fear of offending the southern states, the more recalcitrant the latter became in not just retaining the practice themselves, but demanding it be extended to new states incorporated into the US. Abraham Lincoln (1809-1865) became President with the pledge that he would not allow slavery to be extended anymore. Seven of the pro-slavery states declared they would secede from the US. When that was rejected by the US Government, South Carolina's attack on Fort Sumter set off the American Civil War[88]. It was April 1861, a month

---

[88] For a general history of the war, see McPherson, JM, *Battle Cry of Freedom: The Civil War Era*, Penguin: 2001.

after Tsar Alexander II had proclaimed the emancipation of serfs in Russia.

Lincoln became convinced that attempts to contain slavery had only given it succour to continue when it should have no place at all in communities guaranteed equal respect for everyone who lived within them. While his Emancipation Proclamation of 1862 actually only extended to slaves in states rejecting the Union (hence applicable to slaves who managed to escape into Union jurisdiction but not those left behind), he came to see that the institution of slavery was fundamentally incompatible with the true meaning of freedom. By 1864, he concluded that the contest was about nothing less than what it was to be free in America. On the side of the anti-slavery North, freedom entailed each and every person being able to enjoy "the product of his labor", whereas for the pro-slavery states, freedom meant those with the power could "do as they please with other men, and the product of other men's labor."

The defeat of the pro-slavery states marked the beginning of a long process to enable all people to attain true freedom. Discrimination on the grounds of colour and the determination of the powerful to exploit the product of others' labour continued to pose challenges to progressive reformers. Ironically, while the Republican Party had retained its name and basked in the reputation of Lincoln as the vanquisher of slavery, its modern descendants increasingly left it to the Democrats to battle unjust power structures, while they criticised such attempts as undermining hierarchical arrangements, which should be allowed to operate as they had done in the past.

When Lincoln was targeting the objectionable power to exploit other people and the product of their labour, he was following on a wave of criticisms directed at the spread of irresponsible control exerted by a minority over others. The notion of 'wage slavery', emerging in America and Britain from the nineteenth century on, developed out of reactions against below-subsistence wages, job insecurity, disregard for health and safety, and opposition to workers unions. From this perspective, the problem of slavery on plantations was only the tip of the iceberg. Beneath it were other forms of exploitative control, which would get worse unless the power inequalities that gave rise to them were rectified.

Lincoln's assassination in 1865 left his successors with the task of

Reconstruction, which offered an opportunity to curb the power of those who had acquired unchallenged control over the livelihood of others. But instead they paved the way for the Gilded Age when America came to be dominated by large businesses with concentrated wealth, capable of instigating political corruption to bend the rules to suit them, and delimiting the influence of government institutions while they continued with their oppressive actions.

Where Comte wanted to entrust power to the quasi-priestly class of technocrats, and Nietzsche celebrated those who cared for no one besides their own strength and achievement, Herbert Spencer represented another major anti-progressive current of thought in the nineteenth century. Crudely interpreting Darwin's theory of natural selection as suggesting that all living things evolve to a better state when those most capable of improvement strive against and survive at the expense of others, Spencer leapt to the conclusion that human beings would most effectively attain progress if they were left to compete with each other. The main model Spencer had in mind was that of the business world wherein everyone had the chance to become successful entrepreneurs. Those who lost out should accept that they were simply not fit enough to prosper, and those who were able to build their own business empires should not be held back, least of all by government.

Spencer had no understanding of the subtleties of natural selection, how intra and inter species cooperation could assist survival, and it never occurred to him that the evolution of the reflective capacity of human beings meant that instead of letting outcomes be dependent on the unthinking activities of uncoordinated individuals, people could apply their shared intelligence to examine alternatives and plan together for their mutual benefit. For him, the growth of power inequalities resulting from economic competition should not be criticised as a form of wage slavery, but welcome as a sign of success[89].

In reality, the industrial revolution had been accelerating the process whereby those with one particular set of skills – organising

---

[89] Though mostly neglected by contemporary commentators, Spencer developed many of the basic ideas which were to feature in what was to become known as 'neo-liberal' market ideology. For a broader assessment of Spencer, see Francis, M, *Herbert Spencer and the Invention of Modern Life*, Acumen Publishing: 2007.

others to produce goods and services exchangeable for a monetary value, with the greater part of which going to the organiser – were able to become rapidly richer than those who might have made all kinds of contributions via their labour, skills, loyalty, etc. Consequently, the business and professional classes set themselves up as custodians of society's prosperity, while others lacking the abilities to join their ranks were marked as lower classes deserving of their deprivations.

## The threat of concentrated resource power

From mid 19th century on, progressive liberals turned their attention to the new plutocrats and how they abused their expanding resource power against others. The long battle against irresponsible monarchs had shown how rulers could be subject to increasing democratic control. And it was clear that a new breed of 'petty monarchs' and 'robber barons' were more than capable of oppressing those dependent on them for their livelihood as any tyrant of the past. In Britain, a series of Factory Acts brought together reformists and responsible factory owners who were aware that any voluntary code for the shortening of working hours and improvement of factory conditions would be breached by free riders who would then gain an unfair advantage. Their sustained efforts secured better terms for women and children, and in time, for all factory workers.

One of the enlightened factory owners, Robert Owen (1771-1858), believed that a case could also be made by demonstrating how cooperation between those involved in business operations would lead to benefits for all[90]. He provided education for workers and their families, improved their pay, and increased the quality of his products. However, not all of Owen's projects were successful and vindicated Mill's concern that cooperative socialism needed to be tested out in practice, and should not be imposed uniformly. In the case of the Rochdale Pioneers, Owen's experimental practices were codified in 1844 into a democratic and mutualist format so that all those involved would have an equal vote in

---

[90] On Owen's ideas and activities, see Morton, AL, *The Life and Ideas of Robert Owen*, London, Lawrence & Wishart: 1962; and Donnachie, I, *Robert Owen: Social Visionary*, John Donald Publishers: 2005.

determining how their business is run[91]. It did not mean that everyone would have to do the same things or draw out the same in financial terms, but all concerned could determine as equals what the fairest and most productive arrangements should be. Cooperative enterprise thus found a platform from which it would develop into a highly successful business, extending into wholesale, retail, financial services, housing and many other areas. But even here, different parts of the cooperative movement had their ebbs and flows, and the case that all businesses should be turned into cooperatives was not made. It did confirm that there was a viable alternative to competitive arrangements in running businesses, and the myth that limitations on competition would necessarily damage enterprise was exposed.

In addition to showcasing the cooperative model for economic transactions, Owen encouraged the formation of trade unions so that workers could pool their resources to develop their learning and skills, and help each other in hard times. Most businesses did not adopt cooperative arrangements and would not give workers a say in decisions that affected them. To counter attempts to exploit and marginalise workers' interests, unions could provide collective force to bargain with employers for fairer deals. Individuals who would otherwise be vulnerable could amass sufficient power to stand up to owners and managers dismissive of their concerns. This was precisely why many with business interests intimidated workers privately against joining unions and used their influence in Parliament to introduce public policies against the formation of unions.

It was ironic and yet appropriate that in the year of the bicentenary of the British Bill of Rights, the 1889 Great London Dock Strike should erupt. The workers had faced persistent low pay, dangerous working conditions and precarious employment contracts. They had no protection against the abuse they had to endure from employers who were much more powerful than them. Under the leadership of Ben Tillett (1860-1943) of the Dockers Union, and supported by many other unions in Britain and abroad, the strike gradually succeeded in pressurising the dock owners into granting concessions they had no intention of even

---

[91] Bonner, A, *British Co-operation: the history, principles and organisation of the British co-operative movement*, Manchester: Co-operative Union: 1961.

considering at the outset. Many politicians who had previously been divided by class-obsessed prejudices – admonishing middle class and working class reformists to suspect each other and avoid collaboration – began to see a common cause in rebalancing the scales of power in favour of those placed in the most vulnerable positions. On the newly formed London County Council, for example, the Liberal and Labour members formed a progressive alliance to improve the conditions for all the people in the capital, facing up to powerful interests which had resisted reforms for a long time.

1889 was of course also the centenary of the French Revolution and despite Marxist insistence on rejecting cooperation with liberal reformists and persisting with revolutionary tactics, many of the representatives of socialist parties gathering from across Europe for the Second International were coming round to the view that the progressive recipe of extending the franchise, rallying public support for those committed to socio-political reforms, strengthening measures for equality for all, was the way forward. To the extent that they were prepared to test out their policies – especially in relation to state control of the means of production – on an experimental basis, subject to public scrutiny and electoral discipline, they were helping to devise methods to build more inclusive communities.

One of the new political parties formed that year, the Social Democratic Party (SAP) of Sweden, was to embody precisely the reformist spirit with a programmatic commitment to redistribute power across society so that all could function as equal citizens and none would be left to the mercy of state, corporate or religious authorities. Their approach was attacked by radical socialists and communists who not only maintained that total state control of the economy was non-negotiable but rejected liberal concern over such absolute control as mere middle class bias. This class-based authoritarianism not only obstructed the path of reform, in undermining efforts to establish a united front to oppose the threats against inclusive communities, it made it possible for nationalist-racist authoritarianism and corporate authoritarianism to grow in the closing decades of the 19th century, pushing countless communities into prolonged periods of misery and oppression.

# Chapter 6
# Liberal versus Tribal Nationalism:
# Late 19$^{th}$ to early 20$^{th}$ century

The rise of tribal nationalism

Even as social and liberal reformists were helping to build new power relations enabling citizens to interact more inclusively and treat each other with mutual respect, attempts were made to deflect people into a more oppressive and destructive path. Alpha male authoritarianism has from the earliest time included as one of its key features the diversion of subject people to the defeat of 'aliens' – the 'others' – to give them a false sense of pride, so that they would accept their own downtrodden position in the mammoth hierarchy.

Throughout the 19$^{th}$ century, a number of factors brought this element increasingly into an oppressive form of nationalism: the military triumphs of British imperialism – getting rid of rivals, especially France, from overseas territories which would fall under total British control; the spread of the French army and revolutionary rhetoric in the heyday of Napoleonic conquests – leading to the French model of a nation united by the heritage of the people inspiring others to follow the same path; and the idea of the nation as rooted in linguistic bonds and cultural heritage – expounded by, for example, Herder, Fichte, Hegel, who wanted to forge a German identity in the absence of a country for all German-speaking people[92].

What developed was a sense of special worth attached to one's nationality, which would be enhanced by the achievements of one's leader against other nationalities. The oppressive inequalities harming one's society were to be treated as marginal issues compared with the realisation of one's national superiority over others. Like Marx's idealisation of the working class, or Spencer's admiration of the unregulated masters of the market jungle, tribal nationalism romanticises nationality as a uniquely admirable quality, and naïvely (or in the case of

---

[92] For German nationalism, see Schulze, H, *The Course of German Nationalism*, Cambridge University Press: 1991.

its manipulative proponents, cynically) suggests that it would be best advanced by a small group of powerful figures who, freed from tiresome accountabilities to their fellow citizens, would deliver what they alone could see as the 'true' interests of everyone.

By contrast, progressive reformists had wanted people whose real interests – cultural, economic, political – were neglected by a ruling regime, to secure constitutionally guaranteed mechanisms to have their views and concerns taken into account when the national government acts in the name of all citizens. Liberal nationalism was thus diametrically opposite to tribal nationalism. This was exemplified by Giuseppe Mazzini (1805-1872), who championed the cause of a united Italy, freed from the control of foreign princes, so that all Italians could as equal citizens shape their collective destiny[93]. As he made clear in his 1860 book, *Duties of Man*, the development of a liberal nation was important in providing the means for people to fulfil their duties to support each other's wellbeing within their shared borders, and to extend the readiness to build mutually supportive relations with other people living under conditions of liberal nationhood elsewhere.

Like Kant before him, Mazzini saw republican power distribution as the key to peace and cooperation between citizens internally, and between states externally. Mazzini went beyond Kant in actively promoting the republican cause. In 1849, he and Garibaldi succeeded in establishing a republic in Rome, which they hoped would be a model for the rest of Italy. The short-lived republic showed its enlightened intentions by abolishing the death penalty completely and revising its criminal code. But against the forces of the Austrians, the French, and the Catholic establishment, the republic fell. Mazzini vowed to fight on, but Garibaldi decided at that point Italian nationhood was more important than liberal republican institutions, and joined forces with the King of Piedmont to bring about an Italy united under the latter's rule. The triumph of tribal over liberal nationalism was to steer Italian politics towards an authoritarian dead-end in the next century.

In Britain, where liberal nationalism had the best chance of advancing, the jingoistic temptations of tribal glory remained a substantial obstacle. William Gladstone (1809-1898) had already found

---

[93] Mack Smith, D, *Mazzini*, New Haven, Yale University Press: 1994.

his attempts to extend the franchise at home repeatedly frustrated by his Conservative counterpart, Disraeli, but looking beyond Britain, he was to encounter not just Disraeli but also the reactionary Whig, Palmerston, who showed just how easy it was to stir up 'patriotic' feelings against every form of moral propriety[94].

This was well illustrated by the Opium War (1839-1860) waged by the British Government against China for trying to stop the British selling an addictive narcotic to the Chinese population. An exasperated Gladstone declared, "A war more unjust in its origin, a war more calculated to cover this country with permanent disgrace, I do not know." For Palmerston, who ordered gunboats to China to destroy properties and civilian lives alike, the suffering and humiliation of the Chinese were irrelevant since their inferior status meant they should be exploited for the good of those higher up on the global hierarchy. When liberal Members of Parliament disgusted with Palmerston's behaviour tried to censure him, the utterly unrepentant Prime Minister turned the table on his critics for their "anti-English feeling, an abnegation of all those ties which bind men to their country and to their fellow-countrymen, which I should hardly have expected from the lips of any member of this House. Everything that was English was wrong, and everything that was hostile to England was right."

Substitute 'German', or 'American' for 'English', and one would have a ready-made diatribe against liberals who have ever questioned the Reich or the US for their treatment of foreign nationals. Palmerston went on to give a masterclass in alpha male populist leadership by calling for a general election and winning even more support from the country. Disraeli would continue Palmerston's manipulation of tribal nationalism and deployed troops to different parts of the world to assert British interests. Under him the Conservatives consolidated their flag-waving politics. The image of the Union Jack dominating all others abroad helped to halt explorations for a more just distribution of power at home.

When Gladstone, with the support of John Morley (1838-1923), attempted to secure Parliamentary approval for his proposal to give home rule for Ireland, because the Irish people had been deprived of their own national governance, they would be defeated by the Conservative

---

[94] Jenkins, R, *Gladstone*, Macmillan: 1995.

opposition in 1886 and again in 1893. It even split and weakened the Liberal Party, which lost power in 1895 and remained out of office for a decade.

Liberal nationalism's hope in France was dashed, as we have seen, by Napoleon III who with conservative support swiftly dismantled the Second Republic[95]. In 1852, he ordered widespread arrests, exiled 9,000 men to Algeria, sent another 1,500 away from France, bestowed honours on the army, increased the influence of the Church (it was out of deference to Catholic demands that he sent French troops to crush the Roman Republic briefly established by Mazzini), drastically reduced the power of parliament, and made the executive branch of government supreme with him at its head.

Napoleon III did not want to concede to a liberal, republican system of government where citizens would deliberate on what constituted the common interests they should pursue. Instead he wanted to rally the support of the French nation by showing how they were a constant force to be reckoned with all over Europe and beyond. France was not an aggressor, he proclaimed, but French troops could be readily sent to battle any enemy, which the supreme ruler of France deemed a threat to his people. This unaccountable adventurism led Napoleon into an ill-conceived conflict with Prussia in 1870[96]. Defeat by the Prussian army paved the way for the Third Republic to be established in France. This time liberal nationalists built a state that put the protection and development of its citizens at its heart[97]. But tribalist passions were not easily extinguished and there were always authoritarians waiting to exploit them to expand their own powerbase.

Opponents of the Third Republic could not agree on a leader to champion their different causes, but one thing tribal nationalists could readily identify were scapegoats. When it became increasingly likely that the new republican government would last much longer than its predecessors, France witnessed in the 1880s the emergence of

---

[95] Price, RD, *Napoleon III and the Second Empire*, Routledge: 1997.

[96] Wetzel, D, *A Duel of Giants: Bismarck, Napoleon III, and the Origins of the Franco-Prussian War*, University of Wisconsin Press: 2003.

[97] An excellent introduction to the Third Republic is to be found in Nord, P, *The Republican Moment: struggles for democracy in nineteenth century France*, Harvard University Press: 1995.

organisations like the Anti-Semitic League, founded by Edouard
Drumont to advocate an exclusive French Catholic state. In 1894,
Captain Alfred Dreyfus, a Jewish army officer was found guilty of
treason even though there was no clear-cut evidence. Anti-Semites, self-
styled patriots, devout Catholics immediately lined up against the
republican government for its weak handling of a disgraced officer. On
closer examination, the case was found to be based entirely on
fabrication. Liberal statesman like Auguste Scheurer-Kestner (1833-
1899) stood firm in their support for the due administration of justice.
When the charge against Dreyfus had been totally discredited, Scheurer-
Kestner himself would not rest until the wrongly convicted captain was
finally exonerated. His courageous defiance against racist populism
showed how resolute liberal reformists would have to be to prevent
national pride from being appropriated by hate-mongers and
authoritarian leaders.

Diversionary confrontation

In addition to France's own Jewish population, French nationalists were
also filled with ire towards the Prussians and other Germans who helped
defeat France in 1870. Many openly talked about revenge as a patriotic
cause. Despite Marx's dream of workers uniting in the war against the
capitalists irrespective of their national differences, the unfolding of the
nineteenth century proved that the ability of the powerful to manipulate
the powerless to do their bidding would make nationalism a most potent
force in deflecting people from pursuing their own interests. The French
republic was thus sucked into a destructive rivalry with the new German
Empire, when it should be building up a strategic alliance for peace
across Europe.

France had let slip the opportunity in 1866 to support Austria to
prevent Prussia from using its growing military strength to force
German-speaking states in the north into the North German Federation.
Its failure to take action – in part due to its nationalistic animosity
towards the old Austrian enemy, allowed Prussia to embark on its
ambitious course to become the authoritarian superpower Spain and
France had previously been on the continent. The foundations were laid
by Ministers like Otto von Manteuffel in the 1850s who steered Prussia

towards policies of military development, relieving small tenant farmers of their feudal obligations, tight regulations of factory working conditions and limitations of parliamentary accountabilities. In Britain, liberal reformists had sought to rebalance the power between state and citizens, and indeed with new sources of power like business owners, so that those with neglected needs could get their concerns taken into account. But in Prussia, reforms were designed to pacify the masses and make them feel content and proud, so that they would not question the concentration of power in the ruling regime.

The likes of Napoleon III and Disraeli could relate to such a strategy, for they too had aimed at consolidating conservative power structures by undertaking populist initiatives to win over public support. But liberal culture had taken deep roots in France and Britain so that civic suspicion of what the powerful got up to was not so easily brushed aside. Manteuffel spoke for the Prussian establishment when he expressed his contempt for the liberal and progressive minded, "the so called educated class", when he summed up the "one characteristic of this class [as] a combination of arrogance and cowardice, both spring from Godlessness."

Under Bismarck, Prussia's goal was first to become the dominant force of a united Germany, and then for Germany to be the dominant continental power of Europe. He would diplomatically play one potential rival against another so that no efforts were made by France, Austria or Britain to contain his expansion plans. He was aided by the rise of the cult of the German people as a culturally rich and militarily resolute tribe. He engineered wars against German and non-German neighbours until it appeared to most German speaking people outside Austria that their national destiny would be best fulfilled through a united Germany – a German Empire, with the unquestionable ruler looking after the welfare of his people, bringing them martial glory, and acting on their behalf without them getting involved in the complexities of shaping public policies.

Tribal nationalism routed liberal nationalism. By the end of the nineteenth century, Bismarck's determination to create a strong hierarchical state rather than a vibrant democratic society had led to his own dismissal by the absolute ruler at the top of that hierarchy, Wilhelm II, who wanted to use the immense power now at his disposal to realise his personal vision of a great German Empire, regardless of the consequences for Germans or anyone else.

The contest between liberal and tribal nationalism was to be found in the many campaigns and wars for national independence throughout the late 1800s and into the next century. In the US, the liberal political system was put under considerable stress by the spread of the tribalistic animosity against black Americans growing out of many southern whites' yearning for an unrealizable vengeance against their defeat by the northern states in the civil war. The Italian, the Greek, and the Latin American states all fluctuated between citizens-focused and leaders-focused government until they settled more on the side of top-down authoritarian rule, with a mix of paternalism and dictatorship[98]. In Asia, nationalist sentiments were to be harnessed in contrasting ways by Japan and China, leading to major historical shifts in global power relations.

Following the Meiji Restoration of 1868, Japanese statesmen concentrated on turning the many Japanese daimyo into a centralised nation-state, with the Emperor as the absolute head, and in whose name commands could be issued without question[99]. Japan had been shaken by the ease Western intruders could with impunity come and go as they pleased because of their military superiority. At first, the new ruling elite wanted to adopt practices such as industrialisation, parliamentary procedures, and wider access to education to modernise Japan. Reformists like Ōkubo Toshimichi (1830-1878) and Kido Takayoshi (1833-1877) pressed for more democratic arrangements. But as in Germany, those who managed to secure the greatest influence were the ones who cultivated tribal nationalism as the vehicle to rally the support of the people for martial glory and territorial expansionism. Democratisation was increasingly brushed aside in favour of obedience to the authoritarian command structure.

By the end of the nineteenth century, tribal nationalism had taken hold in Japan. While Prussia played on the pride and need for unity of German speaking people across Europe as the basis for carving out a new

---

[98] A useful one volume guide is Bakewell, P, *A History of Latin America*, WileyBlackwell: 2003.
[99] See Jansen, MB, *The Making of Modern Japan*, Harvard University Press: 2002.

empire, Japan presented itself as the leading Asian nation to roll back the Western encroachment on Asia. Its people would accept all that was asked of them because in return their nation would be the conquering saviour of all Asia. The absence of any significant liberal opposition to the ruling regime meant that the rulers of Japan could take the country's inhabitants – not to mention those of their neighbours – towards the most disastrous fate in the next century.

The one country in Asia in centuries past that would have checked Japan's rapid growth in power was China. But China, like the Ottoman Empire and Hindu Kingdoms, had been bypassed by Western development and left in a state of social, economic and technological stagnation. Ignorance, superstitions, disinclination to innovate froze them in time when others willing to learn, criticise, and revise, surged ahead. As for Britain, France and America, which ought to be concerned with the power imbalance emerging in Asia, they were themselves preoccupied with exploiting political and commercial gains they could get out of China. Britain, as we have seen, defended its right to conduct drug trafficking by launching the Opium War and inflicted humiliating defeats on the Chinese people. At the same time it finally emancipated slaves of African descent, the US began in the 1860s to import large numbers of Chinese as basically slave labour to help with dangerous construction projects such as clearing paths with explosives to help laying down new railway tracks.

Nationalist feelings, combining resentment against the 'non-Chinese' Manchurian rulers and fear of being subjugated by Europeans, Americans and Japanese, became a prominent factor in political discussions of the future of China[100]. One of the most important scholar-civil servants, Kang Youwei (1858-1927), advised the Emperor Guangxu of the importance of reform – especially the constitutional monarchy model of Britain and its adoption by Japan before that country's slide into militarism. Kang pointed to the value of science and democracy in advancing Western nations. He recovered Mozi's progressive ideas on reciprocity and opposition to power inequalities, and incorporated these into his highly acclaimed work, the 1884 *Book of Great Unity*, which set out how the core Confucian notions of deference and social harmony

---

[100] Hsu, I.C.Y., *The Rise of Modern China*, Oxford University Press: 1983.

should be developed into a comprehensive system of equal respect for all, with unjust differentials between masters and servants, between men and women, between different nations, all eliminated.

Leaving aside the academic point of whether Kang' position was actually more Mohist than Confucian, he persuaded Emperor Guangxu to move towards liberal nationalism and introduce a reform programme which would raise education standards, adopt scientific and technological learning, establish parliamentary accountabilities, and strengthen the country's capacity to meet the needs of the people. Although Guangxu was ethnically non-(Han) Chinese, and there was populist animosity against Manchurians, there was no trace of tribal/racist resentment in Kang's philosophy. Furthermore, it was not military glory but improvement to the living conditions for the people themselves that mattered.

Guangxu's reform programme lasted only one hundred days in 1898. The Empress Dowager Cixi, demonstrating forcefully that women could act like alpha male authoritarians too, detested the notion that absolute imperial rule could be diluted. She placed the emperor – her adopted son – under house arrest within the Forbidden City until his death in 1908. All the reform edicts were rescinded with immediate effect. Kang managed to escape from China, but six of the other leading advocates for the 'Hundred Days Reform' were rounded up and executed in public.

Cixi's short-term defeat of the reformists left the progressive-minded with no choice but to plot the violent overthrow of the Manchurian regime. When the Manchurians invaded China in the 17th century, they took over a country which, since around the middle of the 6th century, had more or less been the most powerful in economic and political terms in the whole world. But the Confucian philosophy which had helped to secure its longevity was ill-suited to prepare it for a culture of continuous improvement through the cooperation of equals before the law. This was precisely the culture that was to flourish with the emergence of progressive thinking in England in the 17th century, spreading to others ready to embrace enlightened practices and liberal governance. By the end of the 18th century China had lost all the advantages it previously had in relation to the West. Its decline reached rock bottom as the 19th century drew to a close.

In the next century, China, along with other countries still clinging to authoritarianism, would have to face up to the consequences of seeking to make oppression a permanent feature of life. It was to be a hard, painful lesson for them to learn that the move towards a more inclusive form of power relations was inherently connected with enabling people to interact with each other more cooperatively. When more people were able to contribute to finding solutions without fear of being persecuted, when fewer people could impose their poorly thought-out ideas on others without due constraints, and when all were encouraged to develop their intellectual capacity to improve the conditions of life, more opportunities would follow for better thinking and practices to emerge. It was the great misfortune for millions of people who had to lose their lives before this lesson was accepted[101].

## The politics of collective protection

As the twentieth century began, progressive reformists in Europe and America turned their attention to how authoritarian threats against the powerless at home and abroad could be dealt with through greater collective action. They were aware that tribal nationalism and plutocratic irresponsibility increasingly endangered the wellbeing of countless people. To enable people, who could make little difference as individuals, to protect themselves from those with far greater power, they began to set out a new role for democratic government, which was to be interventionist in securing the freedom of citizens from neglect and abuse.

Treatment of individuals as workers, suppliers, consumers by powerful businesses was to be subject to tighter scrutiny and controls by the state which must at the same time be made democratically more accountable to citizens, women as well as men. People of all talents, nationalities, religions would be expected to support each other through their contributions to public institutions working to the benefit of all without distinction of wealth or rank. In Britain, New Liberals such as Hobson and Hobhouse challenged both the Conservative and Liberal

---

[101] For an interesting thesis on why some nations prosper more than others, see Landes, D, *The Wealth and Poverty of Nations*, Little, Brown & Co: 1998.

Parties to embrace a more responsible approach to the development of market relations. In America, Progressives such as Le Follette and Dewey pressed Republicans and Democrats alike to check the irresponsible use of corporate powers that were ruining the lives of all too many ordinary citizens. Furthermore, they wanted the reform culture to be pioneered by their countries to be exemplars to the rest of the world[102].

These champions for inclusive communities were not arguing for some abstract ideal, but were seeking to remind wider society what progress had been achieved, and how much more could be attained. Each extension of the franchise had led not to clamouring for ill-conceived policies but a better focus on the problems which society needed to address, especially in relation to the living and working conditions of people trapped by the marginalising effects of unrestrained industrialisation.

In science and technology, the effective challenge against authoritarian control over the use of knowledge power paved the way for unprecedented breakthroughs. In 1900, Max Planck published his quantum theory, followed in 1905 by Einstein with his theory of relativity. Newtonian physics, the glory of 18th century Enlightenment, had in accordance with the progressive commitment of experimental science, been surpassed. The world at the national and global level became more readily accessible with new communications and transport technology. Large-scale car production commenced in 1902, and a year later, the Wright brothers demonstrated to the world the possibility of powered flight. None of this would have happened if a priestly elite, or its equivalent, could use its exclusive power to determine what was true or not without reference to what others discover through critical

---

[102] The best book on these turn of the century thinkers and reformists remains Kloppenberg, JT, *Uncertain Victory: social democracy and progressivism in European and American thought, 1870-1920*, Oxford University Press: 1986. A good survey of the reform ideas being developed during this period is provided by Rodgers, DT, *Atlantic Crossings: social politics in a progressive age*, The Belknap Press of Harvard University Press: 1998. On New Liberalism, see Freeden, M, *The New Liberalism: an ideology of social reform*, Clarendon Press: 1986; and Collini, S, *Liberalism & Sociology: L.T. Hobhouse and political argument in England 1880-1914*, Cambridge University Press: 1983.

discussions and experimentation.

Similarly in arts, the absence of a power to dictate what should or should not be done allowed creativity to flourish in the West. Kandinsky, Picasso, Schonberg, Joyce and others led the way in going beyond representational painting, tonality in music, and conventional literary narrative to experiment with new forms of aesthetic expression while artists in authoritarian societies stagnated within the traditional norms they were confined.

Importantly, the recognition that power inequalities obstructed the moral golden rule of reciprocity was spreading to a wider circle of reformists. For example, progressive Christians such as F.D. Maurice, Charles Kingsley, Mary Ward, Walter Rauschenbusch, Henry George, Vida Scudder, saw it as their duty to expose the iniquities of oppressive power distribution, and tirelessly propounded the Social Gospel of translating the personal love of God into the social love of justice for all[103]. They were not always popular within the church hierarchy – Catholic or Protestant – but against authoritarian rulers who had been co-opting religion to bolster their claim to legitimacy, they made it plain that authoritarian division of people into the mighty and the vulnerable was not compatible with authentic faith. Power relations between the haves and the have-nots must henceforth be rectified.

The social Christians and liberal reformers were joined by social democrats, who were as keen to detach the process for progressive improvement from Marxist ideology about a communist utopia as their religious allies were with theological dogma about a heavenly after-life. What was important was the steady, unrelenting redistribution of power from those who made virtually all the key decisions to more and more people across society, especially those who had been most marginalised up to now.

Eduard Bernstein (1850-1932) was particularly influential in shifting the thinking of social democrats, in Germany and across Europe more widely, away from aiming for the collapse of prevailing socio-political arrangements for the sake of an idealized future, and towards

---

[103] Phillips, P.T., *A Kingdom on Earth: Anglo-American Social Christianity, 1880-1940*, Pennsylvania State University Press: 1996.

working for day-to-day reforms[104].

The programmes of social democrats increasingly reflected this approach which crucially relied on citizens in general to work out what needed to be changed as they became less divided by power imbalance, rather than counting on a revolutionary elite to wield concentrated power to deliver what they alone considered to be for the good of all (or the proletariat). They summed up the emerging progressive consensus in every country where it had established a foothold. In broad terms, they sought to secure universal suffrage (for women and men) under the system of proportional representation which distributed power most evenly; the separation of Church and State particularly in terms of the educational curriculum; devolution of power to spread decision-making centres more widely; protection of the freedom to gather for discussions, to express opinions, and to form trade unions; free healthcare and education for all; progressive taxation on income and unearned wealth to fund public services; regulation on working conditions; and state-funded insurance for all workers to mitigate against unemployment.

The Liberals in Britain and the Radicals in France led reforming government to bring about a fairer distribution of power, moving those countries forward in building more inclusive communities[105]. The Liberal Government introduced Infants' Welfare Centres to provide help directly to mothers and infant death-rate at last began to fell. It also brought in insurance against unemployment, ill health and old age, ensuring that collective provisions would be put in place to deal with problems that had hitherto afflicted individuals unable to cope with them on their own. In criminal justice, its policies shifted the focus to prevention and significantly reduced the prison population. Imprisonment of young people was prohibited up to the age of 14 and strictly limited for 14-16.

---

[104] Steger, MB, *The Quest for Evolutionary Socialism: Eduard Bernstein and Social Democracy*, Cambridge University Press: 2006.

[105] The reformist agenda in both countries focused on how to secure greater protection for people who would otherwise be relatively powerless to get their needs and concerns taken seriously. See Packer, I., *Liberal Government and Politics: 1905-1915*, Palgrave Macmillan: 2006; and Stone, J.F., *Sons of the Revolution: Radical Democrats in France, 1862-1914*, Louisiana State University Press: 1996.

In France, the Radical Government managed to bring in a tax on income to facilitate the distribution of wealth in the face of strong opposition. It also established arbitration tribunals to deal with workers' disputes with employers, set minimum wages and introduced maximum hours for work undertaken by public authorities. However, the Radicals could not go further because the Socialists (not to mention the Communists) would not support them. Working on the misguided assumption that unless their agenda for wide ranging reforms could be totally implemented, the Socialists refused to support anyone who might be able to bring in some of those reforms. Any socialist, like Alexandre Millerand, who agreed to serve in the Government (in his case as Minister for Commerce), was condemned as a traitor.

The experience in France reflected a wider problem in the progressive struggle. A key consequence of the commitment to avoid allowing any group to have the absolute power to change society (regardless of their ideological credentials) is that change could then only be brought about with the help of a coalition of diverse citizens and distinct groups. And although liberal reformists had through the 19th century taken significant steps forward in connecting a variety of initiatives to an overall theme of containing those who were too powerful, many people still did not see, let alone embrace, the full implications of the struggle for inclusive communities.

In essence, power inequalities could not be dealt with in a compartmentalised manner with some areas addressed and others left to fester. Revolutionary socialists railed against the excessive power of the capitalists but they had no concern about concentrating power in the militant vanguard acting in the name of the proletariat. At the same time, the many campaigns for extending the vote showed that shifting alliances could hold back progress because some who supported the vote for men did not consider the issue relevant for women, while others backed extending the franchise to white women in the belief that it would strengthen the popular base to continue excluding non-whites.

In Britain, the Conservatives blocked Gladstone's attempt to give more people the right to vote until liberal reformists' call for change was backed by widespread demonstrations by workers' representatives. Gladstone went even further than the 1867 Act passed reluctantly by the Conservatives and brought in the 1884 Act, but even that still left out

40% of adult males. And with Gladstone totally against giving women the vote, it took the Suffragette Movement and sacrifices by campaigners like Emily Davison, who was killed in 1913 as a result of her attempt to disrupt Derby Day at Epsom Downs Racecourse by running onto the course and grabbing the bridle of a horse owned by the King, to keep the pressure on until the Representation of the People Act 1918 for the first time enfranchised women over 30 who met minimum property qualifications (at the same time abolishing practically all property qualifications for men from the age of 21). Full electoral equality was only secured in 1928[106].

But even as women were finally beginning to turn the tide against the power imbalance that had for centuries been in favour of men, the great majority of women and men were finding themselves increasingly powerless in relation to the large business corporations that had grown inexorably since the 19th century. Many liberal critics of overbearing government denying citizens the right to influence its decision-making put the issue of corporate power in a separate compartment altogether. They could not see that large businesses were exerting greater and greater control over people's lives – what they could eat, what price they had to pay, where they could work, what wage they might earn – without ordinary people having any practical means to make businesses take their interests seriously into consideration.

In America, where the breeding ground for giant corporations was most fertile, someone like William Graham Sumner, President of the American Sociological Association, who was ready to condemn his country's inaction in the face of racist atrocities against a black postmaster and his family in South Carolina, and its military bullying of a weaker nation in the Spanish-American War, would nonetheless defend economic inequality because it did not breach any "law of nature, religion, ethics, or the State." Wealth-based power was regarded as something as legitimately earned by those with the drive and skills to build up their business empire. But the conditions of legitimacy were determined by arbitrary rules, and the struggle for inclusive communities was precisely about questioning the legitimacy of those rules in view of the growing concentration of power in a few. The ability to direct others

---

[106] Whitfield, B, *Extension of the Franchise 1832-1928*, Heinemann: 2001.

to make money for oneself, no more than the talent for commanding others to fight and bring new territories under one's control, did not confer any inherent right to put other people under abject dependency.

Sumner's more consistently progressive contemporaries saw the urgent need to curb corporate power. Ernest H. Crosby warned of the rise of an economic aristocracy, which would undermine democratic government. Henry Demarest Lloyd called for a new democracy of industry with unions and cooperatives playing a more prominent role in spreading decision-making powers. They were supported by a new generation of activists like Mary 'Mother' Jones (1830-1930) who helped to rally miners' defiance against coal companies which had hired private police forces to suppress attempts to form unions, and Louis D. Brandeis (1856-1941) who would provide free legal advice to workers and other campaign organisations in their fight for a minimum wage and union rights. In the absence of a social democratic party organisation by now common in Europe, they showed how the curtailment of the powerful in the economic realm could nonetheless be integrated into the wider opposition to the abuse of power in America[107].

Most significantly, Theodore Roosevelt (1858-1919) who became President in 1901, strongly believed that corporate power must be limited if it was not to put ordinary citizens, as consumers and workers, at a serious disadvantage[108]. In 1902, when the United Mine Workers of America went on strike over their treatment by the mine corporations, Roosevelt had no time for the laissez faire mantra of telling workers to accept what the market had to offer. Instead he asked the mine owners and the miners representatives to join him at the White House for negotiation. It resulted in a 10% pay increase and a reduction to a 9-hour day (from the previous 10) and helped to end the strike.

Roosevelt understood that monopoly power – like autocracy in politics – deprived people of any real choice, forcing them to accept whatever the business in question wanted to offer, on the terms they

---

[107] For an excellent account of how different notions of 'freedom' competed for government action (or in some cases, inaction) in the US, see Foner, E, *The Story of American Freedom*, Basingstoke, Papermac: 1999.
[108] See Mowry, GE, *The Era of Theodore Roosevelt and the Birth of Modern America 1900-1912*, Harper Torchbook: 1962; and Miller, N, *Theodore Roosevelt: A Life*, William Morrow: 1994.

would dictate.  He issued 44 lawsuits against major corporations and came to be known as the trust-buster.  In 1906, he secured the passing of the Hepburn Act, which empowered the Interstate Commerce Commission to regulate the activities of the railway barons.  The ICC could replace what the railways were charging the public with "just-and-reasonable" maximum rates, and the penalties for violation were increased. It was able to prescribe a uniform system of accounting, require standardized reports, and inspect railroad accounts.  In the same year, he cajoled Congress into passing the Pure Food and Drug Act, which provided for the labelling of foods and drugs so that the public would know what was really being sold to them, and the Meat Inspection Act, which established statutory inspection of livestock and mandated sanitary conditions at meatpacking plants.

Instead of leaving natural resources to businesses to exploit in line with market demands, Roosevelt took land into state control, established the United States Forest Service, and led the argument for conservation. By 1909, his administration had created an unprecedented 42 million acres (170,000 km²) of national forests, 53 national wildlife refuges, and 18 areas of 'special interest', including the Grand Canyon.

Roosevelt's embrace of the progressive reform agenda, however, was not shared by the rest of the Republican Party, and by the time he concluded that Taft, whose succession to him as President he initially supported, was not sufficiently progressive, the Republican Party establishment had decided that they preferred to stick with Taft.  In 1912, even though Roosevelt was the clear winner in Republican primaries, Taft was put forward as the Republican Presidential candidate. Roosevelt agreed with independent progressives to set up the Progressive Party and stand as their candidate.

Given that the Democrats had decided to nominate Woodrow Wilson, who also espoused progressive views, the hope for progressive reforms was running higher than ever.  Never before in any country had the leading candidates for the highest political office been so concerned with promoting their progressive credentials.  Taft the Republican came third because he was the least convincing progressive.  Most of the progressive Democrats gave their support to Wilson, because they did not believe that Roosevelt would deliver on the platform he had set out in his presidential campaign.  This was in spite of the fact that Roosevelt's programme drew inspiration from Herbert Croly's (1869-1930) important argument that progressives needed to move on from the once legitimate reservations about a powerful federal government, to make proper use of the federal government to tackle the powerful forces from which individual citizens could not protect themselves[109]. The New Nationalism of Roosevelt and Croly aimed to build inclusive communities along similar lines to those set out by European social democrats: minimum wage, prohibition of child labour, compensation for workers, social insurance, full disclosure of contributions to political campaigns, and regulatory authority over businesses.

Wilson beat Roosevelt to the Presidency on a platform which sought to appeal to progressives. But not for the first time, upon closer examination, progressives wondered if they had backed the wrong horse. Roosevelt was unequivocal about his support for the vote for women, whereas Wilson claimed that the matter should be left to individual states. And while Roosevelt publicly defended his invitations to African-American reformists like Booker T. Washington to dine with him at the White House, and his appointment of non-whites to government positions, Wilson gave in to pressures from Southern Democrats to segregate federal government workers on racial lines until he was forced by liberals to reverse his decision. Furthermore, he stood Croly's philosophy on its head by insisting, in the name of economic freedom for all, that the federal government would not use its power to help those who were at a particular disadvantage – people living in impoverished rural communities, vulnerable workers, or labour unions.

The First World War

It was not until 1916 when Wilson was seeking his second term that he started to bring in progressive reforms Roosevelt had long been advocating[110]. By that time, the failure of the global community to build

---

[109] Croly, H, *Progressive Democracy*, Transaction Publishers: 1998; and also *Promise of American Life*, Bobbs-Merrill: 2000.

[110] Link, A, *Woodrow Wilson and the Progressive Era 1910-1917*, Harper Torchbook: 1963; and Milton, J and Cooper, JR, *Woodrow Wilson: A Biography*, Knopf Publishing: 2009.

inclusive international relations had resulted in the crisis of the First World War. Wilson's flawed judgement about maintaining American neutrality – reinforced by his determination to oppose Roosevelt's call to fight on the side of Britain and France – reflected his inadequate grasp of the politics of collective action. He was always guided by the essentially laissez faire outlook that if one ensured a central political power – be it America's federal government in relation to individual states or businesses, or America in relation to other countries – did not confer any advantage on some groups as opposed to others, then everyone would work things out between themselves. He did not see that in a world full of vastly unequal power distribution, some already had huge advantages over others, and unless there was a democratically based political power prepared to intervene to help restore the balance, continued exploitation and oppression would remain the order of the day.

Wilson had remarked that "it would be the irony of fate if my administration had to deal chiefly with foreign affairs." But in an ever inter-connected world, the power relations between countries, and indeed within countries, could not be compartmentalised as issues that could be ignored in the struggle for inclusive communities in one's own country. Since the 1870s, progressive forces through the Liberals and worker representatives in Britain, and the Republican-Socialist allies in France had accelerated the push for reform. But in countries where liberal reformists and social democrats had only minor influence on nationwide policies, divisions grew deeper. In Germany, in particular, the Social Democrats were persecuted, and when Wilhelm II ascended to the throne he followed the tribal nationalist formula of seeking to preserve inequalities within his country by promoting German military superiority over other countries. In Russia, Nicholas II rejected reformist ideas for making his country more democratic and inclusive. Instead, he too assumed that his authoritarian rule was best bolstered by a show of military strength against outsiders. Defeat by Japan in 1905 only stiffened his resolve to find an opportunity to demonstrate Russian might.

Against this backdrop, the assassination of the heir to the Austrian throne, Archduke Franz Ferdinand, in Serbia 1914 was merely a spark in the midst of the explosive tensions authoritarian regimes had already created to deflect their subjects from internal reform movements.

Germany urged Austria to issue Serbia with an impossible ultimatum so that it could provoke a war in which it would emerge as an imperious victor. Russia lined up immediately behind Serbia in the hope that it could demonstrate its power against external enemies. France had not forgotten its humiliation by the Germans in 1870 and was more than ready to honour their agreement to support Russia. German invasion of neutral Belgium brought Britain reluctantly into the war[111].

When war began, few expected it to last very long or that it would bring unprecedented devastation. But three factors had altered the dynamics of the conflict. First, Britain's naval supremacy in the previous two centuries had stoked a burning hubris akin to that of ancient Athens. Like the Athenians, the British assumed both that their military strength should give them an unchallengeable advantage in international affairs, and that peace amongst nations was best secured through ensuring that no single country could attain a significant edge over others in its military capability. But while they pretended that there was no contradiction in this outlook because they were somehow unique, others believed that their disadvantaged position in relation to Britain could only be overcome by either a true balance of power applicable to every country without exception, or an acquisition of military supremacy to rival if not eclipse that of Britain. By the early 20th century, Germany had reached a point where it could seriously consider staking its claim to the latter position. While Britain was still stuck with its outmoded thinking that everyone else was conveniently locked together in a neat balance of power, Germany was in fact capable of overwhelming most of its European neighbours. The same applied to Japan in relation to its part of the world, and yet Britain saw it as a helpful ally instead of a serious threat to world peace.

The failure to recognise German military capability, which was by then far beyond easy containment by the old alliance system, was compounded by the second misjudgement, namely, the impact of technology and advanced weaponry on conventional battle strategy. The radically increased range and destructiveness of missiles, the rapidity and penetration of machine gun fire, the use of chemical materials in

---

[111] Culpin, C and Darby, G, *The Origins of the First World War*, Longman: 1998.

inflicting pain and death, and the accelerated troop mobilisation resulting from improved communication and transportation, all added to far greater number of combatants being maimed or killed often for little territorial gain on either side. When German advancement against France and Russia was eventually checked, it did not lead to a strategic stalemate where opponents eyed each other from afar with practical engagement suspended. Instead, they dug trenches from which the most powerless in the military hierarchy would be sent with callous regularity to face certain death.

One of the key reasons for the war continuing despite its obvious futility was connected with the third factor – the desperate resolution of the authoritarian regimes to bank on military success to help marginalise demands for reforms. Wilhelm II and Nicholas II had not forgotten the fate of Napoleon III of France when his attempt to hold on to personal rule through military glory failed with his army's defeat by the Prussians in 1870, and a republican government took power. And while the Russian Tsar could not contemplate conceding to the Germans, the German Emperor would not pull back to his own borders for fear of being seen as giving grounds to the British and the French who had finally woken up to the threat posed by Germany's new military capability. Authoritarian cowardice was masked for a time with the help of tribal nationalism, diverting the public from the inherent shortcomings of their regimes, and channelling their frustration into hatred of their foreign enemies.

However, tribal nationalism could only be sustained by military success against the 'others'. When military setbacks fuelled anger over economic grievance and social discontent, not even the most oppressive regime would be safe from being overthrown. In 1917, Nicholas II had to abdicate the throne of Russia, but the Provisional Government, which had taken charge, made the mistake of trying to continuing with the war against Germany and its allies. The Bolsheviks under Lenin saw their chance of toppling the Provisional Government and seizing power themselves. The liberals and moderate socialists, ineffective in organising themselves into viable alternative government, were brushed aside by the Bolsheviks who won popular support with their determination to withdraw from the war[112]. Like the Jacobins before them, the Bolsheviks believed they had all the answers and anyone questioning their actions was automatically a counter-revolutionary to be punished. Having won the civil war and secured control of Russia, they had no intention of ever allowing others to seek the right to rule through open elections, or giving anyone the opportunity to hold them to account for their decisions. In the name of bringing about a more equal society, they amassed more power than even the former Tsar could have hoped to have at his disposal. The elite of the Communist Party were to make all the key decisions, assign to themselves special privileges, and subject the general population, but especially those with liberal tendency to question the powerful, to constant threat of arrest, imprisonment or even execution.

Russia's withdrawal gave Germany little advantage as America threw its weight behind Britain and France, and it had to concede defeat in 1919. At Wilson's insistence, Germany became a parliamentary democracy, but as a result of Wilson's wider failure to establish a powerful League of Nations to create a real balance of power across all countries and thus to maintain international peace, the German Weimar Republic did not survive long into the 1930s when it was eliminated by the rise of a militaristic authoritarianism more pernicious than any of its predecessors.

## The consequences of non-intervention

The First World War reminded everyone of the danger of allowing any regime to build up enough power to subject its own population to dictatorial controls and threaten its neighbouring countries with invasion. But pacifists drew from it merely the lesson that war must be avoided in the future, while militarists became more convinced that no one should attain the status of a super power except them. Both strands of thought in America ended up pulling in the same direction – the US should not

---

[112] There are many diverse interpretations of the Russian Revolution. See Ulam, A, *Lenin and the Bolsheviks*, Fontana: 1978; Westwood, JN, *Endurance and Endeavour: Russian History 1812-1971*, Oxford University Press: 1973; Daniels, RV (ed), *The Stalin Revolution*, DC Heath & Co: 1972; and Acton, E, *Rethinking the Russian Revolution*, Bloomsbury Academic: 1990.

get itself embroiled in conflicts abroad, least of all when decisions would be tied up with an international body which could take interests other than those of the US into account, and the safest way forward was to ensure America was so powerful that no one would threaten its security.

Without American leadership to lay the foundations for a worldwide political institution to deal with international issues just as the development of its own federal government was necessary to oversee inter-state matters within the US, nations drifted back into their insular position. In fact, blinkered non-intervention seemed to become the dominant approach. The people of a shell-shocked world did not want to march forward to tackle any more threats. Others would have to take care of themselves. Unfortunately, others, especially those with little power, could not always stand up for themselves, and in the absence of collective action to protect them, those with ruthless ambitions were able to exert their dominance until the damages they caused were beyond repair.

Many with liberal or social democratic leanings who had rallied around a common progressive cause at the beginning of the 20th century now found that they were splintering into factions. Amongst socialists, some came to view the Communist Revolution as an inspirational model, and even when indisputable evidence emerged about Stalin's murderous authoritarian rule with its numerous death camps and executions (estimates range from 10 million to 20 million deaths brought about by Stalin's policies), communist supporters refused to condemn Soviet totalitarianism. Unwittingly they encouraged the noble socialist aims of rolling back power inequalities to be linked with, and thereby debased by, 'Communism' as practised by Stalin.

At the same time, the interventionist stance of the Liberal Government in Britain and Roosevelt's Presidency in America was rejected by many of the post-1919 generation who gravitated towards the market libertarian outlook long championed by the likes of Herbert Spencer. Instead of recognising that individual freedom, in a world of gross power inequalities, could only be secured through collective action to counter exploitation, they returned to the blinkered view that everyone, especially businesses, should just be left to get on with their activities. Powerful businesses took advantage of the freedom they were granted to increase the gap between themselves and the rest of society.

In America, in particular, with Europe weakened by the war, unprecedented economic growth created opportunities for those running large businesses to amass every form of power. A succession of Presidents from a Republican Party which had resolutely rejected Teddy Roosevelt's progressive programme - Harding, Coolidge, Hoover – ran the country from 1921 to 1933, and they were completely content with growing inequalities. From 1923-1929 the average output from each worker increased 32% in manufacturing, while the average wages for manufacturing jobs increased only 8%. During the same period, corporate profits rose 62% and dividends went up 65%. By 1929, the top 0.1% of Americans had a combined income equal to the bottom 42%, and they controlled 34% of all savings, while 80% of Americans had no savings at all.

In the name of reining in government intervention, Republican Presidents distributed more and more power to those who already had the greatest influence in society[113]. Coolidge's Administration reduced federal income and inheritance taxes dramatically. For example, a man with a million-dollar annual income had his federal taxes reduced from $600,000 to $200,000. In 1923 the Supreme Court ruled in the case of Adkins v. Children's Hospital that minimum-wage legislation was unconstitutional.

But as the earning and hence spending power of an increasing number of people continued to fall, those depending on the masses buying their products to sustain their wealth were concerned with the emerging problem of insufficient demand. Instead of solving it by agreeing to even a slightly improved share of business profits to be passed on in higher wages, they concocted a strategy with their allies in the finance and banking sector. They decided to entice the population with credit opportunities. People borrowing money would then use it to pay manufacturers and retailers for the products on sale, but they would also have to pay interest to the lenders. People without an adequate income would fall more and more into debt, and businesses would continue to make money from the sale of goods and credit. By the end of the 1920s 60% of cars and 80% of radios in America were bought on

---

[113] See chapter 14 of Carroll, PN and Noble, DW, *The Free and the Unfree: a new history of the United States*, Penguin Books: 1977.

instalment credit. Between 1925 and 1929 the total amount of outstanding instalment credit more than doubled from $1.38 billion to around $3 billion.

The polarisation between the powerful rich and the marginalised poor taking place in America was replicated at a global level. While big American corporations were expanding their turnover and profits, the economy of Europe was struggling after the devastation of the First World War. There was no prospect of any real support being given to strengthen European productive capability. In fact, tariffs against imports into America rose by more than 100% in many cases. Instead of sharing out economic opportunities more fairly, the US Government followed the example of corporate America and provided credit to the Europeans who spent over 90% of the loans they received on buying American goods. The 'non-interventionist' stance of successive Republican Administrations thus enabled a hyper wealthy corporate elite to sit atop a power pyramid propped up by ever thicker layers of financially weak people in America and beyond.

Against this background, people who led an otherwise hopeless life were attracted to gambling what money they had on get-rich-fast schemes, and none seemed more promising that speculating on the stock market. It was seen as a short-cut to get a share in the super-rich corporations. Financial brokers again encouraged people to borrow money, this time to pay for shares on the assumption that the share prices would rise. In many instances, the mere fact that lots of people could be persuaded to invest in a company would be enough to convince others to buy shares in it as well, and thus helped to push those share prices up. However, ultimately, the actual performance of those companies could not be ignored.

By the end of the 1920s, it was becoming clear that even the most successful companies were facing a downturn as demands for what they had to offer began to shrink. Domestically, people who had already borrowed a large amount of money to buy a car and a radio for their family, and now having to cut back on meeting their everyday needs to pay the interest on the loan, were not willing or in any case able to borrow more money to buy another car or radio. From abroad, the lack of opportunities for other countries to develop their own purchasing power through export sales to America meant that they in turn were increasingly unable to buy goods from America.

In 1929, share prices started to drift downward. Some thought they could recover their losses with one more gamble, but those who understood the underlying weakness of the American economy realised they must sell the shares they owned before their value really plummeted. The critical point came on 24 October that year. After that day, nobody believed the market could recover and share value went into freefall. Between then and the end of the year, industrial output fell by nearly 10%. The mirage of a rich society sustained by the concentrated wealth of an unaccountable minority evaporated. Within a year, five million were without a job. By 1932, the number of unemployed had spiralled to 13 million. People defaulted on their interest payment. Warehouses were filled with repossessed goods. Demand for new products collapsed. Bankers and investors concentrated on cutting their loses and reined in lending at home and abroad. The world, which had become dependent on the American economy, plunged into the Great Depression[114].

Scapegoats had to be found. Apart from agitators for socialist reforms who were all too easily attacked as communist sympathisers, racially marginalised groups also became an easy target. It was an integral part of the 'non-interventionist' approach to ensure that the government would not be used as an instrument to correct the imbalance and abuse of power. If people would direct their suspicion and animosity towards those weaker than themselves, rather than challenge the rich and powerful, it would help those with power to stay in control. This was confirmed by the trend since the late 1910s. Racist organisations like the Ku Klux Klan grew in influence in America, openly anti-black riots broke out in Britain after the war, the blatantly racist regime in South Africa pressed ahead with its policy of segregation and discrimination against black people, and the Nazis gained recognition as a political force in Germany by launching the most vicious verbal and physical attack on Jewish people.

As chaos spread in the 1930s, the struggle for inclusive communities was beaten back by aggressive fanatics who either propagated or embraced authoritarianism to widen the abuse of people

---

[114] Galbraith, JK, *The Great Crash*, Houghton Mifflin: 1997.

they could oppress. In Spain, Franco toppled the progressive Republican government after it lost the support of the socialists and alienated the Catholics. A government that had wanted to check the concentration of power in traditional groups was destroyed by forces united by their determination to reinforce the absolute power structure of Spain – an unquestionable ruler backed by the religious establishment. In Italy, Mussolini invoked the glory of imperial Rome to present his Fascist Party as the restorer of order and pride, when in truth they were the modern version of Roman thugs who unhesitatingly used force to secure advantages to themselves at the expense of others. In Japan, those who favoured liberal and democratic governance had either been assassinated or forced into retirement, leaving the militarists to promote unchallenged their message of glory through conquest.

## Progressive response to authoritarian chaos

The philosophy of 'non-intervention' was, and will always be, an aid to authoritarians. If practised by the naïve, it would leave the field clear to those with no compunction about building up their power economically, militarily, or culturally so that they could more easily break down the resistance they would face when they asserted their dominance. If practised by the cunning, they would intervene selectively to protect the interests of the powerful – imposing tariffs, weakening unions, rejecting minimum wage, cutting taxes for the rich. The result would inevitably be an undermining of trust, harmony and security. Any hope for the cooperation of equals in enhancing the common good would be replaced by fear, suspicion, and the spread of mutual neglect. Into this vacuum, authoritarians perennially present themselves as the only saviours, when in fact they would just prolong the chaos and suffering.

We have seen that in the second half of the 19th century, J. S. Mill's liberal philosophy provided a systematic basis for the development of the progressive challenge to power inequalities. It was taken further forward in the early 20th century by New Liberal thinkers such as L. T. Hobhouse (1864-1929) and John Hobson (1858-1940)[115]. Mill had argued that human wellbeing stood the best chance of improving if safeguards against the concentration and abuse of power were vigilantly put in place. He stressed that it applied not just to governments, but also to other relationships across society such as economic ones between businesses and their employees and cultural-legal ones between men and women.

What the New Liberals did was to develop this outlook into a coherent reform programme. Without relaxing on the need to keep tight democratic reins on how the government should behave, they set out what the government should do to move society from its prevailing iniquities towards one based on genuine reciprocity. Hobhouse explained that this was not about each individual having to give something in return for some form of payment – as that kind of exchange could be based on the unequal bargaining positions – but about according each other respect and acting on that respect no matter what unfortunate circumstances should befall anyone. Hobson explicated this further in terms of the social and economic interdependence of citizens, and how in disregarding the conditions of some – such as their inability to function as productive workers or regular consumers – would lead to problems for the whole community.

With reforms grounded on a conception of citizenship as mutual protection, the New Liberals set out how in addition to giving people the basic capacity to influence collective decisions through the vote and a decent education, disparity which risked turning one's fellow citizens into pathetic supplicants must be removed by everyone accepting their collective responsibility to defend their common wellbeing. This pointed to a two-prong attack on power inequalities. On the one hand, even if income distribution could not be made fairer through cooperative enterprise arrangements in the short term, the impact of low income must be minimised. Hence proposals to provide free meals to school children and the granting of old age pension for all. On the other hand, everyone should contribute to funding the economic security of all citizens.

---

[115] See Hobhouse, LT, *The Elements of Social Justice*, George Allen & Unwin: 1922, and *The Rational Good*, George Allen & Unwin: 1921; and Hobson, J, *The Social Problem*, Thoemmes: 1996.

Everyone would pay in through a national insurance scheme; a progressive income tax system would ensure that a greater proportion of the larger and larger increments of additional earnings is shared with the public; and those without any opportunity to contribute should be provided with meaningful work along with a reasonable wage so that they too could participate as givers as well as recipients. For Hobhouse, "the 'right to work' and the right to a 'living wage' are just as valid as the rights of person or property. That is to say, they are integral conditions of a good social order."

The New Liberals showed how the struggle for inclusive communities could be advanced without conceding either to the capitalist non-interventionists who in effect allowed the wealthiest business people to amass more authoritarian power, or the communist interventionists who in practice concentrated power in an authoritarian one-party state. Their philosophy encouraged progressives like La Follette (1855-1925) and Brandeis (1856-1941) in America to see collective action to restrain corporate powers as not only compatible with the pursuit of liberty, but indeed as essential to safeguarding the freedom of all citizens.

It also strengthened the resolve of social democrats like Ernst Wigforss (1881-1977) in Sweden to ignore the call to take over the control of all productive organisations, but to focus on minimising power inequalities by systematically cutting down social and economic divisions. From 1932 on, Sweden laid the foundation for one of the most effective political systems to support inclusive community life, and in the face of a worldwide depression sustained 6% economic growth through to the end of the Second World War[116]. During the same period, F. D. Roosevelt (1882-1945) led the New Deal reform programme to rescue America from plutocratic 'non-interventionism' and give citizens real hope of recovering a decent life[117].

FDR shared his distant cousin's – the first President Roosevelt – commitment to use the democratically accountable power of the national

---

[116] See Misgeld, K, Molin, K and Amark, K (eds), *Creating Social Democracy: a century of the Social Democratic Labor Party in Sweden*, Pennsylvania State University Press: 1992.

[117] Leuchtenburg, WE, *Franklin D Roosevelt and the New Deal*, Harper Colophon Books: 1963.

government to change the power relations across society so that there was a real prospect for citizens to live without fear of being arbitrarily marginalised. He faced a far greater challenge, though, when 12 years of anti-progressive Republican rule left America in a state of socio-economic chaos when nobody would tame the selfish and reckless behaviour of business giants. After rallying the public to place their trust in the government to restore stability, he soon found that he could only deliver on his promise if he was to take on the corporate authoritarians. Businesses were not going to volunteer to help bring about a fairer society. Instead of placating them – a mistake to be made by many reformists in the 1990s – FDR concluded that he must drive through the reforms despite the opposition of the rich and powerful.

From 1934, midway through his first term as President, FDR signalled his determination to redistribute power on an unprecedented scale. He helped push through the Social Security Act which required employers as well as employees to contribute to a federal fund which would then give financial support to all those who could not earn a living because of their old age or other circumstances beyond their control. He gave his decisive backing to the National Labor Relations Act (the Wagner Act), which guaranteed workers the right to collective bargaining, and compelled employers to accept without obstruction the unionisation of their workforce. His radical proposals to redistribute wealth led to the Wealth Tax Act, raising taxes on estate, gift and capital stock, levying a tax on excess profits, and pushing marginal tax rates to the highest level yet. Against the holding companies, which used their control of the public utilities to exploit vulnerable people's total dependence on them for their energy needs, FDR successfully pressed for the Public Utilities Holding Company Act. As a result of the new federal regulatory intervention, electricity was to become available to many more Americans in the following decades. Finally, to curb the irresponsible behaviour of banks, he backed the Banking Act, which brought open market operations and all state banks under the jurisdiction of the Federal government. In return for the benefits of being part of the federal deposit insurance system, the state banks had to accept national control over currency and credit.

FDR's New Deal and the Scandinavian model of social democracy showed in the 1930s how the chaos created by authoritarian businesses could be brought under control. Alongside the assertion of the power of a democratic national government, progressives were also promoting ideas and practices on the diffusion of power through workers-led, cooperative, and local community-based organisations. Mill had pointed out the importance of having a multiplicity of decision-making arenas both to facilitate more opportunities for truth claims to be contested, and to enable a wider range of citizens to learn from experience how to discharge the responsibility for taking collective decisions for the common good.

These ideas were further developed by reform advocates such as G. D .H. Cole (1889-1959), who explained how a wide range of important decisions and services should be shared between cooperative organisations instead of being centralised into a single state system[118]; and Jane Addams (1860-1935), who stressed the importance of giving people the opportunities to learn from experience to determine shared priorities and joint actions[119].

Following the founding and development of Toynbee Hall, Samuel Barnett (1844-1913) and others inspired more settlement centres to be set up in Britain and America (including notably, Hull House, founded under the leadership of Jane Addams), where university-educated reformists met with citizens in the poorest communities and learnt together what could be done to improve living conditions. Workers education and shared participation in planning and delivering local initiatives helped all involved to deepen their understanding of how problems could be solved through cooperation.

The possibility of an ever increasing number of citizens capable and ready to add their informed views to shaping progressive actions became a core theme of political thinkers like John Dewey (1859-1952) and Mary Parker Follett (1868-1933). Dewey focused particularly on the education of the young, in developing their critical and cooperative abilities so they would not blindly accept or reject prevailing

---

[118] For a selection of writings by thinkers such as Cole, see Hirst, P. Q. (ed), *The Pluralist Theory of the State: selected writings of GDH Cole, JN Figgis, and HJ Laski*, London, Routledge: 1993.

[119] A helpful collection of Jane Addams' writings can be found in Johnson, E. C. (ed), *Jane Addams: a centennial reader*, New York, The Macmillan Company: 1960.

arrangements, but instead explore intelligently how they could be made better[120]. Follett argued that the deliberations of workers groups, social centres, neighbourhood organisations must not be separated out as self-contained activities unconnected with decisions concerning the country as a whole. For her, mere focus on a group or a local community was not enough for two reasons. Individual group interests, similar to the interests of individual citizens, had to be reconciled with the interests of others. Where they were found to be legitimate from the perspective of the wider society, they stood a better chance of being realised if they were pursued with the support of the national government, and not in isolation by themselves[121].

Follett looked to a deeper form of federalism to enable a multi-channel engagement between citizens, groups and government. Citizens would be able to identify with different groups at different levels, and contribute to and expect support in return from society as a whole. She applied this concept to international relations and rightly foretold that the League of Nations could never work if it relied on either a hollow ideal of all nations ignoring their differences or a laissez faire system of shifting alliances reflecting individual national interests. For Follett, the federal principle of unity through differences had to be established at the global level. Nations, like citizens, should have the freedom to assess and pursue their own interests, provided it was within a common framework where the world community would act in unison to deal with transgression against any single country.

Follett's arguments pointed to an urgent need for an international system of collective action to underpin a global inclusive community where the interests of all as equal citizens would be protected. Alas, such a system was far from ready when authoritarian threats from

---

[120] Dewey's philosophy exerted considerable influence over progressive reforms. Two of the best overviews of his ideas are: Westbrook RB, *John Dewey and American Democracy*, Cornell University Press: 1991; and Campbell, J, *Understanding John Dewey*, Chicago, Open Court: 1995. See also Morris, D and Shapiro, I (eds), *John Dewey: the political writings*, Indianapolis, Hackett Publishing: 1993.

[121] Follett, M. P., *The New State: Group Organisation, the Solution of Popular Government*, Pennsylvania State University Press: 1998. See also Mattson, K., *Creating a Democratic Public: the struggle for urban participatory democracy during the progressive era*, Pennsylvania State University Press: 1998 (Ch.5).

Germany, Japan and Italy were escalating in the 1930s. Instead of electing a progressive President such as FDR to tackle their problems, these countries had come under the rule of dictatorial regimes, which responded to the world's economic crisis – brought on by the growth of power inequalities – by embarking on a ruthless campaign to widen power inequalities even further. Britain and America might not have hitherto taken heed of Follett's advice, but over the next decade, they would become convinced that collective protection for all must be secured not just at the national, but also the international level.

# Chapter 7
# Progressive Triumphs and Setbacks:
# 1940s – 1970s

<u>Towards a more inclusive world community</u>

In the absence of a federal system operating at the global level, there was no effective means to hold back authoritarian regimes seeking to advance their interests by crushing those of others. In the 1930s, Germany in Europe and Japan in Asia pressed forward with their military adventurism as no one internationally exhibited the understanding or courage to contain either of these powerful and oppressive regimes. By 1941, Germany had overrun most of Europe and was locked in an attempt to crush the Soviet Union, while Japan had conquered most of Asia and held back only by the resistance they encountered in China. The only countries left with the capability to stop the aggressors were the US and the UK and the latter's Commonwealth allies. Against this background, Roosevelt and Churchill met to agree the Atlantic Charter, setting out their underlying aims in opposing the Axis powers and building a new world order. The key points of the Charter echoed Mary Follett's conception of international relations. These included a commitment not to seek territorial gains, while any territorial adjustments must be in accord with the wishes of the people affected; economic cooperation between nations should advance social welfare for all so that no one needed to fear not being able to make a living; and disarmament of the aggressor nations should be followed by general disarmament to end the threat and burden of wars.

The Anglo-American based alliance brought together the resources of the countries which had more than any other up to then embraced Enlightenment values and applied them in liberal and democratic reforms, and directed them at demolishing the ultimate antithesis of inclusive community life. The German and Japan authoritarian regimes detained, tortured, experimented on, and murdered millions of defenceless civilians; they promoted theorists who reinforced their prejudices but marginalised philosophers and scientists whose independent judgement was anathema to them; and their sole guarantee for order was the threat of ruthless repression. The more it was known what their rule meant, the more resolute the Allies became in stopping them, and any other country in the future, from having such power over the fate of others.

The defeat of Germany and Japan (and their fascist allies) marked a major milestone in the struggle for inclusive communities. The progressive ideas, which had been informing reforms since the turn of the century and articulated in the Atlantic Charter, were translated into the institutional form of the United Nations. It promised a new world order capable of tackling the causes of powerlessness and resultant suffering[122].

First, the devastation of military conflict must be prevented by the federal mechanism of creating a collective power strong enough to stop aggression between nations, and responsive enough to be held to account by member nations. As Germany and Japan had shown, allowing countries to build up their military capability, and not restraining them when they invaded their neighbours would lead to an escalation of deaths and destruction for those not able to defend themselves. Through an international Security Council, military build-up could be deterred, potential conflicts tackled by diplomatic interventions, wars which had broken out could be countered by sanctions or armed response, and ceasefire could be sustained with the help of peacekeeping forces. The UN security system would go on to play a key role in reducing the number of international conflicts. Most notably, whereas a belligerent state like Germany swiftly embarked again on armed campaigns after the First World War, the instigators of World War Two – Germany, Japan, Italy – ceased to pose a military threat against others. For the first time in history, fewer countries lived in dread of being invaded by a more powerful neighbour. The federal arrangements of peace and

---

[122] It is easy to superficially dismiss the UN as ineffectual when its ability to act is constantly held back by the most powerful nation states concerned above all with guarding their power advantages on the world stage. One must not overlook the importance of building on the UN framework through further reforms (see, e.g., Urquhart, B and Childers, E, *A World in Need of Leadership: Tomorrow's United Nations*, Uppsala, Dag Hammarskjold Foundation: 1990), or the range of its actual achievements (Ferguson, J, *Not Them But Us: in praise of the United Nations*, East Wittering, Gooday Publishers: 1988).

disarmament, however, did not become federal enough. At the centre, the collective centre was not sufficiently strong, and the tension between pro-America and pro-Soviet factions meant the stringent accountability requirement led to inaction in too many cases, especially in the increasing number of civil wars which broke out with rival forces supported by the Americans and the Soviets respectively[123].

Secondly, the economic turmoil, which precipitated the Second World War by fuelling disaffection and the spread of extremism, should not be allowed to erupt again as a result of leaving business powers to do as they pleased. As FDR had shown with US Federal regulation of utilities, currency and credit, the economic interests of individual states and corporations had to be considered in the context of wider interests of all affected communities. International cooperation to develop communications, transport and energy provisions could secure more reliable improvements rather than leaving it to individual firms which for the sake of their own short term profits deprive people dependent on them of the most vital services. Trading between nations could take advantage of the division of labour and benefit all those involved, but only if no country or large corporation established one way trading barriers or exploited the weak bargaining positions of others to force them to accept unfavourable terms. An Economic and Social Council took on the responsibility for advising on global policies, and at the 1944 UN Monetary and Finance Conference, the International Monetary Fund (IMF) was set up with the remit to support economic stability[124].

Thirdly, in parallel with minimising the likelihood of economic chaos, it was recognised that all people should regardless of their economic or social status be able to count on decent standards of support

---

[123] For an account of the many conflicts around the world since 1945, see Brogan, P, *World Conflicts*, London, Bloomsbury Publishing: 1998.

[124] Although the global finance system started in the immediate post-war period as a tool to assist economic recovery in war-torn countries, it came to be dominated by plutocratic interests which subordinated the wellbeing of the poorer countries to the rich and powerful ones. See, e.g., Pieper, U and Taylor, L, 'The revival of the liberal creed: the IMF, the World Bank, and inequality in a globalized economy' in Baker, D, Epstein, G and Pollin, R (eds), *Globalization and Progressive Economic Policy*, Cambridge University Press: 1998; and Fox, JA and Brown, LD, *The Struggle for Accountability: the World Bank, NGOs, and Grassroots Movements*, MIT Press: 1998.

in meeting their basic needs. From its inception, the UN set up in quick succession a number of international organisations dedicated to reduce the vulnerabilities of people who might otherwise be hopelessly dependent on the arbitrary decisions of others for their survival. The Food and Agricultural Organisation would take a global overview on how malnutrition and potential inadequate food supply were to be addressed. The International Labour Organisation would continue the role it took on from the League of Nations to involve workers representatives in improving job security and working conditions. UNICEF would provide on-going support as well as emergency relief to children suffering from abject poverty, natural disasters or military conflicts. And WHO (World Health Organisation) would apply to the global level the understanding that public health required widespread immunisation and sanitation, ensuring that the fight against disease was comprehensively carried out and not confined to the richer countries.

Fourthly, the General Assembly formally enshrined the respect for all nations in treating them as equal irrespective of their economic strength or population size. The process of decolonisation was expected to accelerate. However, just as ancient Athens neglected to apply its internal commitment to democracy to its dealings with other states, modern democracies such as the US, UK and France did not readily adapt to treating other nations as equals in their foreign policies[125]. Ever since carving up the old Ottoman Empire between them following the defeat of Turkey in the First World War, the Western powers had left the Muslim population in the region increasingly disillusioned. Their natural resources were being systematically exploited while the great majority of them remained poor, repressive regimes close to the West would be supported by them instead of being made to reform, and their grievances were neglected, especially when a Jewish state was established in 1948 with the agreement of the Western powers in territories which in recent centuries had been under Arab control.

---

[125] For an overview of how developed nations exploited weaker countries around the world, see Stavrianos, LS, *Global Rift: the Third World Comes of Age*, New York, William Morrow & Co: 1981; and for how Britain and America conducted their foreign policies since the Second World War, see Curtis, M, *The Great Deception: Anglo-American Power and World Order*, London, Pluto Press: 1998.

In other parts of the world, Western countries which had firmly accepted the democratic equalisation of domestic power through the system of one person one vote continued to be insistent in denying similar equalisation for people under their colonial control. In India, it took Mahatma Gandhi's (1869-1948) non-violent but widespread campaign of civil disobedience to change British public opinion and made it possible for the post-war Labour Government to end imperial claims to sovereignty over the sub-continent. Yet India's gradual transition to democracy was far from smooth. Hindu advocates of tribal nationalism, attachment to the caste system, and the growth of Islamic separatism fuelled divisions and violent confrontations. Gandhi himself was to be assassinated, and Pakistan became a separate state that would become all too susceptible to military coups.

In the Philippines, the US maintained its de facto colonial rule over the territories and only agreed to grant independence in 1946, but even then, it was reluctant to support real democratic development. Its resolute backing for the Marcos' dictatorial regime meant that it would be almost another half a century before democratic politics found a foothold in the country.

Unlike Britain and America, France would not even take the first step in granting Vietnam independence, and the ensuing military conflicts gave those who had little respect for inclusive power distribution, in the north or south of the country, to build up their powerbase to the detriment of the wider population. When the French finally retreated, the Americans stepped in to thwart any chance of the Vietnamese people securing autonomy for their country. They sent arms and troops to back the thoroughly corrupt South Vietnam regime and prolonged the bloody conflict until it became clear that they had mired themselves in a war they could not win.

In Africa, without any significant resources or geopolitical advantages to sustain their long term attention, the Western powers pulled out without any thought of post-colonial development, leaving hundreds of millions of people facing exploitation by large corporations, oppression by ruthless dictators, and violent attacks fuelled by boundaries inherited from colonial powers with no understanding of the heritage of diverse groups on the continent[126].

In general, without a federal form of global support for de-colonised regimes, a laissez faire approach prevailed and people living in newly independent states were all too often at the mercy of unaccountable government. The pattern was to take hold across Latin America, Africa, Asia and the Middle East.

Inevitably, the development of democratic states and societies would take time, and the fifth area of countering power imbalance across the world involved a long term commitment to improve people's grasp of the problems they faced and how these could be solved through rational discussions and not military action. UNESCO was created to promote learning through universal education, scientific research, and wider cultural understanding. Irrationality, prejudices, miscomprehension which prolonged avoidable suffering, or superficially justified the poor treatment of some sections of the world's population, had to be overcome by spreading the ethos of cooperative inquiry and increasing the access to reliable information and analysis.

To anchor the efforts to strengthen mutual understanding, the legitimate expectation of all human beings to be accorded equal respect was enshrined in the Universal Declaration of Human Rights, signed by members of the United Nations in 1948, exactly 300 years after the Levellers Petition to the English Parliament set out the rights of all people to be treated as equal before the law. After the atrocities committed by the genocidal regimes in Germany and Japan, the world agreed that all human beings must be given the same respect and protection wherever they happened to be. The Declaration, developed under the leadership of Eleanor Roosevelt (1884-1962) who chaired the Commission for Human Rights, provided an important framework for defining what every member of the global human community should expect as minimum standards in how he or she was to be treated by others. Regardless of the power anyone might hold, it set the limits for what could be done without violating the rights of others. It could not of course by itself end all abuse and neglect of human beings, but it established a universal rallying point to challenge ill treatment.

---

[126] Davidson, B, *Africa in History*, London, Paladin: 1985 (Chapter 8).

## Post-war building of inclusive communities

For almost three decades after the end of World War II progressive hope was on the ascendancy. The paralysing disillusionment which afflicted many reformists following the First World War was largely absent. There was a real sense that lessons had truly been learnt the second time around. The building of inclusive communities could only be achieved by tackling the deception, threats, chaos unleashed by those who believed they were too powerful to be held to account – be they ruthless giant corporations or aggressive military regimes. Individual citizens, groups or nations stood little chance of securing their wellbeing if they did not find democratic means to act together for their common good.

Britain and America, having set out the progressive aims in the Atlantic Charter, maintained their commitment to empower all to improve their lives in ways they could never do on their own. Drawing on the experiences of the social democrats in Sweden, the New Deal in America, and its own Liberal reform heritage in the 1900s and 1910s, Britain elected a Labour Government under Clement Attlee to deliver a comprehensive welfare programme along the lines set out by William Beveridge (1879-1963). Beveridge had from his earlier involvement with the Liberal reform agenda been deeply concerned with how unemployment and poverty left people in a state of utter powerlessness, dependent on the small mercies of the charitable. Instead of relying on private philanthropic acts – which were blatantly inadequate – he sought to devise a collective system which would cut the gap between the well-off and those at risk of being left behind.

Beveridge presented his system in terms of five obstacles – or 'five giant evils' – that needed to be overcome: ignorance, want, disease, squalor, and idleness[127]. In tackling ignorance, the Labour Government relied on the Education Act, which had been proposed by the Conservatives and passed by the war-time Coalition government. It made secondary education compulsory until the age of 15 years and provided meals, milk and medical services at every school so that no family would be deterred by the burden of having their children at

---

[127] Timmins, N *The Five Giants – a biography of the welfare state*, London, Fontana Press: 1996.

school. However, in differentiating between children who were able to pass a critical examination at age 11 and those who could not, with only the former expected to stay on after age 15, possibly go to university and get white collar jobs, it did not go very far in giving all children the education to become equally equipped for life's challenges.

When Labour had time to develop its own legislation, it moved more boldly. To curb the debilitating dread of want, it passed the 1946 National Insurance Act to extend the Liberal Act of 1911 to provide comprehensive insurance for all adults against most eventualities through sickness and unemployment benefit, retirement pension and widow and maternity benefit. Further cover was guaranteed through the Industrial Injuries Act, which required employers to take out insurance against industrial injury for all employees. Importantly, industrial injury benefits would henceforth be paid at a higher rate than for ordinary sickness. For those who did not have enough to live on but were not covered by the provisions of these two Acts, the 1948 National Assistance Act set up National Assistance Boards. For many progressives, the benefits were set too low to give citizens enough to attain a decent standard of living, but critics felt that people should ultimately rely on themselves and not the state to meet their basic needs.

What the critics ignored was that the socio-economic structures determining how people could make ends meet were not suited to everyone. While the market fundamentalists insisted that those who could not thrive in the marketplace should accept their pathetic marginalisation by those successful at making money, and the communists asserted that they alone could exercise absolute power in determining all transactions without people suffering from their unquestionable diktats, the progressives recognised that power relations had to be kept vigilantly under review, and the gap between the powerful and the powerless must be reduced, incrementally but unremittingly. This was particularly evident in relation to people's security over their own and their family's health. With the advancement of medical knowledge and practice, the prospect of avoiding and overcoming all forms of disease was rapidly improving. Infant survival rates and life expectancies in general could rise for all, but only if they could equally access what the latest medical care had to offer. The 1946 National Health Service Act ensured that every British citizen could receive medical, dental and optical services free of charge. Examination and treatment by doctors in general practitioner surgeries and in hospitals would also be free.

Closely related to ill-health was the problem of squalor. Labour set a target of building 200,000 houses a year, and tackled over-crowding with the 1946 New Towns Act, which laid the plans for 14 new towns. The Conservatives in the 1950s, accepting the then prevailing progressive consensus, continued the house-building programme and gave many individuals and families real hope of having a decent home.

The substantial investment in housing and other infrastructure after the severe bomb damages of the war helped to deal with the scourge of unemployment. Encouraged by the Liberal economist, John Maynard Keynes (1883-1946), that public spending could help rebalance supply and demand to give people productive jobs when private decisions in the market alone would lead to recession, the Government pressed ahead with national projects, reducing unemployment to just 2.5% while enabling all citizens to have access to affordable utilities such as water, energy and public transport.

By the 1950s, the UK was becoming a key model for the development of inclusive communities – all citizens were to be treated with respect under the law, enabled to have a say about decisions that affected them, and given support to lead a decent life through resources redistributed from the more wealthy. The rising standards of social and liberal protection of all from the irresponsible actions of the powerful, would be seen across the Commonwealth, covering almost a third of the world's population, including many which had recently secured their independence from Britain.

The US also stayed true to the Atlantic Charter's progressive vision. With the Marshall Plan for Europe and the MacArthur reconstruction of Japan, Americans eschewed the futile, indeed counter-productive, approach adopted by the victorious nations at the end of the First World War, and prioritised the rebuilding of vanquished and impoverished countries as essential to attaining a peaceful and prosperous future. Politically, democratic institutions were to be put in place so that citizens would have regular and effective opportunities to question and replace those in government. Socially, the basic needs of all citizens would be met without discrimination. Economically, citizens could run businesses, large and small, through competitive or cooperative arrangements so long as they did not use accumulated power to take unfair advantage against consumers, workers or trading partners.

Both Germany and Japan gave up military ambitions to focus on economic development. Germany, working with France and other neighbouring nations, developed the European Economic Community, which fostered social and economic cooperation to the point that within just twenty years of the ending of the war, it had become inconceivable that members of the EEC (and later the European Union) would go to war against each other. Internally, welfare provisions and long-term job security would prevent citizens from being marginalised within their own country. Externally, developmental investment would ensure that poorer countries would be given the support to develop their economic capacity so that their citizens would not be permanently disadvantaged in relation to those of the richer countries.

Similarly, America's assistance to Japan in establishing it as a liberal, democratic country which provided both the conditions for economic innovation and development, and good employment opportunities for all, transformed an aggressor nation into an anchor for peace and prosperity across south east Asia[128].

America's defence of South Korea against North Korea in the 1950s was vindicated by the divergent development of the two countries subsequently. While the North stagnated with an authoritarian state repressing the people and depriving them of opportunities to improve their quality of life, the South was able to move steadily forward in economic and political terms so that like the people of post-war Japan, they would benefit from living in a more open and inclusive society.

By the 1960s, Britain and America were established global leaders in advancing the progressive cause. Intellectually, the thorough experimentalism, which had characterised their philosophical traditions since the 18th century, informed their scientific development and their capacity for innovations. Dogmas and prejudices were largely swept aside whenever they could not stand up to the scrutiny of empirical analysis. From medical breakthroughs to new product designs, the

---

[128] Galbraith, JK, *The World Economy Since the Wars*, London, Sinclair-Stevenson: 1994.

experimentalist mindset ruled the Atlantic and Pacific waves.

Culturally, the confidence that scientific rationality and liberal democracy could underpin a worldwide quest to protect people from those with excessive power was translated into a new generation of mass media output designed to appeal to the young in particular. Television series such as 'The Man from U.N.C.L.E.', 'Thunderbirds', and 'Star Trek' all presented international (or indeed inter-galactic) institutions bringing people together to carry out a shared mission to secure a better world. Marvel Comics launched a series of comic books featuring superheroes who were vastly different in their abilities and characters but shared a commitment to battle irrationality and injustice no matter how powerful the perpetrator might be. Popular music was transformed by Bob Dylan into a vehicle to rally protest against oppression.

The young growing up in the 1960s were presented with a sense of liberation which, though some would confound it with the irresponsible libertarianism of doing as one pleased, was above all about taking collective action to free others from unacceptable shackles[129]. Far from rebelling blindly against everything represented by the older generation, teenagers looked to progressive leaders to show how they could play their part in defending the human rights of everyone.

The most pressing cause undoubtedly concerned the treatment of blacks in America – blatantly marginalised as second class citizens in southern states, and routinely discriminated against throughout the union. It took activists like Martin Luther King (1929-1968) to encourage Americans of African descent to stand tall and demand the respect they were entitled to from their fellow Americans, and politicians like Robert Kennedy (1925-1968) who put civil rights at the top of his reform agenda to press the establishment, including his brother the President, to take immediate action. When J. F. Kennedy was assassinated, Lyndon Johnson who succeeded him as President managed to use the shift in public opinion to help him tackle head on the invidious practices of segregation, and deal with the problem of poverty which afflicted black communities in particular when the country as a whole was getting more prosperous.

---

[129] Marwick, A, *The Sixties: Cultural Revolution in Britain, France, Italy, and the United States, c. 1958-1974*, Oxford University Pres: 1998.

King's campaign, in sharp contrast to narrow identity politics which, as we will see, was to contribute to the fragmentation and weakening of progressive politics, was grounded on a vision of inclusive communities. He did not want to turn blacks into a state of antagonism against whites, but for all to work together for their common good. This was reflected in the marches and public meetings he organised, as he recalled how when he "stood with them and saw white and Negro, nuns and priests, ministers and rabbis, labor organizers, lawyers, doctors, housemaids and shopworkers brimming with vitality and enjoying a rare comradeship, I knew I was seeing a microcosm of the mankind of the future in this moment of luminous and genuine brotherhood."[130] For him, the struggle was not just about the injustice done to one racial group, or the injustice in one country. For him, it was about resolutely refusing to accept the fate handed down to the powerless everywhere:

"Let us be dissatisfied until rat-infested, vermin-filled slums will be a thing of a dark past and every family will have a decent sanitary house in which to live. Let us be dissatisfied until the empty stomachs of Mississippi are filled and the idle industries of Appalachia are revitalized. . . . Let us be dissatisfied until our brothers of the Third World of Asia, Africa and Latin America will no longer be the victims of imperialist exploitation, but will be lifted from the long night of poverty, illiteracy and disease."[131]

In Britain, improvement to public welfare provisions was accompanied by reforms to tackle prejudices against vulnerable groups. The Home Secretary, Roy Jenkins, gave the Government's backing to legislation which liberated women from being trapped in servile marriages by improving the law on divorce, and from unwanted pregnancies by allowing women to resort to abortion as a legal option. He also ended the criminalisation of homosexuality. Attacked for removing traditional restraints on unacceptable behaviour, Jenkins argued that in any civilised society, people should not be forced by law to conform to expectations which would only make them endure a life of misery. People might disagree as to what decisions individuals should

---

[130] *Where Do We Go from Here: Chaos or Community?*

[131] 'Honoring Dr. Du Bois' in *Freedomways,* VIII, s (Spring 1968), pp. 110-111.

make in their private lives, but so long as those decisions did not harm another person (admittedly, at what point a fertilised human egg became a person was contested), no one should be able to use the law to insist on one course of action only.

The rights to live a decent life, to decide for oneself on the available evidence, count on the respect and support of one's government and fellow citizens, became the focal point for rolling back the power of those who could otherwise trample on such rights. From the 1960s through to the 1970s, progressive reformists campaigned for the rights of racial minorities, women, homosexuals, former colonies, workers, consumers, and people with disabilities. Each category was at risk of being treated with, at best, systemic negligence or at worse, callous disdain by people more powerful than them and needed collective action to ensure their interests would be taken into account.

Under the Democrat and Labour Government of Lyndon Johnson and Harold Wilson respectively, community development programmes were devised to engage with marginalised groups, especially those living under long-term poverty, so that they could be actively involved in shaping the improvement of their neighbourhoods. The empowerment of citizens as equals, irrespective of their differences, to contribute to and benefit from public policies seemed almost to have become the norm.

## Seeds of authoritarian resurgence

The progressive determination built up in the 1930s had gained momentum through the war and become an inspirational force to cut back power inequalities at every level up to the early 1970s. Yet in the subsequent decades anti-progressive forces were able to overturn what many had momentarily, and wrongly, thought was a permanent consensus.

Power equilibrium could not be attained, let alone sustained, if there were concentrations of power left unchecked so that sooner or later they could hold others to ransom. When the ruthless authoritarian regimes of Germany and Japan were defeated at the end of World War II, that defeat was made possible by two other powers that had no greater respect for liberalism or democracy. The Communist Parties of the Soviet Union and the People's Republic of China believed they could make all the key decisions for their respective country without allowing any individual or group to contest the claims they deemed indubitable. Indeed any questioning of the Communist authority was to be treated as a counter-revolutionary threat and punishable accordingly. The war had consolidated Stalin's Soviet rule, expanding his sphere of influence across Eastern Europe. It also provided the opportunity for Mao to eject the Nationalist Party from mainland China, leaving him the indisputable ruler of the country.

Stalin's and Mao's paranoia about security, arrogance in running their government, and deeply flawed judgements on economic matters caused many to be interned and millions more to be left to starve[132]. The existence of their regimes undermined the progressive cause in three ways. Their refusal to cooperate with Britain and America meant that numerous opportunities to intervene to end civil wars and rebuild war-torn areas around the world were lost through their opposition to international action. Often they even prolonged conflicts by backing whichever side happened to be fighting those receiving assistance from the US or UK. Their treatment of their own citizens – arbitrary arrests and show-trials – was an affront to the very notion of an inclusive community. And because they were so unrepentant in their repressive actions, it led many in Britain or America to focus exclusively on criticising the Communist enemies.

Since their proclaimed ideal of equality did, after the death of Stalin and Mao, lead in some cases to better support in terms of education, healthcare and employment for their people, especially when compared with those suffering from the worst deprivation in America, some progressive advocates in the West publicly expressed their approval of those achievements under Communist regimes. That was enough to establish the basis for the standard Cold War *ad hominem* argument – progressive reformists are socialists who are (totalitarian) communists who are a threat. Instead of rebutting this line of attack by challenging power inequalities in the Soviet Union and China as well as

---

[132] To learn more about Stalin and Mao, see Service, R, *Stalin: A Biography*, Pan: 2005; Montefiore, S, *Stalin: The Court of the Red Tsar*, Weidenfeld and Nicolson: 2003; Short, P, *Mao: A life*, John Murray Publishers: 2004; Lynch, M, *Mao*, Routledge: 2004.

the West, a misguided and vocal minority went so far as suggesting the West was on the whole inferior to the Communist regimes and thus adding substance to the charge that they sought to replace democratically elected governments by Communist-backed radicals.

The threat of Communism gave many in the West, especially in America, who had long resented progressive reforms a vital opportunity to regroup. The Communist regimes were foreign, atheistic, anti-business, so decades of conceding to the progressive advocacy of cooperative internationalism, ethical humanism, and business regulation could be reversed on a patriotic, god-fearing and enterprise-loving platform. The ideological structure of the Cold War was foreseen by George Orwell (1903-1950) as he illustrated in his novel, *1984*, how regimes solely concerned with preserving their power advantages would demonise their external enemies and intimidate internal dissenters[133]. Double-speak was not surprisingly used to condemn the infiltration of Communists in the West, the military build-up by the Soviets, the arming of pro-Communist groups in developing countries; and at the same time to praise the deployment of spies from the West, the targeting of an increasing number of missiles at Communist countries, and provision of economic and military aid to any anti-Communist group in the world.

Added to the mix of alpha male confrontation were nuclear weapons with immensely greater destructive capability than anything else humankind had known. In the 1940s/1950s the US and UK, along with their ally, France, had developed their own nuclear bombs, and so had the Soviet Union and China. By the 1970s, these five countries had enough firepower between them to destroy the entire planet many times over. With them making up the permanent members of the UN Security Council, it was apt that the strategy for avoiding a third world war was to be dubbed M.A.D. – mutually assured destruction.

But not entering into direct conflicts did not mean that they would not sponsor proxy wars involving the poorest nations in the world. Minor disputes which could have been easily dealt with by the United Nations if it had the financial and political support of its member states, were instead escalated into protracted and gruesome battles maiming and killing soldiers and civilians alike. Economic development policies

---

[133] Crick, B, *George Orwell: A Life*, Penguin Books 1992.

would no longer be focused exclusively on building vibrant and well-regulated markets to meet local people's needs, but increasingly tied up with geopolitical calculations regarding how to gain military grounds against those backed by the other side. A large slice of foreign aid would in turn have to be earmarked for paying for imported weapons. Having stockpiled their respective arsenals and yet holding back from launching their own wars, the big five made it a priority to sell arms to those who would fight against others on the 'wrong' side. In time, it did not even matter whose side they were on, provided overall they were selling more to those they officially backed than those they publicly denounced. The permanent members of the Security Council rapidly established themselves as the top five arms exporters in the world.

With the fear of external enemies a constant feature of the Cold War, intimidation was used to root out any 'sympathisers'. The Communists continued where the Jacobins had left off – trial without evidence, conviction without cross-examination, and punishment without appeal. But the oppressive practices were contagious. America thus launched its House Committee on Un-American activities, and Joseph McCarthy led the Senate persecution against anyone he suspected of being a communist sympathiser. Anyone critical of American policies came under suspicion. But those who could help with undermining the Communists, even if they posed a threat to the wellbeing of ordinary Americans (like the organised crime lords, who resented Castro for overthrowing the Cuban dictatorship which had granted them special privileges) were enlisted as allies.

Despite the considerable achievements of progressive reformists in the post-war years, the widening power gaps in military capability were stoking new threats to security and stability across the world. From the 1950s to 1960s, North America and Western Europe were enjoying the benefits of socio-economic power redistribution so that citizens as workers and consumers were able to get a reliable income enabling them to acquire a steadily improving quality of living[134]. What they helped to

---

[134] For changing trends in income inequalities across the world, see Mann, M and Riley, D, 'Explaining macro-regional trends in global income inequalities, 1950–2000' in Socio-Economic Review 2007 5(1).

produce would increase the range of goods and services at home, and boost exports abroad, generating more money to fund investment and economic expansion. This led to a sense of complacency about the further need for tackling power inequalities. It came to be assumed that the structure of society was more or less correct and that life would continue to improve year on year for everyone – and with nearly 98% of working age people in employment, it was virtually everyone.

However, the virtues of the progressive vision were grounded on their universal application. For the virtuous circle of continuous improvement to work, it must not be cut off at the borders of the developed countries. Every person, every country, should be able to produce something of benefit to other people, other countries, whose productive activities would offer them something valuable in return. If the exchange of goods and services were not distorted by power inequalities, people would find the most mutually favourable terms to apply their division of labour to raise their respective standards of living.

If, however, the conditions were structured to favour only the developed countries, then they would be able to rely on their actively engaged working population to produce more to buy manufactured goods from other developed countries and just raw materials from non-developed countries. With the manufactured goods set at a higher value than raw materials, the developed countries would get richer at the expense of the non-developed ones. Eventually, the limited purchasing power of the non-developed countries would not be able – without risking long term unsustainable borrowing – to add much to the demands for the output of the developed countries. With the developed countries not being able to generate more income themselves to buy more products, the point was reached in the late 1960s that the good times of ever-rising standards of living were coming to an end.

In the 1920s, the dwindling purchasing power of the marginalised poor in the West was ignored until the West was plunged into the economic depression of the 1930s. In the 1960s, the dwindling purchasing power of the marginalised non-developed countries of the world was ignored until the world headed towards recession at the beginning of the 1970s. In 1971, all the major industrial countries began to experience slowdown in their economic growth, and with supply running ahead of demand, unemployment also started to rise.

Progressive intervention would have necessitated addressing the poverty and underdevelopment in most parts of the world. Instead, the West decided to focus on the spending power of the rich parts of the world. By reflating their own economies in 1972, they were doing what the Republicans of the 1920s thought would help their rich supporters – increase their spending power and everything else would follow. Except that without the spending power of the poor being rectified, only chaos followed.

In 1973, the artificial boom pushed up demand for raw materials to such an extent that their prices began to rise steeply. This led to rising costs of the manufactured products and constant inflationary pressure. Workers demanded wage increases to keep pace with anticipated price rises and made inflation even more difficult to control. At this volatile juncture, the ripples of global insecurity turned into a tidal wave[135]. On 6 October 1973 Soviet-backed Egypt and Syria launched an attack on Israel, which with military and economic aid from America, fought back. The conflict destabilised the region which had been supplying oil to literally fuel the economic growth of the industrialised countries in the post-war period. That growth, and the ill-conceived attempt in 1972 to boost private and public spending, escalated the reliance on oil supply. Sensing their opportunity to exploit their economic power in the absence of any effective global controls, the Organisation of Petroleum Exporting Countries (OPEC), dominated by the Arab nations, announced two days after the Arab-Israeli War broke out a rise of 70% in the price of oil. Another ten days on, the Arab group within OPEC decided to cut oil production to put pressure on the West to get Israel to withdraw from the former Arab territories it was occupying. In December, OPEC announced a further price increase of 130%.

In the West, with the exception of America which at that time was self-sufficient in oil and West Germany which had a robust balance of payment surplus as a result of its in-demand exports, countries were hit by a combination of high inflation, workers' unrest in the face of wage restraints to combat inflation, more expensive imported goods, high energy costs, economic slowdown, and declining levels of employment.

---

[135] Cairncross, F and McRae, H, *The Second Great Crash*, London: Methuen Paperback: 1975.

The purchasing power in the world had suddenly come to be concentrated in the hands of a small number of countries with little engagement with progressive reforms. Their concern was above all to use their oil-based power to consolidate the control of their respective countries, and buy assets and influence around the world. Their astronomical balance of payment surplus attracted the arms exporters – for whatever strategic interests Britain and America might otherwise have in relation to peace in the Middle East, their weapon manufacturers wanted to get their share of the billions sitting in the reserves of the Arab oil producing countries.

The progressive hope of the post-war years was dashed. Voices for power redistribution fell silent. Full employment was no longer to be a policy objective. America and Britain, which had formulated the Atlantic Charter to rally the drive towards a more inclusive global community beyond the conflicts of World War Two, turned their backs on progressive reforms. Between December 1968 and April 1992, the anti-progressive party won control of the British Parliament and the American Presidency in virtually every election held (the only exceptions being Labour's parliamentary victories under Harold Wilson in 1974, and the Democrats' retaking the White House under Jimmy Carter in 1976).

## Fragmentation of the progressive challenge

When the progressive consensus was at its high tide during the postwar years, even those who did not enthusiastically support power redistribution went along with social and political reforms to reduce the divisions between citizens at every level. Neither the Republican President Eisenhower nor the Conservative Prime Minister Macmillan sought to repudiate the programmes put in place by their political opponents. But from the 1970s on, when the once united progressive front increasingly fragmented into distinct strands, their ideological enemies began to explore how they might together fight back. This fragmentation could be seen around four clusters of activities.

First, there was the anti-discrimination agenda. Groups which had traditionally been disadvantaged by laws and customs were increasingly conscious of the barriers they faced. They acknowledged the efforts of the 1960s but felt that changes were too slow. However, instead of building a coalition to empower all discriminated groups to overturn the unjustifiable restrictions placed upon them, each of them believed that the best way to get results was to concentrate on their particular grievance and campaigned relentlessly to secure the changes they wanted. Feminism rightly challenged rules which limited women's ability to choose the life they wanted – divorce arrangements favouring the husband, illegality of abortion forcing them to bear unwanted pregnancies, restricted job opportunities, and so on. Although alpha male social arrangements needed to be comprehensively dismantled, the movement also attracted authoritarian advocates who did not see the problem in terms of general power equilibrium, but wanted to present all men as intrinsically oppressive. Yet in the mid 20th century, it was not unknown for there to be power relations in which men and women were under the exploitative control of female property owners or bosses. It was neither men nor women who by virtue of their sex should be given more or less power over other people, but none of them as equal citizens should be deprived of the opportunity to choose the way they live so long as they would not be harming others. This became problematic when the more extreme campaigners demanded greater freedom for women regardless of the consequences for children, whose powerlessness in relation to their parents, male or female, was a key issue that needed to be addressed in any genuinely inclusive community.

The legitimate battle for minority rights also intensified. With Ronald Reagan in his successful campaign to become Governor of California in 1966 denouncing legislation against racial discrimination in the sale of real estate, defending the right of homeowners to, in his words, "discriminate against Negroes", it was not surprising that many felt that racism had to be more fervently combated. But instead of a coalition of minorities battling those who tried to retain their traditional levers of domination, they increasingly launched their own confrontation. For some black activists what was most important was to assert their identity. If they could do that by linking their identity with fundamentalist religious views which called for opposition to the liberation for women or homosexual people, they would do so. This was taking place at a time when the movement for gay rights was itself gathering momentum.

Marginalising people with divergent sexuality as immoral deviants had been an integral part of many authoritarian hierarchies which aimed to give their core male population a sense of righteous superiority (over women, ethnic minorities, and anyone not conforming to standard customs) in return for their abject subservience to the unquestionable leadership. It was the indefensible power relation that needed to be challenged, and not, as it at times appeared, the very notion of heterosexuality itself. The problem with identity-based protest is that it diverts the focus from the struggle to correct power imbalance for all people, to promoting a rivalry between groups on the basis of just one identity definition when, on other definitions, those groups have more important concerns in common.

One such identity is defined by the ethno-religious heritage people grew up with even if they do not fully subscribe to its prescriptions. The Arab-Israeli War of 1973, apart from contributing to the oil crisis, focused emotional reactions around Islamic/Jewish identities even more. Lobbying for support for Israel in the face of pan-Arab hostility became the priority for Jewish activists, which weakened the strong ties they had previously shared with black activists. In their search for religious underpinning for their cause, some black activists turned to fundamentalist Islamic teachings, which further alienated them from previous Jewish allies in the battle for civil rights. The heightened Muslim identity would also in decades to come draw more and more people who would not otherwise have taken theological dogmas too seriously into a diversionary battle between Muslims and non-Muslims.

A second cluster of activities developed in response to the threat posed by the business sector. The power of large corporations meant that they could pursue what was in their interest even if it was harmful to others. With every piece of legislation introduced to curtail the irresponsible exercise of their power, they responded by hiring the best legal experts to find loopholes, lobbyists to relax future regulation, and public relations firms to show that they were in fact very responsible in looking out for the interests of others. The 1970s' drift away from full employment commitment made protecting the terms and conditions of workers all the more urgent. Yet the unions fighting for their workers at home did not establish a joint front with activists who were beginning to expose the appalling conditions under which workers, including children, were placed abroad. Firms like Nike bypassed the challenge of having to deal with unions in their treatment of domestic workers by contracting out work through intermediaries abroad. When the corporate sector was making full use of global networks, there was no sign of any effective global unions. The consumer movement was similarly myopic. It objected to companies' disregard of the risks for their consumers and succeeded, for example, in campaigning for improved safety features on cars and exposing the harm tobacco did to those who smoked cigarettes. But the lack of global action meant businesses such as the tobacco companies could turn their attention to increasing production and sales in developing countries.

The only area where opposition to corporate irresponsibility took on a global dimension was that of environmental protection. In 1984, a Indian subsidiary of the US firm, Union Carbide Corporation, mismanaged its toxic waste so badly that nearly 4,000 people in the city of Bhopal were killed instantly by the escaped poisonous gas, with another 4,000 dying in the following weeks. The impact of corporate pollution and using up non-renewal resources was clearly not confined to individual countries. In addition to the direct harm, there was growing awareness that the burning of fossil fuel produced ozone depleting gases which caused rapid climate change, leading to more extreme droughts and floods around the world. However, the positioning of a distinct 'green' platform meant that it was not well connected with workers' concerns, and in some cases, calls for reductions in energy consumption and hence related production were seen as threatening to job prospects.

Thirdly, there was a cluster of activities directed at military and security policies. After the McCarthy-led persecution of suspected Communist supporters in the 1950s, the reaction against Communist threat escalated in the sixties. Following the Cuban crisis which was resolved by the Soviet Union and the US both backing down on missile deployment, the two superpowers decided to intensify their support for North and South Vietnam respectively. But whereas the Soviet limited their involvement to weapons and military advice, America sent an increasing number of troops to fight the North Vietnamese. In fact, when North Vietnamese troops evaded American offensive by withdrawing into neighbouring Cambodia, a country not at war with America, Republican President Nixon authorised secret bombing raids into

Cambodia which killed over 600,000 people, mostly Cambodian civilians.

In the name of combating the Communist threat, America generated such widespread resentment that many in Cambodia started to support the hitherto fringe Communist group, the Khmer Rouge, which was able to seize power and like all too many totalitarian regimes before it, slaughtered many of its own people (estimated to be over 1 million). Against the futile, indeed counter-productive war in south east Asia, and the ruthless use of secrecy to deceive the American people (confirmed by the Watergate operation which brought an end to Nixon's Presidency), many protested until American troops were finally withdrawn from Vietnam. By then, many in the West were beginning to question the use of the nuclear deterrent, with the stationing of nuclear weapons in Britain and Germany undermining, rather than enhancing, people's sense of security. In isolation from a wider coalition to tackle the abuse of power, the anti-military/security cluster of activities was all too easily depicted by its opponents as essentially the acts of unpatriotic or (if they resided abroad) anti-American people whose motives alone should discredit them.

Finally, there was the anti-establishment cluster of activities, covering those who for different reasons wanted to challenge the way things were done in society. There were the anti-censorship campaigners who believed that everyone should be able to, not just express an opinion, but to say, show, present anything in any manner without any kind of state restrictions whatsoever. In so far as state censorship might be used to prevent the publication of research information or the debate of issues in the light of objective evidence, it was important to overturn restrictions. However, to seek to place a blanket ban on state intervention which might be necessary to protect the vulnerable from those in a powerful position to promote addictive behaviour via alcohol consumption, gambling, pornography, or the spreading of lies, innuendos, misleading information about individuals who sought to expose irresponsible corporate behaviour, was to hand more power to many who had too much already. There were also those who with sound progressive motives wanted to prevent those in positions of authority in schools from turning their pupils into blind conformists, or worse, frightened victims who were unjustifiably punished for not following absurd orders. But if the limits of authority were not sensibly drawn, and they ended up being anarchically rejected, the result would be little sustained learning, and in some cases, the collapse of discipline altogether. Similarly, advocates of drop-out, counter culture were right about pointing out the dangers of commercialism and the profit-driven routine infecting one's work and home life. Yet obsessive promotion of a 'we should do as we please' ethos was ultimately as self-indulgent as the consumerist society it claimed to reject.

Throughout the 1970s and 1980s, the progressive political parties, which had formerly led the struggle for inclusive communities following the Second World War, failed to provide a rallying point to bring coherence to these diverse protest movements, expose irrational tendencies, root out authoritarian elements, and draw them into a unified political programme. They particularly failed to recognise the need to develop the global dimension in tackling power inequalities. It was critical to develop robust alliances across national frontiers. What took place instead was continuous fragmentation which left citizens, who ought to have stood together to challenge the powerful, splintering into conflicting identity groups – women v men, homosexuals v heterosexuals, consumers v workers, blacks v non-blacks, Christians v Muslims v Jews, traditionalists v 'anything goers'.

In the absence of a sustained and unified platform to curtail power inequalities, those with powerful positions began to find ways, not only to resist further reforms, but also to roll back the progress that had been achieved up to that point. Corporate elites, theological reactionaries, weapon-worshiping militarists started to collaborate in undermining the progressive agenda for developing more inclusive communities. The acceleration of information technology advancement was rapidly exploited from the 1980s on to widen the power gap on a global scale.

# Chapter 8
# Power & Globalisation:
# 1979 – 2000

<u>The intensification of authoritarian threats</u>

As the progressive coalition continued to fragment in the 1970s and 1980s, authoritarians in different fields sensed the growing opportunities to stake out their positions. Initially, they occupied quite distinct territories and indeed were often as hostile to each other as they were to progressive reformists. For example, thinkers like Hayek, Friedman and Nozick concentrated on attacking the use of state power to bring about a fairer society on the grounds that it deprived people of their freedom[136]. For them, those who had gained the most power in society, preferably through market transactions operating with minimal state intervention, should be left alone to enjoy the control they had gained over other people's lives. To minimise the chance that the state had to tackle power inequalities, most activities carried out by public bodies should be privatised as much as possible.

By contrast, others following the leads of writers like Richard Weaver and Russell Kirk showed little faith in markets and commercial dealings. Instead they supported the revival of traditionalist beliefs in what they took to be core Christian values. What they picked out as core values confirmed their underlying interest in defending the alpha male social hierarchy. Subordination of women and exclusion of non-heterosexual underpinned their notion of self-respect, while compassion, forgiveness, sacrifice were despised as signs of weakness. Patriotism was redefined as the embodiment of this narrow, self-righteous outlook. These moral crusaders and the free marketers had at this point little in common.

---

[136] They attacked the notion of the state intervening to pursue the common good on different grounds: Hayek believed such a state would become too arrogant and powerful in controlling people's lives; Friedman was convinced that the economy would function more efficiently if the state would do less; while Nozick argued that the state had no right to insist how society should work other than securing basic law and order.

Yet another group comprised followers of the realpolitic approach to American hegemony. Representative of their thinking was Henry Kissinger who shaped Nixon's foreign policy with the guiding principle that the enemies of the US must be systematically undermined. Moral or religious ideas had nothing to do with policy decisions. Innocent civilians who might get in the way of an attack on enemy soldiers should be killed without hesitation, as they were in Cambodia. Repugnant regimes which might cause problems to the enemies of the US should be supported regardless of what they did to their own people, and so they were given economic and military aid all over South America, the Middle East, Africa, and Asia.

The decline of progressive unity persuaded many who had embraced diverse forms of authoritarian power to consider working towards the establishment of a common anti-progressive front. Frank S. Meyer was one of the first to promote "fusionism", to bring together libertarian and conservative ideas. The prospect of rallying opposition to progressive concerns with tackling power inequalities in every sphere was further developed by William F. Buckley, who founded the influential magazine, *National Review*, and the organisation Young Americans for Freedom, both of which combined lobbying for change across society and advocating for politicians like Ronald Reagan who were dedicated to putting an end to the struggle for inclusive communities.

By the early 1980s, an alliance of market authoritarians, moral authoritarians and military authoritarians had been forged under the banner of the New Right, with Margaret Thatcher and Ronald Reagan shifting the UK and US away from those countries' progressive concern with the development of inclusive communities, to become the most formidable champions of power inequalities[137]. The righteous trinity of 'Wealth', 'God' and 'Nation' were presented as the foundation of the Anglo-American drive for a global plutocracy. Blessed are those who are able to make money from others, they should be allowed to amass wealth and power and use their unrivalled resources and influence to consolidate their positions. Cursed are those who do not conform to the

---

[137] See, e.g., King, D. S., *The New Right: politics, markets and citizenship*, Basingstoke, Macmillan: 1987.

moral expectations laid down by their betters. Problems in society should be blamed on 'deviants' and 'aliens' who cross either traditional behavioural boundaries or the borders of the rich countries. If financial sanctions could not stop those who threatened the new status quo, the use of force from imprisonment at home to military action abroad should be freely deployed.

Before progressives even began to realise the need to regroup, the noble qualities of enterprise, religion and patriotism had been shamelessly subverted to serve the plutocratic elite. The New Right cunningly diverted the attention of people who were losing out under widening power inequalities towards customised enemies. Small to medium businesses overlooked the unfair advantages large corporations had over them when they came to be preoccupied with the need to curtail the power of the workers and their unions. Enterprising individuals were encouraged to rail against interfering regulators. Taxpayers were told they were ripped off by welfare claimants who were cheats, and not by corporate giants who exploited tax loopholes.

Discussions about morals and decency were directed away from economic exploitation and social degradation to subjects like abortion, sexuality and women's role in the traditional family. Law abiding citizens were warned about the threat of crime as an ever-rising number of people were sentenced to prison. Victims of crime were urged to blame those who wanted to be more understanding about the real cause of crime and were obviously too lenient. Workers getting raw deals from their employers were alerted to the subversive communists who might ruin everything through their negative collective action. They were also told that the biggest threat to them came from thoughtless meddlers who wanted to put an end to the business they worked in just because it produced addictive and life-shortening cigarettes, exported weapons to kill countless innocent people, destroyed the environment, or put people's lives at risk through inadequately tested food or medicine.

Patriots were reminded that their country was undermined by people who criticised the brave efforts of their military in dealing with the enemy by whatever means. Real 'Americans' or 'Brits' were repeatedly nudged to look suspiciously on those who were, or appeared to be, foreign. Religious people were asked to think not about the supposed equality of all before God, but to concentrate on selective rituals and the need to be antagonistic towards secularists.

The dominance of the New Right in Britain and America was to be underpinned by a new role for government. This involved three major changes. First, to reduce the public sector's capacity to deliver collective solutions to help all citizens, government bodies were weakened by cutting down on the services they were funded to provide; required to pass many of their functions to the private sector which would take over their assets and henceforth focus on making a profit for their shareholders; and where full-scale privatisation was not achievable, compelled to invite the private sector to tender for particular services so that over time the ability for public organisations to attract and retain staff would be curtailed. Secondly, the government would shift the balance of power even further to large corporations by cutting back on the 'red tape' which held them back, while imposing more restrictions on workers and unions. Thirdly, investment in public education, health, welfare, transport through taxation was to be presented as an inherent evil to be minimised, to be replaced by the efforts of saintly volunteers and philanthropists who would be given tax relief on their generous donations.

The New Right consolidated alpha male authoritarianism and secured the subservience of the masses by convincing them – or a large enough group of them to prop up the regime – that they could secure the subservience of others down the line. Forget about reaching down to bring everyone up to a shared platform of dignity and solidarity, but focus on climbing over others to get as near to the top as possible.

In the closing decades of the 20$^{th}$ century, it succeeded in blotting out the progressive outlook with their concerted propaganda to paint the world as a God-sanctioned marketplace for the money-makers to rise to the top and rule the rest. The Thatcher-Reagan 'revolution' created a new social and political climate. Their supporters felt good about themselves and their country because they believed they could get 'closer' to the top even though in reality most of them were pushed further down towards the bottom. What they could achieve for themselves as individuals were becoming increasingly more important than what they could bring about with their fellow citizens in terms of a fairer society for all. Progressive aspirations were everywhere on the defensive. 'Liberal' and 'socialist' were turned into pejorative terms in

America and Britain respectively. Welfare for the poor was frowned upon. Tax concession for the rich was celebrated. Everyone needed to have more rigid discipline – school children, workers, foreigners, developing countries, public services; all must be controlled and regulated more, with the exception of business people who knew how to make money – they, uniquely, must be given more freedom. The legacy of Roosevelt and Attlee was at its nadir.

Globalisation & Power Imbalance

Although globalisation is regarded by some as virtually synonymous with a worldwide plutocratic conspiracy against social justice, the intensification of international links was not inherently antithetical to the progressive cause[138]. The establishment of the UN and other related international agencies in the postwar period, followed by the growth of air travel, long distance telecommunications, satellite-assisted worldwide television broadcast, and global distribution of cultural products such as films and popular records all helped to spread awareness of the value and possibility of having more inclusive communities. The difference with the new wave of technology and transnational organisation development from the 1980s on was that they took place under a political culture diametrically opposite to that represented by the Atlantic Charter.

Progressive world leaders, especially in America and Britain, had previously been at the forefront of putting in place institutions which would empower the weak and vulnerable to secure peace, healthcare, just labour conditions, higher education standards and protection against aggression from abroad. But by the 1980s, with the New Right in the ascendancy, the Anglo-American market ideologues were focused on reconstructing the world to make it propitious for a global plutocracy[139].

---

[138] Held and Drew, *Globalization/Anti-Globalization*, Cambridge, Polity: 2002. For a detailed study of the global age, see Castells, M, *The Information Age: economy, society and culture* (in three volumes: *The Rise of the Network Society, The Power of Identity, End of Millennium*), Oxford, Blackwells: 1996-1998.
[139] Alexander, T, *Unravelling Global Apartheid*, Cambridge, Polity Press: 1996. See also Hoogvelt, A, *Globalisation and the Postcolonial World*, Basingtoke, Macmillan Press: 1997.

Advancement in information technology could have facilitated international regulations of financial transactions and taxation on currency speculations. Instead it was primarily exploited to enable corporations to gain more effective control over their operations around the world, and most importantly, to bypass what constraints were still in place at the level of national governments. Investment could thus be moved ever more quickly from one country to another, and governments – irrespective of their democratic mandate – could increasingly be pressured into conceding to the demands of the business giants lest they lost out on investment and jobs, leaving them with a weakened economy and high unemployment.

The ease of moving capital around the world was complemented by three other key factors in the rise of the global plutocratic system. First, a propaganda-consultancy industry had emerged to promote relentless deregulation and privatisation as the essence of 'modernisation'. British and American advisers, building on the credentials they built up over the Thatcher-Reagan years in dismantling state controls and increasing corporate freedom to act at the expense of workers, travelled across the world to promote the 'free market' approach. Secondly, to maximise the chance that governments would in practice be supportive of the plutocratic agenda, the rich and powerful would consistently fund election war chests to support the campaigns of politicians who were least likely to resist the widening of power inequalities. Thirdly, commercial media empires would be lined up to present those who championed the plutocratic agenda as god-fearing, morally decent, patriotic figures who could relate to what ordinary people needed. The New Right – which at its core was about a small elite having greater and greater power over the majority who would become increasingly vulnerable and dependent on the powerful few – would then come across as the ideology of ordinary people.

Globalisation thus became an accelerator for concentrating power at almost all levels in those who were most able to accumulate wealth, and enabling them to secure the media, military and any form of support needed to expand their hegemony. It paved the way for the New Right to shift the world culturally and structurally away from collective provisions to sustain social solidarity, and towards a market individualism that defined human responsibility primarily in terms of what individuals should do to earn more money to improve their own lives. 'Tax cuts' was to be essential to give the richest the greatest benefit and the less well-off more opportunities to look after themselves. To rally support from the wider public who might otherwise see that they were mere pawns to those at the apex of this regime, it cultivated its own version of 'God' by amalgamating macho reactionary dispositions – unforgiving towards the weak and misguided, aggressive in war and punishment, endorsing the strong and wealthy, and suspicious of anyone not conforming to some vaguely primitive sense of 'purity'. Many of the plutocrats did not actually subscribe to such a theocratic worldview, but they used it to vindicate their actions when the evidence pointed to their damaging effects on people unable to defend themselves. From benefit cuts for the poor to air raids on civilian populations, 'God' would be invoked to persuade some sections of society that the regime is not callous but caring and righteous.

## The dominance of the New Right

By the end of the 20th century, the New Right appeared to have consolidated a global plutocratic system[140]. Communist regimes had on the whole collapsed or given in to the ethos of individual wealth-generation. Russia allowed individuals with the right connections to build up vast business empires. China embraced capitalist economic policies. But neither took sufficient precaution in protecting those who were left at the bottom of the polarising social hierarchy. The European Union was put on the defensive by the constant threat of losing investment to Asia if its member states did not embrace more deregulation to enable the corporate sector to get away with offering poorer pay and conditions. Its efforts in sustaining social solidarity were constantly undermined by the UK, which wanted workers to be more 'flexible' in meeting the demands of employers. America, as the undisputed global superpower, could deal with any threats abroad or at home because its financial clout sustained its military strength. As for

---

[140] Derber, C, *Corporation Nation*, New York, St Martin's Griffin: 2000; Chomsky, N, *World Orders, Old and New*, London, Pluto Press: 1994; Goldman, M (ed), *Privatizing Nature*, London, Pluto Press: 1998.

people who questioned the moral emptiness of market individualism, they would be told to turn their attention to the centrality of faith in giving life meaning and purpose.

At the forefront of the plutocratic revolution, America and Britain were also demonstrating what the rest of the world could expect to experience when the culture of the New Right spread further by the day. As the US and the UK adopted a more authoritarian stance on law and order, the more problems they encountered compared with previous decades and with other countries keeping with their liberal regimes. America reintroduced capital punishment, while Britain overtook Turkey in Europe in putting the highest percentage of its population in prison. Drug addiction, violent crime, and teenage pregnancies rose rapidly in both countries, where a vastly disproportionate number of young black people were being incarcerated.

The much trumpeted growth rates of the 1990s left Britons and Americans working under greater stress, longer hours, with less job security, and higher family breakdown rates than other developed countries. Income inequalities widened as the case for the rich to be taxed less trumped the case to minimise deprivations. By the mid 1990s, compared with other developed countries in Western Europe and North America, the UK and the US had the highest income inequality rates[141]. Furthermore, social attitudes were being shifted from those associated with progressive solidarity in the postwar years to much more self-centred individualistic ones.

According to the Eurobarometer poll (2001) of European Union countries, the UK had the second highest score in believing that people live in want because they are lazy or lack will power (23%). Only Portugal had a higher score (29%) but a higher percentage of the Portuguese attributed the problem of poverty to injustice in society (34%). When asked if it was due to the prevalence of injustice in society, the UK had the lowest score (after Denmark) of 19%. But the Danes might view injustice as a less likely cause of poverty given their much lower income inequality and lower levels of relative poverty. For many other European countries, blaming their fellow citizens' poor personal circumstances on their laziness or lack of will power was

---

[141] Luxembourg Income Study. www.lisproject.org, 9 June 2003.

confined to a very small minority (Spain and the Netherlands had 12% and Sweden just 9%), whereas recognition of injustice in society as a cause of having to live in want was generally high (France had 40% and Finland 43%). The UK was uniquely following the lead of the US. Although America was not covered by the Eurobarometer poll, the World Values Survey (1995-1997) asked its respondents (which include those living in the United States) if they believed people lived in need because of their 'laziness and lack of will power' or because 'society treats them unfairly', 61% of Americans chose the former.

In Britain and America, looking after one's own interests in financial terms rather than working for justice for all had become a greater concern for each new generation. Political idealism was pushed aside by consumer power. Typically, between 1980 and 1990, the proportion of high school seniors in America who believed that "having lots of money" was personally important to them rose from 51% to 70%[142].

A growing number of citizens felt marginalised and alienated from political decisions that affected their lives. Electoral turnout continued to drop, with the poorest the least likely to cast a vote. Fewer and fewer people bothered to join political parties because they believed the parties had all converged on variants of the market-centric ideology. In the 2005 general election in the UK, more people abstained from voting (39%) than those who actually voted for the winning party (36%). According to the British Government's Citizenship Survey (2005) only about 21% of the public believed they had any influence over decisions affecting their country.

The two nations which initiated the Atlantic Charter, far from leading the way in turning swords into ploughshares, made armed conflicts – which in the fifty years *after* the end of World War Two claimed the lives of over 20 million people, mostly civilians – into a vital business of their economy. Even with the demise of the Soviet threat, the world continued to spend $1,000 billion every year on military expenses, with the US and UK between them accounting for almost two thirds of the world's arms trade. Generating wealth was indeed more

---

[142] The US Monitoring the Future Project. Source: Wendy Rahn, University of Minnesota.

important than sparing people from the ravages of advanced weapons. Instead of regulating the rich and powerful so they had to play a more responsible part in sharing their resource and influence with the disadvantaged, the plutocratic world order proclaimed that the weak must learn to cope on their own so that those with money-making talent could throw off governmental shackles and generate more wealth – for themselves. Individuals or countries, which refused to serve the interests of the plutocratic hierarchy, would be marginalised, demonised, and if necessary, dealt with by force[143].

## The failed pursuit of a Third Way

Faced with the concerted onslaught from the New Right, many progressive advocates began to wonder if they should re-position their politics altogether. Many of the people they had managed to engage with in the past on a promise of greater inclusion appeared to have switched to a completely different mindset. For example, Thomas Frank used the transformation of the State of Kansas from progressive stronghold to New Right heartland, where moderate Republicans were chastised as liberals, to illustrate how the people who would lose most under a global plutocracy had been led to reject as godless and elitist those who would tackle such a regime[144]. Drawing on personal interviews, Linda Kintz discovered how the appeal of God, the Flag, and the freedom to make money could be potently mixed to bind a vast number of people to a cause, which offered them a large dose of righteous validation even if the cause actually favoured corporate elites at their expense in practice[145].

The progressives started to doubt what constituted their reform platform. Attacked for being too interventionist (in tackling the powerful), and too liberal (in supporting the disadvantaged), many of them suffered an ideological disorientation that left them looking

---

[143] See, e.g., Pilger, J, *Freedom Next Time*, Black Swan: 2007; and Chomsky, N, *Failed States: the abuse of power and the assault on democracy*, Penguin: 2007.

[144] Frank, T, *What's the Matter with America: the resistible rise of the American Right*, London, Vintage Books: 2006.

[145] Kintz, L, *Between Jesus and the Market: the emotions that matter in right-wing America*, Durham, Duke University Press: 1997.

desperately for a 'new' politics, a 'third' way, to define what they should stand for. Consequently, at every turn, they found themselves on the defensive. At every election, they would be angst-stricken about what their narrative should be. They started to treat voters, not as fellow citizens to engage in the campaign for more inclusive communities, but as consumers of electoral packages of enticement. Even when they ended up on the winning side, they would still be divided over the concessions made to those who craved for authoritarian social policies, unrestricted corporate dominance, and further strengthening of the security establishment.

In the 1990s, progressives in America and Britain were increasingly told that they had to change if they were ever to succeed in taking political power away from the New Right. The old progressive stance in challenging power inequalities was considered out of date. In its place, the New Democrats and New Labour, under the shared banner of the 'Third Way', offered progressives a new direction to address their concerns in the age of globalisation. Their argument was that with a global economy, national governments could not effectively intervene with corporate powers which operated transnationally, and the best they could do was to provide the conditions under which business elites would view as favourable, while at the same time persuading the population in general that there was no viable alternative to developing and adapting themselves to meet the demands of corporate employers.

Anthony Giddens' writings on what the 'Third Way' should be were endorsed by leading political figures on both sides of the Atlantic as a guide to the real alternative to the New Right[146]. Giddens maintained that the progressive social democratic politics of the past had been superseded by neoliberalism since the 1970s, and there was no going back. A third and substantially different approach had to be found. But for over twenty years, many British and American progressive thinkers and politicians had already set out why some of the policies of the past needed to be revised. Disarmament could only be realistically achieved

---

[146] Giddens, A, *The Third Way*, Cambridge, Polity: 1998, and its sequel, *The Third Way & Its Critics*, Cambridge, Polity: 2000. The critique of Giddens set out here is drawn from Tam, H, 'What is *the* Third Way?' in *The Responsive Community*, Spring 2001 (Volume 11, Issue 2).

through multilateral negotiation and not unilateral actions. Nationalisation of industries might not always be the most reliable solution. Community-based politics and cooperative business initiatives should be supported more to complement central government actions. Welfare provision needed to be supplemented by real support in finding long term employment, otherwise it could create permanent dependency. The use of non-renewable resources had to be managed much more effectively to protect the planet from major damages and to preserve natural assets for future generations. There was nothing new in recognising that these issues needed attention.

Giddens' attempt to find something distinctively original about the 'Third Way' revealed the identity crisis at its heart. Whilst acknowledging that European countries with long standing social democratic governments generally had better public institutions and lower levels of economic inequality than Britain and America, he suggested that these countries might nonetheless borrow ideas from the Third Way to deal with crime and family breakdown. Yet these European countries already had lower crime rates, fewer teenage pregnancies, and lower divorce rates than their Anglo-American counterparts. The only reason why they might have to be prepared for social problems on the Anglo-American scale would be if they were pressured into embracing the deregulation of the market to give more power to corporate giants. Perhaps that was what was unusual about the Third Way – aiming to replace the progressive struggle against power inequalities by a permanent accommodation with global plutocracy.

In his exposition of the Third Way, Giddens wrote about the importance of free choices for consumers but made no reference to the plight of workers. He maintained that "as private companies downsized, adopted flatter hierarchies and sought to become more responsive to customer needs, the limitations of bureaucratic state institutions stood out in relief." But private sector downsizing was all too often about making people redundant, raising profit margins, destabilizing community life, and forcing the remaining employees to concentrate on working more hours and spending less time with their families. As for public sector management, the real challenge was to develop a citizen-focused approach, not to ape the private sector[147].

Tellingly on the issue of equality, Giddens declared that "equality of opportunity typically creates higher rather than lower inequalities of outcome. ... Rather than seeking to suppress these consequences, we should accept them." Many progressives would argue that there ought to be a clear limit to the growth of such outcome inequalities, beyond which the state should take action to redress the balance. One reason why Third Way advocates hesitated to endorse state engagement in any activities that might reduce growing inequalities in wealth distribution was that "the better-off sections of the electorate have become resistant to paying very high taxes." Their underlying concern was clearly with not upsetting the powerful. From a moral point of view, there are all kinds of state action that criminals, irresponsible corporations, or racists may resent and seek to evade, but that does not in itself offer an argument why such state action should be abandoned. It is only from an electoral point of view that it might be ill-advised for the state to press for tax-based redistribution, because those with financial power could – by threatening to move jobs to other countries, providing campaign finances, and buying media airtime – influence voting patterns considerably and stop any party with such policies from winning power.

Indeed a defining feature of the Third Way was above all that "social democrats should continue to move away from heavy reliance on taxes that might inhibit effort or enterprise, including income and corporate taxes." And lest this position should become completely indistinguishable from that of the New Right, Giddens added that the loss of fiscal revenue could be compensated by a shift to eco-taxation on energy, waste, and transport. But if the aim of taxing environmentally unfriendly activities were to obtain significant new sources of revenue, then achieving it would mean that those activities had not been effectively reduced. On the other hand, if the aim were to reduce those activities substantially, then securing that aim would mean that the loss of tax revenue from other sources would not be compensated.

---

[147] See, e.g., Ranson, S and Stewart, J, *Management for the Public Domain*, Basingstoke, Macmillan Press: 1994; Tam, H (ed), *Marketing, Competition and the Public Sector*, Harlow, Longman: 1994; and Stewart, J and Tam, H, *Putting Citizens First*, London, Municipal Journal: 1997.

Ultimately, the Third Way was not concerned with raising enough taxes to tackle social and economic inequalities. It was unequivocal that governments should move away from redistribution towards wealth creation. It quickly became clear that the Conservative and Republican parties had little to fear from this 'new' kind of politics. A decade into the 21st century, the two-term Presidency of George W Bush showed how the 'Third Way' had allowed the global plutocracy to grow and wreck havoc around the world. The New Democrats positioned themselves as business-friendly, and regained Congress in 2006 when they started to field candidates who backed the social conservative agenda. New Labour, despite being in government and opposed to many of the military, energy, and trading policies of America, found their Prime Minister – a key Third Way champion, Tony Blair – consistently supportive of the US plutocrats. The Anglo-American mantra for privatisation and deregulation continued to spread and put the profits of the business sector ahead of ordinary citizens. Bonuses for the rich continued to increase while pension entitlement of most workers further dwindled. Faith-based practices, however irrational, from the teaching of creationism in schools to anti-contraception policies in the fight against AIDS, were privileged against evidence-based approaches. All the while, the power gap continued to widen.

What Clinton and Blair managed to do was to take forward policies where they could be convincingly presented as helpful in meeting corporate interests. For example, tackling discrimination against women and ethnic minorities in the workplace helped to provide a wider pool of talent for employers. Investing in schools and increasing testing made it easier to sift out those with not enough talent to thrive in a modern economy. Shifting support to job-seeking as a pre-condition for benefits enlarged the supply of applicants for low paid positions. Improving the health services (where Clinton was much less successful than Blair) meant that less in terms of productivity would be lost through people lying on their sick bed.

By contrast, any regulatory attempts to strengthen the position of workers in relation to their employers would not find favour with Third Way advocates. Across Europe, the UK continued to slow the pace of Europe-wide social reforms. In Germany, Schroder embraced the approach of the Third Way under the slogan of the 'New Middle' to win power for the Social Democrats after decades of dominance by the Christian Democrats. In so doing, he merely consolidated the drift towards the outlook of the New

Right, and the Christian Democrats swiftly returned to power. In France, Jospin and the Socialists resisted the Anglo-American ideology of deregulation and privatisation, protected pension rights of workers, and shortened the working week. Yet for that very reason they came under attack from international economic commentators for their refusal to 'modernise', and Sarkozy not only succeeded in continuing to keep the French Presidency from the left, he shifted France more than ever in the direction of the New Right. It was in Italy that the influence of the New Right had become most visible with the archetypal plutocrat, Berlusconi, third richest man in Italy, owning large media and finance businesses, and running the country as Prime Minister.

## The impact of widening power inequalities

The New Right subversion of enterprise, religion and patriotism into an Idol for money grabbing, weapon-wielding devotees helped to consolidate the spread of global plutocracy. A tiny elite of plutocrats – comprising the wealthiest business leaders, their supporters occupying key executive positions in government, the media and financial institutions – would make rules and decisions which favour them and the continued expansion of their power, leaving the vast majority of humankind unable to do much to change the arrangements under which they must live.

In the past, the arbitrary rule of the few had always been tamed by what could be viewed broadly as a three step process – constraining the exercise of the ruler's power by a political body accountable to the people, strengthening that accountability by extending the franchise to all adults, and using the universal franchise as a basis for systematic democratic deliberations in deciding who and what policies to support. But under the global plutocracy, most of the international regulatory bodies for trade or finance are accountable, not to the world's population, but to America and its closest allies. Where there is even a modicum of accountability, such as through the United Nations General Assembly, the US frequently undermined it by operating unilaterally, not paying its contributions, and defying the views of the majority. There is no equivalent to any form of electoral franchise, let alone a universal one, to ground a democratic global government.

From the 1970s to the end of the 20th century, power inequalities, especially in terms of wealth distribution, widened in the US and UK, and countries like Russia which bought into the ideology of the New Right. For Third Way politics, such a growing gap posed no problem at all[148]. To counter such complacency, researchers around the world accumulated evidence to show the unremitting harm caused by the relentlessly divisive system.

They demonstrated that those with lower socio-economic status generally had shorter life expectancy than those with higher status[149]. Within organisations, death rates increased steadily from the those at the top to those nearer the bottom, with the death rates from heart disease in one case study with 17,000 staff rising to four times as high amongst the most junior workers as amongst the most senior managers working in the same offices[150]. So much for people being paid much more at the top to cope with the heavier stresses and strains. In fact, people should be paid more for being lower down the hierarchy to compensate for their life-shortening status.

The widening income gap de-motivated the poor because it meant that however hard they worked they would be stuck with their lower social status. It deprived more and more people any chance of attaining even the average standards of health and living conditions as a minority soaked up more of the wealth around. At the same time it made the rich elite more remote from and disdainful of others who they could make to do anything with money.

It became increasingly clear that people living in more unequal societies at the national or sub-national level were more likely to live a shorter and less decent life. For example, a study of 528 cities in US, UK, Canada, Australia, and Sweden found that working age men in cities with higher income differences tended to have higher death rates. The age-

---

[148] A leading British Third Way politician summed up the outlook when he said, "we are intensely relaxed about people getting filthy rich" (Peter Mandelson speaking to computer executives in California in 1998). He subsequently pointed out to media reporters who quoted him that his sentence finished with "... so long as they pay their taxes." Yet tax avoidance has been one of the growth industries in the age of deregulation – for example, one UK bank paid its head of tax avoidance at least £40 million a year.

[149] Donkin, A, Goldblatt, P and Lynch, K, 'Inequalities in Life Expectancy by Social Class 1972-1999', *Health Statistics Quarterly* 52 (2002): 15-19.

[150] Rose, G and Marmot, MG, 'Social class and coronary heart disease', *British Heart Journal* (1981) 45: 13-19.

adjusted death rates for the highly unequal New Orleans were twice as high as those of Melbourne, one of the cities with the lowest income differences[151]. The same applied to infant mortality rates. Although a country's overall GNP has an impact on reducing infant mortality, the reduction is greater where the country's income inequality is lower[152]

Within countries, income disparity could be translated directly into disparity in life expectancy. A boy living in the deprived Glasgow suburb of Calton will live on average 28 years less than a boy born in nearby affluent Lenzie. And the average life expectancy in London's wealthy Hampstead was 11 years longer than in nearby St Pancras[153].

By reducing income inequalities, life expectancy rates could be improved. For example, between 1960 and 1977, most communist countries as well as the high growth early capitalist countries of Taiwan, South Korea, Hong Kong and Singapore, all succeeded in narrowing income differentials over this period, and they out-performed other countries in extending their populations' life expectancy rates[154]. Unfortunately, the trend with the expanding global plutocracy is in the opposite direction. The rise of income inequalities across central and Eastern Europe from 1989 to 1995 was correlated with a decline in life expectancy. Notably, the drop in life expectancy was marginal (less than a year) in Hungary and Romania where the change was small, but it worsened by 4 and 6 years in Moldovia and Russia respectively where income inequalities had increased substantially[155].

---

[151] Ross, N, and Dorling, D, etc. 'Metropolitan income inequality and working age mortality', *Journal of Urban Health*, quoted in R. Wilkinson, *The Impact of Inequality*, London: Routledge 2005. It was hardly surprising that when Hurricane Katrina hit New Orleans, the city with the worst income inequalities in America, the rich had by and large moved out of the city, and the poor were left behind to suffer the devastation. Nearly 2,000 people died, and thousands remained displaced from their homes five years after the disaster.

[152] Hales, S, Howden-Chapman, P, and Salmon, C, etc 'National infant mortality rates in relation to GNP and distribution of income', *Lancet* 354 (1997): 2,047.

[153] Report by WHO's Commission on the Social Determinants of Health, 2008.

[154] Sen, A, 'Public action and the quality of life in developing countries', *Oxford Bulletin of Economics and Statistics* (1981) 43: 287-319

[155] Marmot, M and Bobak, M, 'International comparators and poverty and health in Europe', *British Medical Journal* 321(2000):I, 124-128.

Apart from the effect on people's health, inequalities had been strongly linked to destructive attitudes and behaviour. From studies which found that the US states with the highest income inequality had four times the homicide rates than US states and Canadian provinces with the lowest income inequality[156], to research which drew from international data from thirty-nine countries from different continents and concluded that homicide rates were also higher in countries where income inequalities were greater[157], the pattern is beyond dispute. Indeed according to J.L. Neapolitan, "[T]he most consistent finding in cross-national research on homicides has been that of a positive association between income inequality and homicides."[158]

The plutocratic reinforcement of alpha male hierarchies was designed to revive the old authoritarian outlook whereby men stuck low down on the socio-economic pyramid would secure a sense of self-worth through being able to dominate others who were physically or culturally vulnerable – women, foreigners, defenceless neighbours, non-believers, etc. By deflecting their frustration and anger towards those placed even lower down, the likelihood of confronting those at the top would recede. Studies in America confirmed that average hostility levels were higher in cities where a lower proportion of income went to the poorest half of the population[159], and that racial prejudice levels were higher in those American states with greater income inequality[160].

Power inequalities have also been measured in terms of pay differentials and political participation (in terms of proportion of elected representatives) between female and male. It was found that the more women were left behind, the higher the mortality rates were for *both*

---

[156] Daly, M, Wilson, M, and Vasdev, S, 'Income Inequality and Homicide Rates in Canada and the United States' *Canadian Journal of Criminology* 43 (2001): 219-36.

[157] Fajnzylber, P, Lederman, D and Loayza, N 'Inequality and violent crime', *Journal of Law and Economics* 2002; 45 (I): 1-40

[158] Neapolitan, JL, 'A comparative analysis of nations with low and high levels of violent crime', *Journal of Criminal Justice* 27 (3): 259-274.

[159] Williams, RB, Feaganes, J, and Barefoot, JC, 'Hostility and Death Rates in 10 US Cities', *Psychosomatic Medicine* 1995; 57 (I): 94.

[160] Kennedy, BP and Kawachi, I etc. '(Dis)respect and black mortality', *Ethnicity and Disease* 1997, 7:207-214.

women and men[161]. Where men and women were more able to live as equals in society, the greater mutual respect and harmony they could expect. According to Richard Wilkinson, "Why men's health improves even more than women's where the status of women is better is because dominance hierarchies are power competitions among men. Men do more of the fighting and striving for dominance and suffer more of the injuries, anxieties, and stresses of these social processes. The costs are shown in their increased levels of violence, more risk-taking behaviour (from car crashes to sexually transmitted diseases), excessive drinking, drug taking, and cardio-vascular diseases. .... Women also suffer because men who feel subordinated will often try to regain a sense of their authority by subordinating women, particularly their partners. This is part of a much wider process of downward discrimination in which people who feel humiliated try to repair their sense of selfhood by demonstrating their superiority over any more vulnerable group, whether women, ethnic minorities, or low status minorities."[162]

The growth of income inequalities under the global plutocracy was corrosive of cooperative relationships at every level. The states in US with the highest income inequalities had the highest proportion of people who did not trust each other – as much as four times the proportion in the least unequal states[163]. The same pattern has been found internationally with people trusting each other far less in countries with larger income differences[164]. Conversely, participation in community life was found to be much stronger where income differences were smaller, both in relation to regions in Italy[165], and states in America[166].

---

[161] Kawachi, I, etc. 'Women's status and the health of women: a view from the States', *Social Science and Medicine* (1999) 48 (1): 21-32.

[162] Wilkinson, R, *The Impact of Inequality*, London: Routledge 2005, 218-219.

[163] Kawachi, I, etc. 'Social Capital, Income Inequality, and Morality', *American Journal of Public Health* 87 (1997): I, 491-498.

[164] Uslaner, E, *The Moral Foundations of Trust*, New York: Cambridge University Press, 2002.

[165] Putnam, R, Leonardi, R, and Nenetti, RY, *Making democracy work: civic traditions in modern Italy*, Princeton, Princeton University Press: 1993

[166] Putnam, R, *Bowling Alone: the collapse and revival of American community*, New York, Simon and Schuster: 2000

Henry Tam

## Communitarian warnings against socio-economic divisions

As the global plutocracy expanded its sphere of influence, it drained human interactions of the potential to develop collective democratic solutions to their common problems, and more and more people ended up thinking the only way out of their predicament was to try to push past others to get a rung or two higher up on the ever-extending socio-economic ladder. As the rich nations and corporations got richer, the poorest not only got even poorer, but were told that the world could no longer afford the 'over-generous' support which the post-war consensus for social solidarity sustained for almost three decades.

In the 1990s, the social fragmentation caused by deepening power inequalities prompted a number of progressive thinkers to formulate a unified platform to oppose plutocratic trends. Drawing on the tradition of inclusive community development, a group of British and American political critics adopted the 'communitarian' name to describe their shared concern with the spread of self-centred individualism in splitting communities into the powerful with no sense of responsibility, and the powerless deprived of all rights. The communitarians wanted progressives to join forces once more in countering the effects of relentless marketisation and the deterioration of social bonds. They warned that these problems would continue to worsen unless policies were urgently introduced to curtail power inequalities and rebuild cooperative community life at every level[167].

Instead of seeking accommodation with plutocratic powers as

---

[167] This group included Jonathan Boswell, Philip Selznick, Robert Bellah, Henry Tam, Amitai Etzioni, and William A. Galston. A good introduction to their core views can be found in the following key texts: Boswell, J. *Community and the Economy: the Theory of Public Co-operation.* London, Routledge: 1990; Selznick, P. *The Moral Commonwealth*, Berkeley, University of California Press: 1992; Bellah, R., et al, *The Good Society.* Vintage Books: 1995; Tam, H. *Communitarianism: a new agenda for politics and citizenship.* Basingstoke, Macmillan: 1998; and Tam, H. (ed), *Progressive Politics in the Global Age*, Cambridge, Polity Press: 2001. William Galston was an advisor to President Clinton. Henry Tam set up the Civil Renewal Unit for the UK Government in 2003 to run the seven-year nationwide 'Together We Can' campaign (http://www.hbtam.blogspot.co.uk/2013/06/find-our-more-about-together-we-can.html).

Third Way advocates had done, the progressive communitarians focused attention on the utmost priority of closing the power gap that was tearing society apart. They warned that corporate power and irresponsibility, if left unchecked, would push more and more people into a life of futility at best, and of wanton destruction at worst.

In the name of 'modernisation', plutocrats had already remodelled society so that all values and concerns were subordinated to the ability to make money. Children were to be tested from an early age and regularly thereafter to see if they were fit for market competition. This would be replicated in adult life to see if they were worthy of being recruited to join the elite or if they should remain amongst the highly dispensable. The stresses and strains in keeping up with the demands of the corporate decision makers would then put pressures on family relationships, transmitting a pervasive sense of insecurity to old and young alike.

To cope with life under the global plutocracy, many have gone along with the false hopes of the plutocratic race, cushioned by consumerist indulgence and debt accumulation. Just as poorer people are more likely to play the lottery even though the chance of a substantial winning is remote, most people who work hard and put in the time to rise in the business world will not actually make it to their organisational apex. They will more likely suffer from poor health and family tensions. Year in, year out, they watch the very few hit the corporate jackpot, not appreciating their own turn will never come. Addictive consumerism numbs the setbacks. In the meantime, drained of their energy just to stay where they are, they have little time left for wider collective concerns.

Then there is the opt-out route. Through ill health, disillusionment, or plain mental fatigue, many just cannot be bothered to keep up with the competition to gain some paltry recognition anymore. They withdraw, apathetically absorbing accusations that they take things out of society without putting anything back. Some may turn to superstitions, 'new age' fantasies, or quiet religious comfort to get through their day. What they have in common is a weary rejection of society under the management of the plutocrats.

Thirdly, the relentless depletion of self-esteem can cause some to feel so frustrated and angry that they lash out against themselves as well as others. They see through the hollow promise that everyone would have a fair chance of getting on when in fact it applies only to those with a talent for impressing the corporate world. So they drift into self-destructive behaviour. Consuming alcohol and drugs to deactivate their minds, using weapons to validate their own importance but ending up risking more serious injuries to themselves and others, having unprotected sex with no regard to transmission of AIDS or unwanted pregnancies. Their downward spiral is often portrayed as a sign of moral decline when in fact it is a symptom of a dysfunctional power structure which robs people without money-making skills of dignity and hope.

Fourthly, there is the door to parallel power structures. This appeals to those who believe they can make money and establish their own top-down organisations, provided they can make up their own rules. They form gangs, trade in stolen goods, narcotics and victims who have been forced into prostitution. Like their 'legitimate' counterpart, they are quick to hire lawyers to defend their interests against public prosecutors. Their underworld creates a space in which many who would otherwise be castigated as failures can find a degree of respect – even if it is a concept often confused with fear in their violent universe.

Finally, there is the extremist refuge for those who think they can restore their broken egos by focusing their minds through intense hatred and aggression towards a scapegoat. Their victims could be anyone: ethnic minorities; refugees and immigrants; believers in another religion or no religion; people who give abortions to women in distress; people with different sexual orientation; or people connected with carrying out experiments on animals to advance medical knowledge. In all these cases, their anger and fear are transferred to the designated scapegoat group, and a self-deluding sense of righteousness drives them to condemn, protest, hate, and in extreme cases, injure and kill.

Through their callous actions, they escape into a world of imagined purity where they are deemed heroes and martyrs. This was tragically the route taken by those who signed up for the September 11 terrorist attack on America, marking the opening of the 21st century with the senseless killing of nearly 3,000 people, devastating their families in over 100 countries.

Not only had communitarian warnings gone unheeded, plutocratic polarisation across the world was about to get even worse.

# Chapter 9
# Plutocracy in the 21<sup>st</sup> Century

Plutocratic hegemony & global irresponsibility

In 2001, Bush, Cheney and their New Right Administration turned the
September 11 tragedy into a springboard to launch a War on Terror,
dividing the world into terrorists and regimes prepared to collaborate
with America in crushing terrorists and their sympathisers. Such a
division conveniently blurred the fact that many of the leading
protagonists shared a commitment to use wealth-based power to stir up
fundamentalist hatred and deploy arms to torture and crush one's
opponents (even in cases where suspects were targeted with little
evidence of any kind of terrorist involvement).

Osama bin Laden was not the first to resort to the familiar
technique of inciting animosity against those marginalised in traditional
societies and funding violent actions to bolster his leadership. Like many
right-wing extremists in America, he was anti-Semitic, anti-homosexual
and utterly contemptuous of women equality. His readiness to use his
accumulated wealth as the basis to deploy force to intimidate ordinary
people and destroy innocent lives, far from suggesting that his outlook
came from an alien civilisation, confirmed that he was from that common
authoritarian stock of unaccountable leaders who use religious
propaganda and violence to get others to live according to their preferred
vision of the world.

With Al-Qaeda stepping into the Orwellian slot of arch demonic
enemy, left vacant by the demise of the Soviet Union, global plutocrats
could rally around Bush in attacking a common foe. With attention
diverted to the danger the ubiquitous terrorists posed, Bush and his
backers could go on making irresponsible decisions to benefit themselves
and undermine the wellbeing of others. This enabled the Bush
Presidency to deploy the full economic and military resources of the
world's undisputed superpower to enhance the interests of the rich.

Using the War on Terror as cover for its neglect of the poor and
vulnerable, it launched the invasion of Iraq in the name of the regime's
alleged links with Al-Qaeda, which turned out to be tenuous at best, and

to prevent its use of weapons of mass destruction, which turned out to be non-existent. Death of Iraqi civilians through bombing raids long after Saddam's capture and execution was dismissed as inconsequential; the loss of lives amongst the American forces was cited as the reason why people should not criticise the war; and while the occupation continued to add nothing to bring down Al-Qaeda, it helped the recruitment drive for the fugitive terrorists. In the meantime, liberal protection of all people under the American political system was undermined by new powers of surveillance and detention without charge.

The unilateral military initiatives (backed by the UK) alienated former allies and even at home started to cause erstwhile supporters to question the drawn-out occupation of a foreign country. But the New Right was above all concerned with securing plutocratic interests – oil deals, arms sales, reconstruction contracts – under the guise of military glory (except the glory was not so forthcoming)[168]. Similar commitment to the corporate agenda steered Bush to implacably oppose the demands for action against the emission of green house gases, which were accelerating destructive climate change.

As a result of industrialisation and the profit to be made from using non-renewable resources on an unprecedented scale to fuel the production of consumer goods, the level of $CO_2$ had gone up radically depleting the ozone layer to such an extent that harmful climatic changes had become more rapid and intense. For over 600,000 years up to the dawn of the industrial revolution, $CO_2$ levels in the earth's atmosphere fluctuated between 180ppm (parts per million) and 280ppm. In the last two hundred years, it went up to 380ppm and at the current rate of rise of 3ppm a year, the level could reach nearly 700ppm by the end of the 21st century. If the world's temperature is not to rise by more than 2.4 degrees Celsius, the $CO_2$ levels must be stabilised between 350 and 400ppm[169].

To do that, businesses would have to cut down drastically on their

---

[168] See, Klein, N., *The Shock Doctrine*, London, Penguin Books: 2007.

[169] See, for example, Gore, A, *An Inconvenient Truth: The Planetary Emergency of Global Warming and What We Can Do About It*, Rodale Books: 2006; and Stern, N, *The Economics of Climate Change: the Stern Review*, Cambridge University Press: 2006.

use of energy resources, especially those producing $CO_2$. But as that would reduce their short-term profits and hence their powerbase, they pressed their plutocratic partners in the White House to resist change. Together they plotted their defence strategy: they were only responding to consumer demands; they wanted the world to be aware that there were researchers (supported by their corporate funding) who dismissed the evidence on industrial causes of climate change as misconceived; they were worried that jobs would be lost if production was cut; and they recognised that to the extent there was a problem it could in any case only be tackled by resorting to greater use of nuclear power (though that would cause even more difficulties for the planet with the proliferation of radioactive waste)[170].

Not surprisingly the Bush Administration pulled America out of the Kyoto Agreement to reduce the emissions of greenhouse gases by industrialised countries. From the New Right's perspective, by refusing to cooperate with others, they could go on making profits while those acting more responsibly would lose grounds to them. If the damages to the environment could be contained by the action of others without US firms having to do anything, they would have had a free ride. But even if their refusal to play their part should lead to disasters around the world, the global plutocracy might still be able to exploit the situation to its advantage.

Their guiding assumption was that although persistent increase in the use of non-renewable energy would lead to problems, it would hit the poorest and vulnerable most immediately and severely. In those circumstances, they could advance their interests even further by exploiting the suffering into which others would have been plunged. So they stuck to their course as warmer climate started to melt the polar ice caps, raising sea levels and threatening millions with the loss of their homes, farmlands and supplies of drinking water in coastal areas. Other problems proliferated. With warmer air currents, storms were becoming more frequent and violent, and food crops were increasingly destroyed

---

[170] A fallback strategy has been to argue that businesses were already doing as much as they could to 'look after' the environment. See Karliner, J, *The Corporate Planet: ecology and politics in the age of globalization*, San Francisco, Sierra Club Books: 1997.

by persistent rainfall in some parts of the world and extended periods of drought in others. Tropical insects and diseases such as malaria and yellow fever, instead of being eradicated, would spread to temperate regions of the world.

Over-fishing had already led to huge drops in fish stocks. Food source on land was suffering from a similar fate, with over-exploitation of topsoil reducing the land available for food cultivation. Problems of desertification and decline in productivity were affecting over half of the world's arable lands. With potentially millions of people starving and homeless, conflicts would be more likely than ever to break out. For the New Right, this would mean an increase in three types of people: warlords who would buy weapons from the world's leading arms suppliers; terrorists who could be invoked to justify the suspension of liberal protection at home and military operations abroad; and refugees and economic migrants who could be blamed as foreigners competing for jobs and other limited resources, and would serve as useful scapegoats for the problems caused by the plutocrats.

Appealing to corporate social responsibility to act for the common good would not be sufficient. As in 19$^{th}$ century Britain, industrialists who wanted to do the responsible thing found that they would be undermined by others who were solely concerned with exploiting the weak for their own profit. The enlightened business owners pressed the government to take action so that *all* would be regulated in the same way. In the 21$^{st}$ century, there is no global government to turn to.

Bush's reign of irresponsibility continued despite the growing number of Iraqi and Afghanistan civilians and American soldiers killed in the Middle East; more babies born with AIDS in Africa after America actively stopped programme which would have educated the young about birth control; the poorest in America itself sinking further after funds to help them were withdrawn to pay for tax cuts for the richest; and non-renewable resources dwindling while climate change threatened millions with homelessness and starvation around the world.

Too many Americans were living under the illusion that for all the woes befalling the poorest in their country and the countless victims in foreign lands, they would be safe in their own privileged 'God Bless America' position, enjoying their economic prosperity, moral righteousness and military superiority. They did not want to question the

New Right orthodoxy. This allowed Bush to secure a second term of office and pressed on with policies so inimical to the wellbeing of everyone across America and the rest of the world that his Administration finally imploded.

Financial Mismanagement

Like Al Capone, who for all his violent crime was finally brought down by his violation of tax regulation, the dominance of the New Right was disrupted by their gross financial mismanagement. The Republicans inherited a $128 billion federal surplus from the Democrats in 2001 and turned that in eight years into a federal deficit approaching $480 billion. Instead of investing public resources into a fair structure for inclusive community life where everyone would contribute to a meaningful safety net for all, champions of the New Right preferred to squander public money on misguided military adventures and tax gifts for the rich.

As if they wanted to defiantly rekindle the spirit of the successive Republican Presidents who ruled America on behalf of plutocratic interests from 1921 to 1933, they embarked on a systematic programme to concentrate even more power in the rich corporations and business leaders so that they could make even more money for themselves. Regulations to make businesses behave responsibly towards their workers were dismantled in the name of flexibility and competitiveness. Job security, real wage levels, protection against redundancy, pension benefits all plummeted. As the rich got richer and more powerful, the only thing they needed was for those left behind to be able to borrow enough money to buy their products – and earn them interests as lenders. Any sustainable realignment of the economy through a fair system of wealth redistribution was out of the question.

Turning a blind eye to the fact that the plutocratic irresponsibility of the Republican trinity of Harding-Coolidge-Hoover led to the Great Depression, the US, and the other outpost of the New Right, UK, carried on with their obsessive deregulation. The more people were losing out under growing inequalities, the more they found that the only way they could keep up was by borrowing money, and the more businesses were supported by the American and British governments in lending more aggressively and irresponsibly than ever before. In 2008, it dawned on the lenders that the debt they were counting on collecting had reached breaking point[171].

They swung from one extreme of pushing loans to all and sundry to the other extreme of cutting drastically back on their lending. The tightening of credit for people who were dependent on borrowing to keep going meant they could not afford to buy as much as they had before. Consumption dropped, production capacity went into surplus, and jobs were cut leaving an increasing number of people with nothing to fall back on. Those of a working age were told that benefits would depend on how committed they were in finding another job when employment opportunities were drastically reduced. Those who might otherwise contemplate retirement discovered that Anglo-American style deregulation had led to businesses stripping down their pension scheme so that retirement was not an option either.

True to their absolute focus on their own interests, the plutocrats who had argued that governments must leave business leaders to make as much money for themselves when there was plenty of profit to be made, switched to demanding state support to bail them out with billions of pounds and dollars of public money so they could keep paying themselves huge bonuses even as they sacked more of their workers. The fallout engulfed the world economy and brought deep anxiety to all citizens. Many people who had previously voted for Bush in the US or stayed silent in the face of relentless deregulation in the UK began at long last to question if governments should not be much more forthright in holding the powerful to account.

By the time the first decade of the 21st century drew to a close, a young senator with one of the most liberal voting records in Congress was elected President in America. Barack Obama was even able to withstand the ultimate 'silver bullet' attack from the Republicans who charged him with wanting to redistribute wealth. In Britain, the language of progressive change was being adopted by leaders across the political

---

[171] Many commentators had throughout the late 1980s and 1990s written about the mounting dangers of the global plutocratic system for both the developed and developing countries. See, e.g., Soros, G, *The Crisis of Global Capitalism*, Little, Brown & Company: 1998; and Culpeper, R, Berry, A, and Stewart, F (eds), *Global Development Fifty Years after Bretton Woods*, Basingstoke, Macmillan: 1997.

spectrum in expressing the need to curb the powerful in society.

In practice, however, plutocratic power structures remained firmly in place despite the fact they had been directly responsible for the banking crisis, which drained public finances to bailout corporate failures and destablised the world economy.

In the US, Obama brought an end to the wars Bush launched in Iraq and Afghanistan, and turned his attention instead to the objective Americans were really concerned with after the September 11 attack, namely, to track down the leader of Al-Qaeda and prevent him from plotting any more terrorist offensive against the US. He also introduced the Affordable Care Act to give millions more Americans the chance to access healthcare, despite the ferocious attempts of Republicans to stop him. But with Republican control of Congress, Wall Street dominance over financial policies, and billionaire corporate leaders funding the Tea Party push to tilt the Republican Party even further to plutocratic extremes, Obama could only secure the support to go so far in mending the severe damages inflicted by two terms of Bush. Income inequalities continued to widen. And the recovery of the stock market benefited the richest, while the poorest continued to struggle to make a living[172]. Republicans in Congress not only decimated support for the poorest civilians in the US, but they had a surprise for the country's armed forces too. Having pushed for military actions abroad, Republicans cut support for war veterans when they returned home.

In the UK, the Conservatives dropped all pretence to being progressive as soon as they were in control of the government in 2010. They cut the top marginal rate tax for the wealthiest from 50% to 45%. They fought the European Union's attempt to limit bonus payment to bankers. They drastically cut benefits to the poorest in society. Homelessness in England rose by 21% in the two years since they took charge of housing policies, while rough sleeping in London went up by 62% in the same period[173]. Meanwhile, public provisions such as the

---

[172] See Stiglitz, J, *Freefall: free markets and the sinking of the global economy*, London, Penguin: 2010; and Reich, R. *Supercapitalism: the battle for democracy in an age of big business*, London, Icon Books, 2009.
[173] Source: Crisis, the national charity for homeless people, http://www.crisis.org.uk/pages/homeless-def-numbers.html

National Health Service, Legal Aid, and children centres were resolutely denied the funding to meet demands[174]. Although they had promised to support renewable energy and tackle environmental degradation, once in office they cut support for solar energy, opposed wind power, and poured public money into supporting established corporations in relation to nuclear power stations and fracking for shale gas. Like their Republican counterparts, they embarked on a thoroughly anti-progressive campaign to give even more financial and statutory support to large corporations, attack worker rights, and stir up fear and hatred of immigrants and welfare claimants.

Plutocrats had managed to cover up the connection between the deregulation of the banking sector championed by the New Right and the financial chaos it brought about. They had deflected enough people into thinking that the problem was the government trying to spend money on helping people who could not cope with all of life's difficulties on their own. In reality, the resources needed to help people to cope with the difficulties that might arise in life could be distributed in a number of ways. Plutocrats preferred to persist with the distribution that favoured them at the expense of everyone else, and their political priority was to ensure that governments would continue to protect them, and not do anything to close the power gap between them and the multitude they were thus able to exploit.

The plutocratic deception concerning what caused the global financial meltdown would inevitably lead to more banking catastrophes. Instead of recognising that more people should be given the purchasing power they needed to sustain a healthy economy, the prevailing view was that bankers should be left to lend as they saw fit. But lending to people who could not pay it back was not so much a solution as a disaster waiting to happen.

In China, where decades of economic growth were supposed to have helped keep the global economic engine running when corporate financial mismanagement caused chaos in Europe and America, the rise of powerful financiers had already steered that country towards a similar credit bubble that would one day burst. The Chinese government,

---

[174] Tam, H., 'The Big Con: reframing the state-society debate', *PPR* Journal, March-May 2011, Volume 18, Issue 1.

instead of investing in public provisions such as healthcare and old age pension, had left its citizens fearful that unless they saved up enough money, they would not be able to cope with sickness or ageing. With the majority of the working population not earning enough to buy the goods they helped to produce, the banks had tried to drive 'growth' by lending to corporations with large-scale capital projects. Hotels, leisure complexes, luxury apartments were built without sufficient demand to make them viable, and it was highly likely that many of these loans would never be paid back. When these loans had to be written off, another crisis would be unleashed, and once again, the poor would suffer the most[175].

The need to recover reciprocity

The social and economic fault-lines opened up by gross power inequalities could not be mended unless those divisive gaps were substantially closed. Without equal respect, there would be little mutual support. Every institution that has a role to play in the distribution and exercise of power should be structured to enable everyone involved to participate on equal terms.

Government at all levels must work in partnership with community organisations and lifelong learning providers to give citizens the confidence, skills and opportunities to shape public decisions and prioritise community needs. Governments have to learn to involve communities in meaningful deliberations about options to raise and deploy public resources. Community groups need to build their capacity and resource base so that they can have a significant input into the activities that affect the future of their constituent members.

People disengaged from public deliberations are prone to suspect that their interests are disregarded, and are susceptible to being misled into thinking that their interests would only be safeguarded if they focus on pursuing their personal goals irrespective of others. In reality, cooperative endeavours bringing people from diverse backgrounds to

---

[175] See Chu, B. 'The Chinese have re-invented capitalism' in *Chinese Whispers: why everything you've heard about China is wrong*, pp166-192, London, Weidenfeld & Nicolson: 2013.

think and act together offer the best hope for cultivating shared understanding and civic collaboration[176].

Contrary to claims that citizen participation would be too cumbersome or ineffectual, late 20th and early 21st century experiments in deliberative engagement have consistently found that with the appropriate techniques of involvement, citizens are highly motivated to participate, better results are achieved compared with cases without public input, and people are more satisfied with the outcomes[177]. People's confidence in venturing out after dark has been boosted; mental and physical health have improved; trust in public agencies has been raised; and repairs have been carried out to housing estates more effectively – all because arrangements were put in place to make sure all those concerned were given the respect, support, and opportunities to have an informed input in the decision-making process.

In Latin America, progressive political leaders ignored 'Third Way' thinking and relied on community-based deliberative engagement with the people to build up support for a shared agenda for change. They insisted that those with least power should be given support in analysing the problems they faced and formulating appropriate solutions. These practices became increasingly widespread in Brazil, Mexico, Uruguay, Venezuela, Guatemala, and many other Latin American countries[178]. Mass media propaganda, which the rich could buy and control, were countered by mass civic engagement, which empowered the poor to draw their own conclusions. By the turn of the century, political parties with substantial social reform objectives began to gain electoral victories across the continent. Starting with the election of Hugo Chávez in Venezuela in 1998, leftist parties or coalitions won the presidency across

---

[176] Sirianni, C and Friedland, L, *Civic Innovation in America: community empowerment, public policy and the movement for civic renewal*, University of California Press: 2001.

[177] Tam, H 'Civil Renewal: the agenda for empowering citizens' in Brannan, T, John, P and Stoker, G (eds) *Re-energizing Citizenship: strategies for civil renewal*, Basingstoke, Palgrave Macmillan: 2007.

[178] See Selee, A. 'Deliberative Approaches to Governance in Latin America', 2008, available at: http://www.deliberative-democracy.net.

South America throughout the 2000s and 2010s[179].

In a region where plutocratic rule, often allied with military intimidation, had for decades dominated, it might have been thought that any reform campaign which relied on engaging people in determining what really needed to be done for their common good – as opposed to what plutocrats disguise as the 'national' interest – would inevitably fail. But Latin American activists have proven that it could be done, and progressives everywhere should take heed.

Apart from the government, the culture of cooperation needs to be promoted and sustained so that democratic collaboration becomes the norm in all spheres of human interaction. Commercial and voluntary organisations, which take decisions affecting their own employees and the wider communities, should give the latter a meaningful say in setting their priorities and structuring their decision-making. Petty monarchs and arrogant emperors used to decry democratic power sharing as an affront to their divinely sanctioned authority. Contemporary plutocrats would like to make a similar claim on behalf of their status, which had been conferred on them by their accumulated wealth. But cooperative working is a more effective alternative to authoritarian management. From Semco in Brazil to the John Lewis Partnership in Britain, businesses thrive for all those involved where workers are given an equal say in their shared destiny. The same trend can be detected in diverse community and cooperative enterprises, schools and resident groups[180].

The evidence accumulated over decades from across the world has proven time and time again that where people are treated as fellow participants in a shared enterprise, where their views and talents are valued, they work more effectively, and they think not just about what they can get out of the organisation themselves but how they can help the organisation maximise its positive impact[181]. This is crucially not

---

[179] Presidential elections were won by left-of-centre candidates in Brazil (2002, 2006, 2010), Argentina (2003, 2007, 2011), Uruguay (2004, 2009), Bolivia (2005, 2009), Chile (2006, 2013), Ecuador (2006, 2009, 2013), Peru (2006, 2011), and Paraguay (2009, 2013).

[180] For an extensive range of examples, see Tam, H. 'Rejuvenating Democracy: lessons from a communitarian experiment', *Forum* (the journal for promoting 3-19 comprehensive education), Volume 53, Number 3, 2011, pp 407-420.

[181] See, e.g., Lewis, M. and Conaty, P. *The Resilience Imperative: cooperative*

because of some hidden altruism breaking through, but simply down to the fact that with cooperative working, people can see that the benefits they generate together will be shared out in accordance with their own informed assessment of how that should be done. Instead of a small elite taking a disproportionately large share for themselves, people who work on making things happen deliberate on how to distribute the fruits of their labour. On that basis, constructive cooperation with others is simply the most reliable strategy to secure the best outcome one can hope for.

A new generation of progressive advocates are beginning to build on the successful experience of cooperative working to set out an agenda for the politics of the commons[182]. Instead of getting mired in the distorted debate about whether top-down corporations can only function if governments keep backing off to allow them to act as they alone see fit, the new agenda focuses on the more important task of rebuilding power relations in society.

Power inequalities have escalated whenever common resources are captured by some who then impose exclusive control rights over them. From land, forest, water and other natural resources, to virtual though vitally important resources created in cyberspace covering computer networks and intellectual property, exclusionary structures open the door to exploitative underpayment of workers and overcharging of users. The development of enterprises that abide by the founding principles of democratic decision-making and reciprocal sharing will help to advance the ethos of inclusive community life.

This trend can be seen with the continued emergence of credit unions and the revival of mutual finance institutions. It is being applied

---

transitions to a steady-state economy, New Society Publishers: 2013; and Alperovitz, G., America Beyond Capitalism: reclaiming our wealth, our liberty, and our democracy, John Wiley & Sons: 2004.

[182] For example, Bauwens, M., 'The Political Economy of Peer Production', published on CTheory: 2005 - http://www.ctheory.net/articles.aspx?id=499; Restakis, J., Humanizing the Economy: cooperatives in the age of capital, New Society Publishers: 2010; Walljasper, J., All That We Share: a field guide to the commons, New Press: 2010; Bollier, D. & Helfrich, S. (eds), The Wealth of the Commons: a world beyond market and state, Levellers Press: 2012 - http://wealthofthecommons.org/home; and Bollier, D., Think Like a Commoner, New Society Publishers: 2014.

to the development of mutually owned renewable energy supplies when these opportunities are seen as threats by corporations dependent on either profits from the depletion of fossil fuels or public subsidies for the disposal of nuclear waste. It is exemplified by the growth of open source knowledge technology so that the benefits of new designs and inventions can be maximised without access to their use being artificially restricted by conventional proprietary measures.

Activists for co-operative housing and community land trusts are joining forces to secure common resources to be democratically run by the people who are seeking affordable homes[183]. Examples of effective user-controlled health and social care are drawn together and extensively promoted by the cooperative movement to support their wider adoption[184]. Meanwhile, community groups in town and cities are setting up local and sustainable food systems. Some have even used local growing and healthy eating as a platform to reclaim unproductive land for communal use and build larger networks of cooperation to address social and environmental concerns[185].

For these diverse initiatives to reach the level where they are no longer the minority practices, but become the norm for how community and business interactions are conducted, education in the broadest sense – from schools to adult learning – must help to raise awareness of why and how cooperative problem-solving offers practically feasible means to achieve consistently better ends for everyone[186]. People of all ages need to cultivate pro-reciprocal dispositions towards others in any social context. By inculcating what may be termed the Cooperative Gestalt[187], they will have the confidence and inclination to work with others to find

---

[183] Bliss, N. and Lambert, B., *New Cooperative and Community-led Homes*, Manchester, Confederation of Cooperative Housing: 2014 - http://www.cch.coop/newcoophomes/docs/new-co-operative-and-community-led-homes.pdf.

[184] Conaty, P., *Social Cooperatives: a democratic co-production agenda for care services in the UK*, Manchester, Cooperatives UK: 2014.

[185] Warhurst, P. and Dobson, J., *Incredible! Plant Veg, Grow a Revolution: the story of Incredible Edible Todmorden*, Troubador: 2014.

[186] Tam, H. 'Cooperative Problem-Solving & Education', *Forum*, Volume 55 Number 2, 2013, pp.185-201.

[187] Tam, H. 'The Cooperative Gestalt', posted on *Question the Powerful*, 2013 - http://henry-tam.blogspot.co.uk/2013/11/the-cooperative-gestalt.html

collaborative and inclusive ways forward, rather than assume that they will have nothing to gain, and everything to lose, if they enter into any form of cooperative venture.

Alongside the input of progressive reformists in local and national government, advocates for cooperative enterprise and the commons agenda, and enlightened educators, we should recognise that a major challenge remains that can only be tackled by institutional changes at the global level.

## The need for global democratic governance

Transnational corporations have built up the global plutocratic system to bypass the control of national governments and reject all democratic accountability to the people whose lives they affect in countless ways. If corporate barons are to be effectively regulated for the common good, a worldwide system of democratic governance, building on the UN, will have to be put in place[188].

International institutions, which now serve the plutocratic interests of the most powerful counties, must be brought under the control of political representatives with a mandate from the citizens of all nations. Such a system would make it possible to probe into cross-border business dealings, put an end to off-shore devices to by-pass public scrutiny, and regulate currency and other financial speculations. It would also provide a basis to bring people who are truly accountable to citizens together to consider and coordinate actions to deal with military and environmental threats against any member of the global community.

As part of this development, the case for global political infrastructure has to be effectively made. Authoritarians have always invested in efforts to rouse people's suspicion and hostility towards collective actions which threaten their ability to do as they please. They are particularly cunning in misrepresenting bodies (e.g., trade unions, the federal government, environmental agencies, the United Nations) designed to restrain irresponsible behaviour as arbitrary meddlers, when in truth they want to be left alone to take advantage of others in a weaker position.

---

[188] See, e.g., Tetalman, J and Belitsos, B, *One World Democracy: a progressive vision for enforceable global law*, San Rafael, Origin Press: 2005.

Global civic education needs to be developed to underpin the construction of global democratic governance. To paraphrase UNESCO's dictum: since enslavement begin in people's minds, it is in people's minds that the defence of freedom and dignity must be constructed. For too long progressives have allowed the New Right to hijack the ideas of 'patriotism', 'enterprise' and 'God' to invoke as if they were uniquely associated with the rule of the global plutocracy. In reality, for people who truly care for their country and the wellbeing of their fellow citizens, people who want to generate wealth and improvement for society in a fair and sustainable manner, and people who seek to live up to the ultimate religious injunction to love others without discrimination, they need to be aware that they cannot obtain their goals without an inclusive system with the global strength to prevent any powerful elite from manipulating the rules to suit their own vested interests[189].

However, a worldwide form of government can only be entrusted with exercising greater power if it there are guarantees that it will respect the jurisdiction of the constituent states. To concentrate too much power in a single ruling body would risk tyranny. But to concede nothing on any issue to the higher body except on the unanimous support of all members would lead to impotence. In getting this balance right, it is not only necessary to ensure the culture and due process from the most reliable democracies over the last century are introduced into the workings of global political institutions, it is also essential for all countries to meet reform requirements in line with the highest inclusive standards and not the lowest common denominators.

The readiness of the US at its inception to allow the southern states to retain their system of slavery was a near-fatal error, which took a Civil War to correct. The European Union learnt this lesson and insisted that EU membership must carry with it compliance with its core liberal and democratic requirements, including adherence to the

---

[189] The development of a worldwide political system should be built with global civic actions which help to raise awareness and engagement with worldwide problems. See, e.g., Edwards, M and Gaventa (eds), *Global Citizen Action*, Boulder, Lynne Rienner Publishers: 2001; and Ekins, P, *A New World Order: grassroots movements for global change*, London, Routledge: 1992.

European Convention on Human Rights[190]. The process of developing a global democratic system must similarly require a progressive reform programme to bring all countries in line with standards citizens everywhere should be able to count on. In many cases support would have to be provided to implement the reforms and consolidate new inclusive arrangements.

Many critics of attempts to spread Enlightenment values and progressive practices condemn them as an unacceptable form of cultural imperialism. But intentionally or otherwise, they are merely serving to shield authoritarian rulers from pressures to change by branding inclusive reformists as wrong-headed interventionists. Educative and protective action in support of democratic inclusion should not be deflected by such stooges of powerful oppressors.

As anti-Enlightenment critics continue to deny the universal relevance of the progressive values of inclusive communities, regimes that repudiate those values have carried on destroying lives with impunity. In Somalia, teenage girls as young as 13 were stoned to death for breaching Islamic law after they had been raped while the rapists were not brought to justice. In the US, the Government admitted that it had held people for well over a decade without charge in its Guantanamo Bay detention facilities even though they were not enemy combatants and who posed no threat to America. In Cambodia, land activists who sought to oppose arbitrary eviction were regularly subject to arrests and groundless charges from the police and the courts. And in Colombia, the violent actions of both the security forces and paramilitary groups had by 2012 led to tens of thousands of people displaced from their homes, and millions of hectares of land misappropriated[191].

Such abuse of power must be overturned with real democratic accountability established in every country. Furthermore, the undue influence plutocrats could bring to bear on the electoral process through campaign funding, media controls, and the spread of misleading

---

[190] In 2014, the New Right Government of the UK announced its intention to abolish the Human Rights Act, which would entail the country's withdrawal from the European Convention on Human Rights.

[191] Amnesty International 2013 Report on Columbia: http://www.amnesty.org/en/region/colombia/report-2013

information would have to be regulated and monitored with the help of international organisations[192].

Where power is already over concentrated in some at the expense of others, it should be redistributed to minimise the scope for exploitation and oppression, and maximise the potential for cooperative improvement and sustainable growth. One of the most urgent gaps that need to be reduced is that concerning available resources. IMF researchers concluded in a 2011 study that "inequality is an underlying feature that makes it more likely that a number of factors—external shocks, external debt, ethnic fractionalization—come together to bring a growth spell to an end."[193]

To address this, global policies should be developed, for example, to facilitate the sharing out of land for cultivation more equitably where the majority of people depend on what they can grow to survive, or to improve the quality of and access to public housing, healthcare and other social services. In general, through a combination of minimum wage, marginal tax for top incomes and closure of fiscal loopholes for the wealthiest, the disparity should be brought down to no more than sufficient to motivate those with the potential to take on the harder tasks. The power of money itself should be limited with clear restrictions on what it can be used to buy, particularly in relation to corruptive practices to secure influence with public or private institutions.

Other forms of power disparity go beyond income differentials. Authoritarian cultural norms have for a long time conferred the status power to discriminate and act abusively against women, minorities and other vulnerable groups. It is therefore vital to outlaw discrimination and ensure that oppressive customs – however precious they were to those who embraced such norms as part of their identity – are not accepted anymore, anywhere in the world.

Within the framework of an open system for proposing and

---

[192] The reforms to be considered would include many that have been set out by progressive advocates: e.g., Levine, P, *The New Progressive Era: toward a fair & deliberative democracy*, Rowman and Littlefield Publishers: 2000; and Unger, RM, *Democracy Realized: the progressive alternative*, Verso: 1998.

[193] Berg, A. and Ostry, J.D., 'Equality and Efficiency' in *Finance & Development*, September 2011, Vol. 48, No. 3. (Berg is Assistant Director and Ostry is Deputy Director of the IMF's Research Department).

contesting knowledge claims – which requires universal education providing all with the skills and confidence to reason coherently, question responsibly, and draw conclusions based on the available evidence – people should be protected from interference stopping them explore through experimentation what may work. This does not mean that falsehoods – as revealed by the most systematic analysis – should not be restricted or at least made to carry a deception warning. It would be irresponsible to allow, for example, the defamation of innocent individuals, the promotion of 'medication' as completely safe when it has dangerous side-effects, the teaching of how a divine being created a world in which people who blew themselves and others up would be fast-tracked to eternal happiness, the assertion that non-heterosexual people deserve to suffer, the fabrication of stories about particular political candidates to destroy their electoral prospects. Concern with enhancing the freedom to discover the truth is not to be confused with reticence to stop lies being spread.

It would not be easy to develop a global network of government institutions that are robust enough to introduce and enforce these policies, while at the same time enable citizens to have confidence that they can hold such institutions to democratic account. A system of subsidiarity, allowing decisions to be taken at the most appropriate level, and facilitating their scrutiny by those best placed to review their performance, will have to be developed. What needs to be remembered is that the construction of socially responsible and democratically accountable government has been repeatedly dismissed as impossible in the past, and yet has been achieved over and over again in history.

Those who want to keep taking advantage of their ever expanding power in the absence of any effective form of global government will continue to stir up doubts and animosity towards any prospect of it ever coming into being. But the abuse of power is rife precisely because without genuine democratic accountability, transnational deals are being struck by corporations and plutocratic politicians to give the wealthy elite even more power to exploit other people and our common resources without having to answer for the dire consequences.

## Progressives at the global crossroad

It is often claimed that globalisation has changed everything. But one thing it has not erased is the perennial contest between those who press for and those who are against fairer distribution of power. In a corporately integrated, but politically fragmented, world, the plutocrats are in a strong position to divide and conquer. The powerful can impose their agenda on different national governments, and pick politicians off one by one with the incentive of campaign donations (not to mention lucrative board positions), and the threat of withholding investment as well as tactical media attacks. Like their autocratic predecessors throughout history, they are adept at manipulating people into believing that they should go along with the system devised by those who actually care little for others lower down the hierarchy.

If people are to attain true reciprocity in their interactions, the drive to cut down power inequalities must be directed at the real barriers and relentlessly maintained. Individual understanding must be improved, and institutional structures must be reformed. Democratic cooperation has to be re-imagined and instilled in the workings of productive enterprise, community initiatives, and our collective government at not just the local and national, but also the international level.

Where the progressive struggle has had the deepest influence on reducing the gap between the powerful and the rest, it has helped to liberate the human potential for mutual respect and cooperation in building a fairer, happier and more sustainable form of association for all concerned. But where it has been held back – and alas, that is still true in so many parts of the world – the poor end up subsidising the rich, women are at the mercy of men, children are abused as slaves and soldiers, superstitions ruin the lives of the ignorant, minorities are maltreated, innocents have to endure the fear of arbitrary arrest and torture, and dissidents are silenced.

It is distressingly easy for people's grievance at not being treated fairly to be deflected to false targets – liberal-minded politicians, the European Union, public sector workers, immigrants, refugees, working women, jobless single mothers, the 'envious' poor. It is much harder to reach out, engage diverse communities, and unite them in a common cause against the real source of oppression[194].

But having looked back on history, we know that progress is possible so long as its champions maintain their focus on cutting back on power inequalities, use effective educational means to raise public understanding of the underlying problems, build extensive alliances to strengthen public support, and vigilantly resist the emergence of new concentrations of power. Whatever the odds, the progressive struggle has won its share of success in past centuries.

Of course opposition to progressive reforms, at the local, national and global levels, will persist. Short-term concessions from the powerful should not be mistaken for lasting achievements. Where arbitrary power can still be exercised by the rich over the poor, bosses over workers, parents over their children, men over women, wardens over inmates, superpowers over small countries, one ethnic group over another, the weaker groups will remain at the mercy of the strong, and routinely suffer as a result of their malice or misjudgement.

What history has shown is that the progressive struggle for inclusive communities is indispensable if we are to keep iniquity and oppression at bay. Remembering how many obstacles we have already overcome should remind us that we need never surrender to the forces of exploitation or succumb to numbing despair. A better future is possible for those of us ready to stand together in solidarity.

---

[194] For more on this problem, see Westen, D, *The Political Brain: the role of emotion in deciding the fate of the nation*, New York, Public Affairs: 2007.

www.ingramcontent.com/pod-product-compliance
Lightning Source LLC
Chambersburg PA
CBHW030433290526
45786CB00001B/262